European
phrase book

D1413688

Easy to use features
- Handy thematic colour coding
- Quick Reference Section—opposite page
- Tipping Guide—inside back cover
- Quick reply panels throughout

Berlitz Publishing Company, Inc.

Princeton   Mexico City   London   Eschborn   Singapore

How best to use this phrase book

This phrase book is designed to provide you with the essential key phrases you'll need for travelling in and around Europe.

● **Colour margins** will help you locate quickly the language that you require.

● Each language is divided into essential **topic sections**. The following content table will help you find your way around:

Basic expressions	Shops, stores & services
Hotel–Accommodation	incl. bank, post, telephone
Eating out	Time, date, numbers
Travelling around	Emergency
Sightseeing	Guide to pronunciation

● Each expression appears with a transliteration next to it. Simply read this imitated pronunciation as if it were English, stressing the syllables printed in bold type. For further help, consult the **Guide to pronunciation** at the back of each language section.

● In the **Eating out** section, a selection of popular traditional dishes are listed alphabetically, followed by brief explanations, to help you decypher dishes appearing on a menu.

● Throughout the book, this symbol ☛ suggests phrases your listener can use to answer you, simply by pointing to the appropriate answer.

Note: Where languages vary slightly according to gender, parentheses ( ) indicate the feminine version.

8th printing October 2001

Printed in Spain

Danish

Some basic expressions *Anvendelige udtryk*

Yes/No.	**Ja/Nej.**	ya/nigh
Please.	**Vær så venlig.**	vær sāw **vehn**lee
Thank you.	**Tak.**	tak
I beg your pardon.	**Undskyld.**	**oon**skewl

Introductions *Præsentationer*

Good morning.	**God morgen.**	goadh**mōā**ern
Good afternoon.	**God dag.**	goadh**dai**
Good evening.	**God aften.**	goadh**afdern**
Good night.	**God nat.**	goadh**nat**
Good-bye.	**Farvel.**	far**vehl**
My name is...	**Jeg hedder...**	yigh **hehdherr**
Pleased to meet you!	**Det glæder mig at træffe Dem!**	dɛ **glædherr** migh ah **træfer** dehm
What's your name?	**Hvad hedder De/du?**	vadh **hehdherr** dee/doo
How are you?	**Hvordan har du det?**	vor**dan** har doo dɛ
Fine, thanks. And you?	**Tak, godt. Og hvordan har du det?**	tak god. oa vor**dan** har doo dɛ
Where do you come from?	**Hvor kommer du fra?**	vōar **komer** doo fra
I'm from...	**Jeg er fra...**	yigh ehr fra
Australia	**Australien**	owstral**eēe**rn
Canada	**Canada**	**ka**nada
Great Britain	**Storbritannien**	**stoar**britanyern
United States	**USA**	oo ehs ah
I'm with my...	**Jeg er her sammen med...**	yigh ehr hehr **sā**mern mehdh
wife	**min kone**	meen **koa**ner
husband	**min mand**	meen man
family	**min familie**	meen **fa**milyer
children	**mine børn**	**mee**ner børn
parents	**mine forældre**	**mee**ner for**æl**drer
boyfriend/girlfriend	**min kæreste**	meen **kær**sder
I'm on holiday (vacation).	**Jeg er her på ferie.**	yigh ehr hehr paw **feh**ryer

GUIDE TO PRONUNCIATION/EMERGENCIES, see page 16

Questions *Spørgsmål*

When?/How?	**Hvornår?/Hvordan?**	vornawr/vordan
What?/Why?	**Hvad?/Hvorfor?**	vadh/vorfor
Who?/Which?	**Hvem?/Hvilken?**	vehm/vilkern
Where is/are …?	**Hvor er …?**	voār ehr
Where can I find/get…?	**Hvor kan jeg finde/få…?**	voār kan yigh finner/faw
How far?	**Hvor langt?**	voār langt
How long?	**Hvor længe?**	voār længer
How much/How many?	**Hvor meget/Hvor mange?**	voār mighert/voār manger
Can I have…?	**Kan jeg få…?**	kan yigh faw
Can you help me?	**Kan De hjælpe mig?**	kan dee yehlper migh
What does this/that mean?	**Hvad betyder det her/det der?**	vadh bertewdherr dE hehr/dE dehr
I understand.	**Jeg forstår det.**	yigh forstawr dE
I don't understand.	**Jeg forstår det ikke.**	yigh forstawr dE igger
Can you translate this for me?	**Kan De oversætte det her for mig?**	kan dee oᵒᵒerrsehder dE hehr for migh
Do you speak English?	**Kan De tale engelsk?**	kan dee tāler ehngerlsk
I don't speak (much) Danish.	**Jeg kan ikke tale det (ret meget) dansk.**	yigh kan igger tāler dE (reht mighert) dansk

A few more useful words *Nogle flere nyttige ord*

better/worse	**bedre/værre**	behdhrer/vehrer
big/small	**stort/lille**	stoart/leeler
cheap/expensive	**billigt/dyrt**	beeleet/dewrt
early/late	**tidligt/sent**	teedhleet/sEnt
good/bad	**godt/dårligt**	god/dawleet
hot/cold	**varmt/koldt**	varmt/kolt
near/far	**i nærheden/langt væk**	ee nærhEdhern/langt vehk
old/new	**gammelt/nyt**	gamerlt/newt
right/wrong	**rigtigt/forkert**	rigteet/forkehrt
vacant/ occupied	**ledigt/optaget**	lehdheet/optáerdh

Hotel—Accommodation *Hotel*

I have a reservation.	**Jeg har bestilt værelse.**	yigh har berstilt væererlser
We've reserved an apartment.	**Vi har bestilt en lejlighed.**	vee har berstilt ehn lighleeehehdh
Do you have any vacancies?	**Har De nogle ledige værelser?**	har dee nōaler lɛdeeer væererlserr
I'd like a...	**Jeg vil gerne have et...**	yigh veel gehrner ha eht
single room	**enkeltværelse**	ehnkerldvæererlser
double room	**dobbeltværelse**	doberldvæererlser
We'd like a room...	**Vi vil gerne have et værelse...**	vee veel gehrner ha eht væererlser
with twin beds	**med to senge**	mehdh toa sehnger
with a double bed	**med dobbeltseng**	mehdh doberldsehng
with a bath	**med bad**	mehdh badh
with a shower	**med brusebad**	mehdh brōōserbadh
We'll be staying...	**Vi bliver her...**	vee blēēerr hehr
overnight only	**en enkel nat**	ehn ehnkerlt nat
a few days	**et par dage**	eht par daer
a week (at least)	**i (mindst) en uge**	ee (meenst) ehn ōer
Is there a camp site near here?	**Er der en camping-plads i nærheden?**	ehr dehr ehn kampingplas ee nærhɛdhern

Decision *Beslutning*

May I see the room?	**Kan jeg se værelset?**	kan yigh sɛ væererlserdh
That's fine. I'll take it.	**Det er godt. Jeg tager det.**	dɛ ehr god. yigh tar dɛ
No. I don't like it.	**Jeg kan ikke lide det.**	yigh kan igger li dɛ
It's too ...	**Det er for ...**	dɛ ehr for ...
dark/small	**mørkt/lyst**	mørkt/lewst
noisy	**støjende**	stoierner
Do you have anything ...?	**Har De noget ...?**	har dee nōaert
better	**bedre**	behdhrer
cheaper	**billigere**	beelēēerrer
quieter	**roligere**	roalēēerrer
May I have my bill, please?	**Må jeg bede om regningen?**	maw yigh bɛ om righningern
It's been a very enjoyable stay.	**Vi har nydt ophol-det meget.**	vee har newt opholerdh mighert

DAYS OF THE WEEK, see page 15

Eating out *Restauranter*

I'd like to reserve a table for 4.	**Jeg vil gerne bes-tille et bord til 4.**	yigh veel **gehr**ner ber**stiler** eht boar til **fee**rer
We'll come at 8.	**Vi kommer klokken 8.**	vee **komerr kloggern oader**
I'd like..., please.	**Jeg vil gerne have...**	yigh veel **gehr**ner ha
breakfast	**morgenmad**	**moa**rernmadh
lunch/dinner	**frokost/middag**	**froa**koast/**middai**
What do you recommend?	**Hvad kan De anbe-fale?**	vadh kan dee **an**berfāler
Do you have any vegetarian dishes?	**Er der nogle vege-tariske retter?**	ehr dehr **noa**ler vehgeht**ar**isger **reh**derr

Breakfast *Morgenmad*

I'll have a/an/some...	**Jeg vil gerne have...**	yigh veel **gehr**ner ha
bacon and eggs	**bacon og æg**	"bacon" oa æg
boiled egg	**et æg**	eht æg
bread	**brød**	brødh
butter	**smør**	smør
cereal	**cornflakes**	"cornflakes"
eggs	**æg**	æg
fried eggs	**spejlæg**	**spigh**læg
scrambled eggs	**røræg**	**rør**æg
poached eggs	**pocheret æg**	posh**ē**rerdh æg
jam	**syltetøj/marmelade**	**sewl**dertoi/marmerl**ā**dher
rolls	**rundstykker**	**roon**stewggerr
toast	**ristet brød**	**reest**erdh brødh

Starters (Appetizers) *Forretter*

blandet hors d'oeuvre	**blan**erdh "hors d'oeuvre"	assorted appetizers
fyldte tomater	**fewl**der toa**mad**err	stuffed tomatoes
omelet	oamer**leht**	omelet
sildesalat	**seel**ersalat	herring salad
kyllingesalat (**kew**leengersahlāt)		chicken meat, macaroni, tomato slices, green peppers, olives, green pees, lettuce and mushrooms, covered with a tomato dressing
smørrebrød (**smø**rerbrødh)		large, buttered open-faced sandwich covered with one of a variety of delicacies and garnished with various accessories

NUMBERS, see page 15

Fish and seafood *Fisk og skaldyr*

cod	**torsk**	torsk
perch	**aborre**	ahborer
pike	**gedde**	gehdher
smoked herring	**røget sild**	roierdh seel
sole	**søtunge**	søtoonger
trout	**forel**	foarehl

ålesuppe
(**awl**ersoobber)

sweet-and-sour eel soup, with apples and prunes, served with dark rye bread

boiled	**kogt**	kogt
fried	**stegt**	stehgt
grilled	**grillet**	greelerdh
roast	**ovnstegt**	o°°nstehgt
stewed	**stuvet**	stoo͞oerdh
underdone (rare)	**letstegt**	lehtstehgt
medium	**medium**	mehdeeoom
well-done	**gennemstegt**	gehnermstehgt

Meat *Kød*

beef	**oksekød**	okserkødh
chicken	**kylling**	kewling
duck	**and**	an
ham	**skinke**	skeenger
lamb	**lammekød**	lamerkødh
pork	**svinekød**	svee͞enerkødh
veal	**kalvekød**	kalverkødh

flæskesteg med svær
(**flæsg**erstigh mehdh svær)

roast pork with crackling, often served with braised red cabbage, gravy and small browned potatoes

forloren skildpadde
(for**loar**ern **skeel**padher)

"mock turtle": a traditional dish of meat from a calf's head with meat balls and fish balls

Vegetables *Grøntsager*

beans	**bønner**	bønerr
cabbage	**kål**	kawl
carrots	**gulerødder**	goo͞olerrødherr
mushrooms	**champignoner**	shampinyong
onions	**løg**	loi
peas	**ærter**	ærderr
potatoes	**kartofler**	kartoflerr
tomatoes	**tomater**	toamaderr

DANISH

Fruit and dessert *Frugt og nødder*

apple	et æble	eht æbler
cherries	kirsebær	keerserbær
lemon	citron	seetroan
orange	en appelsin	aberlseen
pear	pære	pærer
plums	blommer	blomerr
strawberries	jordbær	yoarbær
eis	ēēs	ice-cream
ost	oast	cheese
Weinerbrød	vēēnerbrødh	Danish pastry

| **bondepige med slør** | "veiled country maid": a mixture of rye-bread |
| (**boan**erpēēer mehdh slør) | crumbs, apple sauce, cream and sugar |

Drinks *Drikkevarer*

beer	øl	øl
(hot) chocolate	(varm) chokolade	(varm) shoakoaladher
coffee	kaffe	kafer
black	sort	soart
with cream	med fløde	mehdh flødher
fruit juice	frugtsaft	froogtsaft
milk	mælk	mælk
mineral water	mineralvand	meenehralvan
tea	te	tE
with milk/lemon	med mælk/citron	mehdh mælk/seetroan
wine	vin	vēēn
red/white	rød/hvid	rødh/veedh

Complaints–Paying *Klager–Regningen*

This is too...	Det her er for...	dE hehr ehr for
bitter/salty/sweet	bittert/salt/sødt	biderdh/salt/søt
That's not what I ordered.	Det har jeg ikke bestilt.	dE har yigh igger berstilt
I'd like to pay.	Jeg vil gerne betale.	yigh veel gehrner bertāler
I think there's a mistake in this bill.	Der er vist en fejl i denne regning.	deh ehr vist ehn fighl ee dehner righning
Can I pay with this credit card?	Kan jeg betale med dette kreditkort?	kan yigh bertāler mehdh dehder krehditkort
Is service included?	Er service inkluderet?	ehr "service" inklood**E**rerdh
We enjoyed it, thank you.	Vi har nydt det.	vee har newt dE

Dansk

NUMBERS, see page 15

Travelling around *Rejse omkring*

Plane *Ifly*

Is there a flight to Rønne?	**Er der et fly til Rønne?**	ehr dehr eht flew til **rø**ner
What time should I check in?	**Hvad tid må jeg checke ind?**	vadh teed maw yigh "check"er in
I'd like to... my reservation.	**Jeg vil gerne... min bestilling.**	yigh veel **gehr**ner... meen be**sti**ling
cancel	**annullere**	annool**ē**rer
change	**ændre på**	**æn**drer paw
confirm	**bekræfte**	ber**kræf**der

Train *Tog*

I'd like a ticket to Copenhagen.	**Jeg vil gerne have en billet til København.**	yigh veel **gehr**ner ha ehn bee**leh**d til købern**hown**
single (one-way)	**enkelt**	**ehn**kerlt
return (round trip)	**retur**	reh**tōōr**
first/second class	**første/anden klasse**	**før**sder/**an**ern **kla**ser
How long does the journey (trip) take?	**Hvor længe tager turen?**	vōār **læn**ger tar **tōō**rern
When is the... train to Århus?	**Hvornår kører det... tog til Århus?**	vor**nawr kø**rerr deht... to^{oo} til **awr**hōōs
first/last/next	**første/sidste**	**før**sder/**sees**der
Is this the right train to Aarhus?	**Kører det her tog til Århus?**	**kø**rerr dᴇ hehr to^{oo} til **aw**hōōs

Bus *Bus*

Which tram (streetcar) goes to the town centre?	**Hvilken sporvogn kører til centrum?**	**vil**kern **spoar**vo^{oo}n **kø**rerr til **sen**troom
How much is the fare to...?	**Hvor meget koster det til...?**	vōār **migh**ert **kos**derr dᴇ til
Will you tell me when to get off?	**Vil De sige til, hvornår jeg skal af?**	veel dee **sē**er til vor**nawr** yigh skal ah

TELLING THE TIME, see page 14

Taxi *Taxa*

What's the fare to...?	**Hvad koster det til...?**	vadh **kos**derr dE til
Take me to...	**Kør mig til...**	kør migh til
this address	**denne adresse**	**deh**ner ah**dreh**ser
Please stop here.	**Stands her.**	stans hehr
Could you wait for me?	**Kan De vente på mig?**	kan dee **vehn**der paw migh

Car hire (rental) *Biludlejning*

I'd like to hire (rent) a car.	**Jeg vil gerne leje en bil.**	yigh veel **gehr**ner **ligh**er ehn beel
I'd like it for a day/a week.	**Jeg vil gerne have den en enkel dag/en uge.**	yigh veel **gehr**ner ha dehn ehn **ehnk**erl dai/ehn ōōer
Where's the nearest filling station?	**Hvor er den nærmeste benzinstation?**	vōar ehr dehn **nær**merster behn**seen**stashon
Give me... litres of petrol (gasoline).	**... liter benzin.**	... **lee**derr ben**seen**
How can I find this place/address?	**Hvordan kan jeg finde frem til dette sted/denne adresse?**	vor**dan** kan yigh **finn**er frehm til **deh**der stehdh/**deh**ner ah**dreh**ser
I've had a breakdown at...	**Jeg har fået motorstop ved...**	yigh har **fāw**erdh **moa**torstop vehdh
Can you send a mechanic?	**Kan De sende en mekaniker?**	kan dee **sehn**ner ehn meh**kan**eekerr
Can you mend this puncture (fix this flat)?	**Kan De reparere denne punktering?**	kan dee reh**par**Erer **deh**ner **poonk**tehring

De har kørt forkert.	You're on the wrong road.
Kør ligeud.	Go straight ahead.
Det ligger der til venstre/højre.	It's down there on the left/right.
overfor/bagved...	opposite/behind...
ved siden af/efter...	next to/after...
nord/syd/øst/vest	north/south/east/west

NUMBERS, see page 15

Sightseeing *Seværdigheder*

Where's the tourist office?	**Hvor er turistbureauet?**	vōar ehr tooreestbewroaert
Is there an English-speaking guide?	**Findes der en engelsktalende guide?**	finners dehr ehn ehngerlsktālernder "guide"
Where is/are the...?	**Hvor er...?**	vōar ehr
art gallery	**kunstgalleriet**	koonstgalerēēert
botanical gardens	**den botaniske have**	dehn botaneesger hāver
castle	**borgen**	bōargern
city centre	**byens centrum**	bewerns sentroom
church	**kirken**	kēērgern
concert hall	**koncertsalen**	konsehrtsālern
market	**torvet**	tōārverdh
museum	**museet**	moosseherdh
palace	**slottet**	sloderdh
square	**pladsen/torvet**	plasern/torverdh
tower	**tårnet**	tawrnerdh
town hall	**rådhuset**	rawdhhōōserdh
What are the opening hours?	**Hvornår er der åbent?**	vornawr ehr dehr āwbern
When does it close?	**Hvornår lukkes der?**	vornawr looggers dehr
How much is the entrance fee?	**Hvor meget koster det i entre?**	vōar mighert kosderr dɛ ee angtrɛ

Relaxing *Forlystelser*

What's playing at the... Theatre?	**Hvad spiller man på... Teateret?**	vadh speelerr man paw... tɛatrerdh
Are there any seats for tonight?	**Er der flere pladser tilbage til i aften?**	ehr dehr flɛrer plasserr tilbāer til ee afdern
How much are the seats?	**Hvor meget koster billetterne?**	vōar mighert kosderr beelehderner
Would you like to go out with me tonight?	**Har du lyst til at gå ud med mig i aften?**	har doo lewst til ah gaw ood mehdh migh ee afdern
Is there a disco-theque in town?	**Findes der et diskotek i byen?**	finners dehr eht diskoatēk ee bewern
Would you like to dance?	**Skal vi danse?**	skal vee danser
Thank you, it's been a wonderful evening.	**Tak, det har været en virkelig hyggelig aften.**	tak dɛ har vāererdh ehn veerkerlee hewggerlee afdern

TELLING THE TIME, see page 14/DAYS OF THE WEEK, page 15

Shops, stores and services *Butikker og servicevirksomheder*

Where's the nearest...?	**Hvor er den/det nærmeste...**	vōar ehr dehn/deht nærmerster
bakery	**bager**	bāer
bookshop	**boghandel**	bo°°hanerl
butcher's	**slagter**	slagderr
chemist's/drugstore	**apotek**	apotehk
dentist	**tandlæge**	tanlǣer
department store	**stormagasin**	stoarmagaseen
grocery	**købmand**	køman
hairdresser's (ladies/ men)	**frisør (dame-/ herre-)**	freesør (damer-/hehrrer-)
newsagent's	**bladhandler**	bladhhanlerr
post office	**posthus**	posthoos
supermarket	**supermarked**	sōōbermarkerdh

General expressions *Almindelige udtryk*

Where's the main shopping area?	**Hvor er forret- ningskvarteret?**	vōar er forrehtningskvartehrerdh
Do you have any...?	**Har De nogen...?**	har dee nōaern
Can you show me...?	**Kan De vise mig...?**	kan dee vēeser migh
this/that	**det her/det der**	dᴇ hehr/dᴇ dehr
Don't you have any- thing...?	**Har De ikke noget...?**	har dee igger nōaert
cheaper/better larger/smaller	**billigere/dyrere større/mindre**	beelēeerrer/dēwerrer størrer/mindrer
Can I try it on?	**Kan jeg prøve den?**	kan yigh prøver dehn
How much is this?	**Hvad koster det?**	vadh kosder dᴇ
Please write it down.	**Vær rar og skriv det ned.**	vær rar oa skreev dᴇ nedh
I don't want to spend more than... kroner.	**Jeg vil ikke bruge mere end... kroner.**	yigh veel igger brōōer mēhrer ehn ... krōanerr
No, I don't like it.	**Det bryder jeg mig ikke om.**	dᴇ brewdherr yigh migh igger om
I'll take it.	**Jeg tager det.**	yigh tar dᴇ
Do you accept credit cards?	**Tager De kredit- kort?**	tar dee krehditkort
Can you order it for me?	**Kan De bestille det til mig?**	kan dee berstiler dᴇ til migh

black	**sort**	soart
blue	**blå**	blaw
brown	**brun**	broon
green	**grøn**	grøn
orange	**orange**	oarangsher
red	**rød**	rødh
white	**hvid**	veedh
yellow	**gul**	gool
light...	**lyse-**	lewser-
dark...	**mørke-**	mørker-

I want to buy a/an/ some...	**Jeg vil gerne have...**	yigh veel **gehr**ner ha
aspirin	**en æske aspirin**	ehn æsger "aspirin"
bottle opener	**oplukker**	op**loog**ger
newspaper	**en avis**	ehn a**vees**
postcard	**et postkort**	eht **post**kort
shampoo	**en shampoo**	ehn "shampoo"
soap	**et stykke sæbe**	eht **stewg**ger **sæ**ber
toothpaste	**en tandpasta**	ehn **tan**pasta
half-kilo of tomatoes	**et halvt kilo tomater**	eht halt **kee**lo to**mad**err
a litre of milk	**en liter mælk**	ehn **leed**err mælk
I'd like a film for this camera.	**Jeg vil gerne have en film til dette kamera.**	yigh vil **gehr**ner ha ehn film til **deh**der kamerra

Souvenirs *Souvenirer*

antiques	**antikviteter**	anteekvee**tēd**err
ceramics	**keramik**	kehra**mēēk**
furniture	**møbler**	**mø**blerr
knitware	**strikvarer**	**streek**vārerr
shag-rug	**et rya-tæppe**	eht **rēw**ataiber

At the bank *I banken*

Where's the nearest currency exchange office/bank?	**Hvor er det nærmeste vekselkontor/bank?**	vōar ehr dɛ **nær**merster **vehk**serlkon**tōar**/bank
I want to change some dollars/pounds.	**Jeg ønsker at veksle nogle dollars/pund.**	yigh **øns**gerr at **vehks**ler **nōa**ler "dollars"/poon
I want to cash a traveller's cheque.	**Jeg ønsker at indløse en rejsecheck.**	yigh **øns**gerr at in**lø**ser ehn **righs**er"cheque"

NUMBERS, see page 15

At the post office Posthus

I'd like to send this (by)...	Jeg vil gerne sende det her...	yigh veel **gehr**ner **seh**ner dE hehr
airmail	**(med) luft**post	(mehdh) **looft**post
express	**ex**pres	**ehks**prehs
A...-øre stamp, please.	Et...-øres frimærke.	eht... **ø**rers **free**mærker
What's the postage for a postcard/letter to Los Angeles?	Hvad er portoen for et postkort/brev til Los Angeles?	vadh ehr **por**tōāern for eht **post**kort/breh°° til "Los Angeles"
Is there any post (mail) for me?	Er der noget post til mig?	ehr dehr **nōā**ert post til migh

Telephoning Telefonering

Where's the nearest telephone booth?	Hvor er den nærmeste telefonboks?	vōār ehr dehn **nær**merster **teh**ler**foan**boks
I'd like a telephone card.	Jeg vil gerne have et telet.	yigh veel **gehr**ner ha eht **teh**let
Hello. This is...	Hallo. Det er...	hal**loa** dE ehr
I'd like to speak to...	Jeg vil gerne tale med...	yigh veel **gehr**ner **tā**ler mehdh
When will he/she be back?	Hvornår kommer han/hun tilbage?	vor**nawr koa**merr han/hoon til**bā**er

Time and date Klokken og dato

It's...	Den er...	dehn ehr
five past one	**fem** minutter over et	fehm mi**nood**err o°°er eht
a quarter past three	kvart over tre	kvart o°°er treh
twenty past four	**ty**ve minutter over fire	**tēw**ver mi**nood**err o°°er **fee**rer
half past six	halvsyv	**hal**sewv
twenty-five to seven	**fem** minutter over halvsyv	fehm mi**nood**err o°°er **hal**sewv
ten to ten	ti minutter i ti	tee mi**nood**err ee tee
twelve o'clock	tolv	toal
in the morning	om morgenen	om **mōā**ernern
in the afternoon	om eftermiddagen	om **ehf**dermiddaern
at night	om natten	om **nadd**ern
yesterday/today	i går/i dag	ee gawr/ee dai
tomorrow	i morgen	ee **mōā**ern

| spring/summer | **forår/sommer** | forawr/somerr |
| autumn/winter | **efterår/vinter** | ehfderawr/vinderr |

Sunday	**søndag**	søndai
Monday	**mandag**	mandai
Tuesday	**tirsdag**	teērsdai
Wednesday	**onsdag**	oansdai
Thursday	**torsdag**	toarsdai
Friday	**fredag**	frehdai
Saturday	**lørdag**	lørdai
January	**januar**	yanooar
February	**februar**	fehbrooar
March	**marts**	marts
April	**april**	apreēl
May	**maj**	migh
June	**juni**	yoōnee
July	**juli**	yoōlee
August	**august**	owgoost
September	**september**	sehptehmberr
October	**oktober**	oktoaberr
November	**november**	noavehmberr
December	**december**	dehsehmberr

Numbers *Tal*

0	**nul**	nool
1	**en**	ehn
2	**to**	toa
3	**tre**	treh
4	**fire**	feērer
5	**fem**	fehm
6	**seks**	sehks
7	**syv**	sewv
8	**otte**	oader
9	**ni**	nee
10	**ti**	tee
11	**elleve**	ehlver
12	**tolv**	toal
13	**tretten**	trehdern
14	**fjorten**	fyoardern
15	**femten**	fehmdern
16	**seksten**	sighsdern
17	**sytten**	sewdern
18	**atten**	addern
19	**nitten**	needdern
20	**tyve**	tewver

21	**enogtyve**	ehnot$\overline{ew}$ver
30	**tredive**	trehdhver
40	**fyrre**	førrer
50	**halvtreds**	haltrehs
60	**tres**	trehs
70	**halvfjerds**	halfyehrs
80	**firs**	f$\overline{ee}$rs
90	**halvfems**	half**ehms**
100/1000	**hundrede/tusind**	hoonrerdher/t$\overline{oo}$sin
first	**første**	førsder
second	**anden/andet**	anern/anerdh
once/twice	**en gang/to gange**	ehn gang/toa **gang**er
a half	**en halv/et halvt**	ehn hal/eht halt

Emergency *Nødstilfælde*

Call the police	**Tilkald politiet**	**til**kal politierdh
Get a doctor	**Tilkald læge**	**til**kal l$\overline{æ}$er
Go away	**Gå væk**	gaw vehk
HELP	**HJÆLP**	yehlp
I'm ill	**Jeg er syg**	yigh ehr sew
I'm lost	**Jeg er faret vild**	yigh ehr f$\overline{aa}$rerdh veel
LOOK OUT	**GIV AGT**	giv agt
STOP THIEF	**STOP TYVEN**	stop **tew**vern
My... has been stolen.	**Min/Mit... er ble-vet stjålet.**	meen/meet... ehr bleh^{oo}erdh sty$\overline{aw}$lerdh
I've lost my...	**Jeg har tabt...**	yigh har tabt
handbag	**min håndtaske**	meen h$\overline{aw}$ntasger
passport	**mit pas**	meet pas
wallet	**min tegnebog**	meen **tigh**nerbo^{oo}
Where can I find a doctor who speaks English?	**Hvor kan jeg finde en læge, der taler engelsk?**	v$\overline{oa}$r kan yigh **fin**ner ehn l$\overline{æ}$er dehr **tā**lerr **ehng**erlsk

Guide to Danish pronunciation *Udtale*

Consonants

Letter	Approximate pronounciation	Symbol	Example	
b, f, l, m, n, v	as in English			
c	1) like **s** in s**i**t	c	**citron**	seetr$\overline{oa}$n
	2) like **k** in **k**ite			
d	1) like **th** in **th**is	dh	**med**	mEdh
	2) as in English	d	**dale**	d$\overline{a}$ler

TELEPHONING, see page 14

DANISH

g	1) as in **go**	g	**glas**	gals
	2) like **ch** in Scottish **loch**	y	**sige**	sēēyer
hv	like **v** in view	v	**hvot**	vōar
j, hj	like **y** in yet	y	**ja**	yǣ
k	1) like **g** in go	g	**ikke**	igger
	2) like **k** in kite	k	**kaffe**	kahfer
p	1) like **b** in bit	b	**stoppe**	stobber
	2) like **p** in pill	p	**pude**	poodher
r	pronounced in the back of the throat; otherwise often omitted	r	**rose**	rōasser
s	always as in **see**	s	**skål**	skawl
sj	usually like **sh** in sheet	sh	**sjælden**	shehlern
t	1) like **d** in do	d	**lytte**	lewder
	2) like **t** in to (at the end of a word often mute)	t	**torsk**	toarsk

Vowels

a	1) long, like **a** in car	ā	**klare**	klārer
	2) short, like **a** in cart	a	**hat**	hat
e	1) as in the French **les**	ē	**flere**	flērer
	2) short, like **i** in hit	E	**fedt**	fEt
	3) like **e** in met	eh	**let**	leht
	4) like **a** in above	er	**hjælpe**	yehlper
i	1) long, like **ee** in bee	ēē	**ile**	ēēler
	2) short, between **a** in plate and **i** in pin	i	**drikke**	drigger
o	1) like the **oa** sound in boat, long or short	ōa / oa	**pol** / **bonde**	pōa / boaner
	2) short, like **o** in lot	o	**godt**	god
u	1) long, like **oo** in pool	ōō	**frue**	frōōer
	2) short, like **oo** in loot	oo	**nu**	noo
y	put your tongue in the position for the **ee** of bee, but round your lips as for the **oo** of pool, long or short	ēw / ew	**nyde** / **lytte**	nēwdher / lewder
æ	1) long, like **ai** in air	ǣ	**sæbe**	sǣber
	2) short, like **e** in get	eh	**ægte**	ehgter
ø	put your lips together to whistle but make a noise with your voice instead; long or short	ø̄ / ø	**frøken** / **øl**	frø̄gern / øl
å	1) long, like **aw** in saw	āw	**åben**	āwbern
	2) short, like **o** in on	aw	**på**	paw

Dutch

Basic expressions *Enkele woorden en uitdrukkingen*

Yes/No.	**Ja/Nee.**	yaa/nay
Please.	**Alstublieft.**	ahlstew**bleeft**
Thank you.	**Dank u.**	dahnk ew
I beg your pardon?	**Wat zegt u?**	√aht zehkht ew

Introductions *Kennismaking*

Good morning.	**Goedemorgen.**	ghooder**mor**ghern
Good afternoon.	**Goedemiddag.**	ghooder**mid**dahkh
Good night.	**Goedenacht.**	ghooder**nahkht**
Hello/Hi.	**Hallo.**	hah**loa**
Good-bye.	**Tot ziens.**	tot seenss
My name is...	**Mijn naam is...**	maiyn naam iss
Pleased to meet you.	**Prettig kennis te maken.**	preh tikh **keh**niss ter **maa**kern
What's your name?	**Hoe heet u?**	hoo hayt ew
How are you?	**Hoe maakt u het?**	hoo maakt ew heht
Fine thanks.	**Uitstekend, dank u.**	ur^{ew}t**stay**kernt dahnk ew
And you?	**En u?**	ehn ew
Where do you come from?	**Waar komt u vandaan?**	√aar komt ew vahn**daan**
I'm from...	**Ik kom uit...**	ik kom ur^{ew}t
Australia	**Australië**	oa**straa**leeyer
Great Britain	**Groot-Brittannië**	groat brit**tah**neeyer
Canada	**Canada**	**kah**naadaa
United States	**Verenigde Staten**	veh**ray**nergder **staa**tern
I'm with my...	**Ik ben met...**	ik behn neht
wife	**mijn vrouw**	maiyn vro^{ow}
husband	**mijn man**	maiyn mahn
family	**mijn gezin**	maiyn gher**zin**
boyfriend	**mijn vriend**	maiyn vreent
girlfriend	**mijn vriendin**	maiyn vreen**din**
I'm on a business trip/vacation.	**Ik ben op zakenreis/met vakantie.**	ik behn op **zaa**kernrayss/ meht vaa**kahn**see

GUIDE TO PRONUNCIATION, see page 31/EMERGENCIES, page 30

Questions *Vragen*

When?	**Wanneer/Hoe laat?**	√ah**nayr**/hoo laat
How?	**Hoe?**	hoo
What?/Why?	**Wat?/Waarom?**	√aht/√**aa**rom
Who?	**Wie?**	√ee
Which?	**Welk/Welke?**	√ehlk/√**ehl**ker
Where is/are...?	**Waar is/zijn...?**	√aar iss/zaiyn
Where can I find/ get...?	**Waar kan ik... vinden/krijgen?**	√aar kahn ik... **vin**dern/ **kraiy**ghern
How far?	**Hoever?**	hoo**vehr**
How long?	**Hoelang?**	hoo**lahng**
How much/many?	**Hoeveel?**	hoo**vayl**
Can I have...?	**Mag ik... hebben?**	mahk ik... **heh**bern
Can you help me?	**Kunt u mij helpen?**	kurnt ew maiy **hehl**pern
What does this mean?	**Wat betekent dit?**	√aht ber**tay**kernt dit
I understand.	**Ik begrijp het.**	ik ber**ghraiyp** heht
I don't understand.	**Ik begrijp het niet.**	ik ber**ghraiyp** heht neet
Can you translate this for me?	**Kunt u dit voor mij vertalen?**	kurnt ew dit voar maiy verr**taa**lern
Do you speak English?	**Spreekt u Engels?**	spraykt ew **ehn**gerlss
I don't speak Dutch.	**Ik spreek geen Nederlands.**	ik sprayk ghayn **nay**derrlahnts

A few more useful words *Nog een paar nuttige woorden*

better/worse	**beter/slechter**	**bay**terr/**slehkh**terr
big/small	**groot/klein**	ghroat/klaiyn
cheap/expensive	**goedkoop/duur**	ghoot**koap**/dewr
early/late	**vroeg/laat**	vrookh/laat
good/bad	**goed/slecht**	ghoot/slehkht
hot/cold	**warm/koud**	√ahrm/ko^{ow}t
near/far	**dichtbij/ver**	dikht**baiy**/vehr
old/new	**oud/nieuw**	o^{ow}/nee^{oo}
open/shut	**open/dicht**	**oa**pern/dikht
right/wrong	**juist/verkeerd**	yur^{ew}st/verr**kayrt**
vacant/occupied	**vrij/bezet**	vraiy/ber**zeht**

Hotel–Accommodation *Hotel*

I have a reservation.	Ik heb gereserveerd.	ik hehp gherrayzehrvayrt
We've reserved 2 rooms.	Wij hebben 2 kamers gereserveerd.	√aiy hehbern 2 kaamerrss gherrayzehrvayrt
Do you have any vacancies?	Hebt u nog kamers vrij?	hehpt ew nokh kaamerrss vraiy
I'd like a...	Ik wil graag een...	ik √il ghraakh ern
single room	éénpersoonskamer	aynpehrsoanskaamerr
double room	tweepersoons-kamer	t√aypehrsoanskammerr
with twin beds	met lits-jumeaux	meht lee-zhewmoa
with a double bed	met een twee-persoonsbed	meht ern t√ay-pehrsoansbeht
with a bath/shower	met badkamer/douche	meht bahtkaamerr/doosh
We'll be staying...	Wij blijven...	√aiy blaiyvern
overnight only	alleen vannacht	ahlayn vahnnahkht
a few days	een paar dagen	ern paar daaghern
a week	een week	ern √ayk
Is there a camp site near here?	Is hier een kampeerterrein in de buurt?	iss heer ern kahmpayr-tehraiyn in der bewrt

Decision *Beslissing*

May I see the room?	Mag ik de kamer zien?	mahkh ik der kaamerr zeen
That's fine. I'll take it.	Deze is prima. Die neem ik.	dayzer iss preemah. dee naym ik
No. I don't like it.	Nee. Die bavalt mij niet.	nay. de bervahlt maiy neet
It's too...	Het is te...	heht iss ter
small	klein	klaiyn
noisy	lawaaierig	laa√aaⁱⁱyerrerkh
Do you have anything...?	Hebt u iets...?	hehpt ew eets
better/bigger	beters/groters	bayterrss/ghroaterrss
cheaper	goedkopers	ghootkoaperrss
quieter	rustigers	rurstergherrss
May I have my bill, please?	Mag ik mijn rekening, alstublieft?	mahkh ik maiyn rakerning ahlstewbleeft
It's been a very enjoyable stay.	Het is een erg prettig verblijf geweest.	heht iss ern ehrkh prehtikh verrblaiyf gher√ayst

DAYS OF THE WEEK, see page 29

Eating out *Uit eten*

I'd like to reserve a table for 4.	**Ik wil graag een tafel reserveren voor 4 personen.**	ik vil ghraakh ern taaferl rayzehrvayrern voar 4 pehrsoanern
We'll come at 8.	**Wij komen om 8 uur.**	vaiy koamern om 8 ewr
I'd like...	**Ik wil graag...**	ik vil ghraakh
breakfast/lunch dinner	**ontbijt/koffietafel diner**	ontbayt/koffeetaaferl deenay
What would you recommend?	**Wat kunt u aanbevelen?**	vaht kurnt ew aanbervaylern
Do you have any vegetarian dishes?	**Hebt u vegettarische gerechten**	hehpt ew vayghaytaareeser gherrehkhtern

Breakfast *Ontbijt*

May I have some...?	**Mag ik... hebben?**	mahkh ik...hehbern
bread	**brood**	broat
butter	**boter**	boaterr
cheese	**kaas**	kaass
ham and eggs	**ham en eieren**	hahm ehn aiyyerrern
jam	**jam**	zhehm
rolls	**een paar broodjes**	ern paar broatyers

Starters *Voorgerechten*

ansjovis	ahnshoaviss	anchovies
aspergepunten	ahspehrzherpurntern	asparagus tips
bitterballen	bitterbahlern	small breaded meat-balls
gevulde eieren	ghervurlder aiyyerrern	stuffed eggs

Soups *Soepen*

aardappelsoep	aardahperlsoop	potato soup
bruine bonesoep	brur^{ew}ner boanernsoop	thick kidney bean soup
bouillon	boo^{ee}yon	clear soup
met groenten	meht ghroontern	with shredded vegetables
erwtensoep (met kluif)	ehrternsoop (meht klur^{ew}f)	thick pea soup (with sausage)
groentesoep (met balletjes)	ghroontersoop (meht bahlertyerss)	vegetable soup (with meat balls)
palingsoep	paalingsoop	cream of eel
soep van de dag	soop vahn der dahkh	soup of the day
vissoep	vissoop	fish soup

NUMBERS, see page 30

Fish and seafood *Vis, schaal-en schelpdieren*

carp	**karper**	**kahr**perr
cod	**kabeljauw**	kahberlyo^ow
crab	**krab**	krahp
eel	**paling**	**paa**ling
kipper	**bokking**	**bok**king
lobster	**kreeft**	krayft
mussels	**mosselen**	**mos**serlern
scampi	**(kleine) zeekreeft**	**(klay**ner) **zay**krayft

baked/fried	**gebakken**	gher**bah**kern
boiled	**gekookt**	gher**koakt**
grilled	**gegrild**	gher**ghrillt**
roasted	**gebraden**	gher**braa**dern
stewed	**gestoofd**	gher**stoaft**
underdone (rare)	**niet gaar/rood**	neet ghaar/roat
medium	**net gaar gebakken**	neht ghaar gher**bah**kern
well-done	**doorgebakken**	**doar**gher**bah**kern

Meat *Vlees*

I'd like some...	**Ik wil graag... hebber.**	ik √il ghraakh...**heb**bern
beef/lamb	**rundvlees/lamvlees**	**rurnt**vlayss/**lahm**svlayss
chicken/duck	**kip/eend**	kip/aynt
pork	**varkensvlees**	**vahr**kernsvlayss
veal	**kalfsvlees**	**kahlfs**vlayss
hete bliksem	**hay**ter **blik**serm	potato, bacon and apple dish
jachtschotel	**yahkht**skhoaterl	meat casserole
rijsttafel	**raiys**ttaaferl	Indonesian rice table
zuurkool	**zewr**koal	sauerkraut

Vegetables *Groenten*

beans	**bonen**	**boa**nern
cabbage	**kool**	koal
carrots	**worteltjes**	√**orterl**tyerss
cauliflower	**bloemkool**	**bloom**koal
mushrooms	**champignons**	**shahm**peeñonss
onions	**uien**	**ur**^ew yern
peas	**doperwtjes**	**dop**ehrrtyerss
potatoes	**aardappelen**	**aard**ahperlern
tomatoes	**tomaten**	toa**maa**tern

Fruit and dessert *Vruchten en nagerechten*

apple	**apple**	ahperl
banana	**banaan**	baanaan
cherries	**kersen**	kehrsern
lemon	**citroen**	seetroon
orange	**sinaasappel**	seenaasahperl
pear	**peer**	payr
strawberries	**aardbeien**	aartbaiyyern
broodschoteltje	broatskhoaterltyer	bread pudding
flensjes	flehnsyerss	thin pancakes
Haagse bluf	haaghser blurf	whipped egg white dessert
ijs	aiyss	ice cream
rijstebrijpudding	raiysterbraiypurding	rice pudding

Drinks *Dranken*

beer	**biertje/pils**	**beer**tyer/pilss
(hot) chocolate	**warme chocolade**	√**ahr**mer
	melk	shoakoa**laa**dermehlk
coffee	**koffie**	**kof**fee
a pot	**een potje**	ern **pot**yer
with cream	**met room**	meht roam
fruit juice	**vruchtesap**	**vrurkh**tersahp
milk	**melk**	mehlk
mineral water	**mineraalwater**	meener**raal**√aaterr
tea	**thee**	tay
wine	**wijn**	√aiyn
red/white	**rood/wit**	roat/√it

Complaints and paying *Klachten en de rekening*

This is too...	**Dis is te...**	dit iss ter
bitter/sweet	**bitter/zoet**	**bit**err/zoot
That's not what I ordered.	**Dit heb ik niet besteld.**	dit hehp ik neet ber**stehlt**
I'd like to pay.	**Ik wil graag betalen.**	ik √il graakh ber**taal**ern
I think there's a mistake in this bill.	**Ik geloof dat er een vergissing is in deze rekening.**	ik gher**loaf** daht ehr ern verr**ghiss**ing iss in **day**zer **ray**kerning
Can I pay with this credit card?	**Kan ik met deze credit card betalen?**	kahn ik meht **day**zer "credit card" ber**taal**ern
We enjoyed it, thank you.	**Wij hebben genoten, dank u.**	√aiy **hehb**ern gher**noat**ern dahnk ew

NUMBERS, see page 30

Travelling around *Rondreizen*

Plane *Vliegtuig*

Is there a flight to…?	**Is er een vlucht naar…?**	iss ehr ern vlurkht naar
What time should I check in?	**Hoe laat moet ik inchecken?**	hoo laat moot ik **in**shehkern
I'd like to… my reservation.	**Ik wil graag mijn reservering…**	ik √il ghraakh maiyn rayzehr**vay**ring
cancel	**annuleren**	ahnew**lay**rern
change	**veranderen**	ver**rahn**derrern
confirm	**bevestigen**	ber**veh**sterghern

Train *Trein*

I'd like a ticket to…	**Ik wil graag een naar…**	ik·√il ghraakh ern **kaar**tyer naar
single (one-way)	**enkele reis**	**ehn**kerler raiyss
return (roundtrip)	**retour**	rertoor
first/second class	**eerste/tweede klas**	**ayr**ster/t√**ay**der klahss
How long does the journey take?	**Hoeland duurt de rit?**	hoo**lahng** dewrt der rit
When is the… train to…	**Wanneer gaat de… train naar…**	√ah**nayr** ghaat der…trayn naar
first	**eerste**	**ayr**ster
last	**laatste**	**laat**ster
next	**volgende**	**vol**ghernder
Is this the train to…?	**Is dit de trein naar…?**	iss dit der traiyn naar

Bus–Tram (streetcar) *Bus-Tram*

Which tram goes to the town centre?	**Welke tram rijdt naar het stads-centrum?**	√**eh**lker trehm raiyt naar heht **stahts**sehntrurm
How much is the fare to…?	**Hoeveel kost het naar…?**	hoo**vayl** kost heht naar
Will you tell me when to get off?	**Wilt u mij zeggen wanneer ik moet uitstappen?**	√ilt ew maiy **zeh**ghern √ah**nayr** ik moot ur**ew**tstahpern

TELLING THE TIME, see page 29

Taxi *Taxi*

Take me to this address.	**Brengt u mij naar dit adresa.**	brehngt ew maiy naar dit aadrehss
Please stop here.	**Wilt u hier stoppen, alstublieft.**	√ilt ew heer **stop**pern ahlstew**bleeft**
Could you wait for me?	**Kunt u op mij wachten, alstublieft?**	kurnt ew op maiy √ahkhtern ahlstew**bleeft**

Car hire (rental) *Autoverhuur*

I'd like to hire (rent) a car.	**Ik wil graag een auto huren.**	ik √il ghraakh ern o^{ow}toa **hew**rern
I'd like it for...	**Ik wil het graag voor...**	ik √il heht ghraakh voar
a day	**een dag**	ern dahkh
a week	**een week**	ern √ayk
Where's the nearest filling station?	**Waar is het dichtstbijzijnde benzinestation?**	√aar iss heht dikhstbaiy-**zaiyn**der behn**zee**ner stah**syon**
Fill it up, please.	**Vol, alstublieft.**	vol ahlstew**bleeft**
Give me... litres of petrol (gasoline).	**Geeft u mij... liter benzine.**	ghayft ew maiy ... **lee**terr behn**zee**ner
How do I get to this place/this address?	**Hoe kom ik naar deze plaats/it adres?**	hoo kom ik naar **day**zer plaats/dit **aa**drehss
I've had a breakdown at...	**Ik sta met autopech bij...**	ik staa meht o^{ow}toapehkh baiy
Can you send a mechanic?	**Kunt u een monteur sturen?**	kurnt ew ern mon**turr stew**rern
Can you mend this puncture (fix this flat)?	**Kunt u deze lekke band repareren?**	kurnt ew **day**zer **leh**ker bahnt raypaa**ray**rern

---

U bent op de verkeerde weg.	You're on the wrong road.
U moet rechtdoor riden.	Go straight ahead.
Het is daarginds...	It's down there on the...
links/rechts	left/right
tegenover/achter...	opposite/behind...
naast/na...	next to/after...
noord/zuid/oost/west	north/south/east/west

NUMBERS/EMERGENCIES, see page 30

Sightseeing *Sightseeing*

Where's the tourist office?	**Waar is het ver-keersbureau?**	√aar iss heht verr**kayrs**bewroa
Is there an English-speaking guide?	**Is er een Engels-sprekende gids?**	iss ehr ern **ehng**erls-spraykernder ghits
Where is/are...?	**Waar is/zijn...?**	√aar iss/zaiyn
art museum	**het museum voor beeldende kunst**	heht mew**zay**yum voar **bayl**dernder kurnst
castle	**het kasteel**	heht kah**stayl**
cathedral/church	**de kathedraal/kerk**	der kahter**draal**/kehrk
city centre	**het (stads) centrum**	heht (**stahts**)sehntrurm
museum	**het museum**	heht mew**zay**yum
What are the opening hours?	**Wat zijn de openingstijden?**	√aht zaiyn der **oa**pernings-taiydern

Relaxing *Ontspanning*

What's playing at the... Theatre?	**Wat wordt er in het ... Theater gespeeld?**	√aht √ort ehr in heht ... tay**aa**terr gher**spaylt**
Are there any seats for tonight?	**Zijn er nog plaatsen voor vanavond?**	zaiyn ehr nokh **plaat**sern voar vahn**aa**vont
Would you like to go out with me tonight?	**Hebt u zin om vanavond met mij uit te gaan?**	hehpt ew zin om vahn**aa**vont meht maiy ur^{ew}t ter ghaan
Would you like to dance?	**Wilt u dansen?**	√ilt ew **dahn**sern
Thank you, it's been a wonderful evening.	**Dank u, het was een heerlijke avond.**	dahnk ew heht √ahss ern **hayr**lerker **aa**vont

Shops, stores and services *Winkels en diensten*

Where's the nearest...?	**Waar is de/het dichtstbijzinde...?**	√aar iss der/heht dikhtstbaiy**zaiy**nder
bakery	**de bakker**	der **bah**kerr
bookshop	**de boekhandel**	der **book**handerl
chemist's/drugstore	**de apotheek**	der ahpo**atayk**
department store	**het warenhuis**	heht √**aa**rernhur^{ew}ss
grocery	**de kruidenier**	der krur^{ew}der**neer**
hairdresser	**de kapper**	der **kah**perr
newsagent	**de krantenkiosk**	der **krahn**ternkeeyosk
post office	**het postkantoor**	heht **post**kahntoar
supermarket	**de supermarkt**	der **sew**perrmahrkt
toilets	**de toiletten**	der t√**aa**lehtern

General expressions *Algemene uitdrukkingen*

Where's the main shopping area?	**Waar is de winkel-buurt?**	√aar iss de √inkerlbewrt
Do you have any...?	**Hebt u...?**	hehpt ew
Don't you have anything...?	**Hebt u niet iets...?**	hehpt ew neet eets
cheaper/better	**goedkopers/beters**	ghoot**koa**perss/**bay**terrss
larger/smaller	**groters/kleiners**	**ghroa**terrss/**klaiy**nerrss
Can I try it on?	**Kan ik het aan-passen?**	kahn ik heht **aan**pahssern
How much is this?	**Hoeveel Kost dit?**	hoo**vahl** kost dit
No, I don't like it.	**Nee, het bevalt mij niet.**	nay heht ber**vahlt** maiy neet
I'll take it.	**Ik neem dit.**	ik naym dit
Do you accept credit cards?	**Neemt u credit cards aan?**	naymt ew "credit cards" aan

black	**zwart**	z√ahrt
blue	**blauw**	blo°ʷ
brown	**bruin**	brurᵉʷn
green	**groen**	ghroon
orange	**oranje**	oarahñer
red	**rood**	roat
white	**wit**	√it
yellow	**geel**	ghayl
light...	**licht...**	likht
dark...	**donker...**	**donk**err

I want to buy...	**Ik wil graag... kopen.**	ik √il ghraakh... **koa**pern
aspirin	**aspirine**	ahspee**ree**ner
newspaper	**een krant**	ern krahnt
postcard	**een briefkaart**	ern **breef**kaart
shampoo	**shampoo**	**shahm**poa
toothpaste	**tandpasta**	**tahnt**pahstaa
half-kilo of tomatoes	**een pond/halve kilo tomaten**	ern pont/**hahl**ver **kee**loa toa**maa**tern
litre of milk	**een liter melk**	ern **lee**terr mehlk
I'd like a... film for this camera.	**Ik wil graag een... film voor dit toestal.**	ik √il ghraakh ern... film voar dit **toos**tehl
black and white	**zwart-wit**	z√ahrt-√it
colour	**kleuren**	**klur**rern

NUMBERS, see page 30

Souvenirs *Souvenirs*

I'd like a/some...	**Ik wil graag...**	ik √il ghraakh
(tulip) bulbs	**(tulpen) bollen**	(turlpern) bollern
china	**porselein**	porserrlaiyn
clogs	**klompen**	klompern
lace	**kant**	kahnt
miniature windmill	**miniatuur molen**	meeneeyaatewr moalern

At the bank *Bank*

Where's the nearest bank/currency exchange office	**Waar is de dichtst-bijzijnde bank/wisselkantoor?**	√aar iss der dikhtst-baiyzaiynder bahnk/√isserlkahntoar
I want to change some dollars/pounds.	**Ik wil graag dollars/ponden wisselen.**	ik √il ghraakh dollahrss/pondern √isserlern
I want to cash a traveller's cheque.	**Ik wil graag een reischeque wisselen.**	ik √il ghraakh ern raiysshehk √isserlern

At the post office *Postkantoor*

I'd like to send this by...	**Ik wil dit graag... verzenden.**	ik √il dit ghraakh verrzehndern
airmail	**per luchtpost**	pehr lurkhtpost
express	**per expresse**	pehr ehksprehss
A...-cent stamp, please.	**Een postzegel van... cent, alstublieft.**	ern postzaygherl vahn... sehnt ahlstewbleeft
What's the postage for a letter/postcard to Los Angeles?	**Hoeveel port moet er op ern brief naar Los Angeles?**	hoovayl port moot ehr op een breef naar "los angeles"
Is there any post/mail for me?	**Is er post voor mij?**	iss ehr post voar maiy

Telephoning *Telefoneren*

Where's the nearest telephone booth?	**Waar is de dichtst-bijzinde telefoon-cel?**	√aar iss der dikhtst-baiyzaiynder taylerfoan-sehl
Hello. This is...	**Hallo. U spreekt met...**	hahloa. ew spraykt meht
I'd like to speak to...	**Ik wil graag... spreken.**	ik √il ghraakh...spraykern
When will he/she be back?	**Wanneer komt hij/zij terug?**	√ahnayr komt haiy/zaiy terrurkh

Days and date *Dagen en datum*

It's...	Het is...	heht iss
five past one	**vijf over een**	vaif **oa**verr ayn
quarter past three	**kwart over drie**	k√ahrt **oa**verr dree
twenty past four	**tien voor half vijf/ twintig over vier**	teen voar hahlf vaiyf/ t√interkh **oa**verr veer
half-past six	**half zeven**	hahlf **zay**vern
twenty-five to seven	**vijf over half zeven**	vaiyf **oa**verr hahlf **zay**vern
ten to ten	**tien voor tien**	teen voar teen
noon/midnight	**'s middags/'s nachts**	s**mid**dahkhss/**snah**khss
in the morning	**'s morgens**	s**morg**hernss
in the afternoon	**'s middags**	s**mid**dahkhss
in the evening	**'s avonds**	**saa**vontss
during the day	**overdag**	oaverr**dahkh**
at night	**'s nachts**	**snah**khts
yesterday	**gisteren**	**ghis**terrern
today	**vandaag**	vahn**daakh**
tomorrow	**morgen**	**morg**hern
spring/summer	**lente/zomer**	**lehn**ter/**zoa**merr
autumn/winter	**herfst/winter**	**hehr**fst/√**in**terr

Sunday	**zondag**	**zon**dahkh
Monday	**maandag**	**maan**dahkh
Tuesday	**dinsdag**	**dins**dahkh
Wednesday	**woensdag**	√**oons**dahkh
Thursday	**donderdag**	**don**derrdahkh
Friday	**vrijdag**	**vrai**ydahkh
Saturday	**zaterdag**	**zaa**terrdahkh
January	**abuari**	yahnew√**aari**
February	**februari**	fabrew√**aari**
March	**maart**	maart
April	**april**	ah**pril**
May	**mei**	maiy
June	**juni**	**yew**nee
July	**juli**	**yew**lee
August	**augustus**	o^{ow}**ghur**sturss
September	**september**	sehp**tehm**berr
October	**oktober**	ok**toa**berr
November	**november**	noa**vehm**berr
December	**december**	day**sehm**berr

NUMBERS, see page 30

Numbers *Getallen*

0	**nul**	nurl
1	**een**	ayn
2	**twee**	t√ay
3	**drie**	dree
4	**vier**	veer
5	**vijf**	vaif
6	**zes**	zehss
7	**zeven**	**zay**vern
8	**acht**	ahkht
9	**negen**	**nay**ghern
10	**tien**	teen
11	**elf**	ehlf
12	**twaalf**	t√aalf
13	**dertien**	**dehr**teen
14	**veertien**	**vayr**teen
15	**vijftien**	**vaiyf**teen
16	**zestien**	**zeh**steen
17	**zeventien**	**zay**vernteen
18	**achttien**	**ahkh**teen
19	**negentien**	**nay**ghernteen
20	**twintig**	t√**in**terkh
30	**dertig**	**dehr**terkh
40	**veertig**	**vayr**terkh
50	**vijftig**	**vaiyf**terkh
60	**zestig**	**zeh**sterkh
70	**zeventig**	**zay**vernterkh
80	**tachtig**	**tahkh**terkh
90	**negentig**	**nay**ghernterkh
100	**honderd**	**hon**derrt
1,000	**duizend**	dur^{ew}zernt
first	**eersste**	**ayr**ster
second	**tweede**	t√**ay**der
once/twice	**eenmaal/tweemaal**	**ayn**maal/t√**ay**maal
a half	**een helft**	ern hehlft

Emergency *In geval van nood*

Call the police	**Roep de politie**	roop der poa**leet**see
Get a doctor	**Roep een dokter**	roop ern **dok**terr
Go away	**Ga weg**	ghaa √ehkh
HELP	**HELP**	hehlp
I'm ill	**Ik ben ziek**	ik behn zeek
I'm lost	**Ik ben verdwaald**	ik behn verr**d√aalt**
LOOK OUT	**PAS OP**	pahss op
STOP THIEF	**HOUD DE DIEF**	ho^{ow} der deef

TELEPHONING, see page 28

My... has been stolen.	**Mijn... is gestolen.**	maiyn... iss gher**stoa**lern
I've lost my...	**Ik heb... verloren.**	ik hehp... verr**loa**rern
handbag	**mijn handtas**	maiyn **hahn**ttahss
wallet	**mijn portefeuille**	maiyn porter**fur**^{ew}yer
passport	**mijn paspoort**	maiyn **pahs**poort
luggage	**mijn bagage**	maiyn baag**haa**zher
Where can I find a doctor who speaks English?	**Waar kan ik een dokter vinen die Engels spreekt?**	√aar kahn ik ern **dok**terr **vin**dern dee **ehng**erlss spraykt

Guide to Dutch pronunciation *Uitspraak*

Consonants

Letter	Approximate pronunciation	Symbol	Example	
f, h, k, l, m, n, p, q, t, u, v, y, z	as in English			
b	as in but; at the end of a word, like p in cup	b p	**ben** **hep**	behn hehp
c	1) like k in keen 2) before e, i, like s in sit	k s	**inclusief** **ceintuur**	in**klew**seef sehn**tewr**
ch	1) like ch in loch 2) like sh in shut	kh sh	**nacht** **cheque**	nahkht shehk
d	as in English, but, at the end of a word, like t in hit	d t	**doe** **avond**	doo aa**vont**
g	1) like ch in loch 2) like s in pleasure 3) like a softer voiced version of ch in loch	kh zh gh	**deeg** **genie** **groot** **zagen**	daykh zher**nee** ghroat **zaag**hern
j	1) like y in yes 2) like s in leisure	y zh	**ja** **jumeaux**	yaa zhew**mo**^{ow}
nj	like ñ in Spanish señor	ñ	**oranje**	oa**rah**ñer
r	always trilled	r	**warm**	√ahrm
sj, stj	like sh in shut	sh	**misje**	**maiy**sher
th	like t in tea	t	**thee**	tay
tj	like ty in hit you	ty	**katje**	**kah**tyer
v	as in English, but often sounds like f	v	**hoeveel** **van**	hoo**vay** vahn
w	like English v, but with the bottom lip raised	√	**water**	√**aa**terr

Vowels

a	1) when short, between a in cat and u in cut	ah	**kat**	kaht
	2) when long, like a in cart	aa	**vader**	**vaa**derr
e	1) short, like e in bed	eh	**bed**	beht
	2) long, like a in late	ay	**zee**	zay
	3) like er in other	er	**zitten**	zittern
eu	like ur in fur, but pronounced with rounded lips	ur	**deur**	durr
i	1) short, like i in bit	i	**kink**	kint
	2) when long (also spelt ie), like ee in bee	ee	**zien**	zeen
	3) like er in other	er	**monnik**	**mon**nerk
ij	sometimes, like er in other	er	**lelijk**	**lay**lerk
o	1) when short, like a very short version of aw in lawn	o	**pot**	pot
	2) when long, something like oa in road	oa	**boot**	boat
oe	(long) like oo in moon and well rounded	oo	**hoe**	hoo
u	1) when short, like ur in hurt, with rounded lips	ur	**bus**	burss
	2) when long, like u in French sur; say ee, and, without moving your tongue, round your lips	ew	**nu**	new

Diphthongs

ai	like igh in sigh	igh	**ai**	igh
ei, ij	between a in late and igh in sigh	aiy	**reis**	raiyss
			ijs	aiyss
au, ou	like ow in now	o^{ow}	**koud**	ko^{ow}t
ieuw	like ee in free, followed by a short oo sound	ee^{oo}	**nieuw**	nee^{oo}
ui	like ur in hurt followed by a Dutch u sound, as described in u 2), but shorter	ur^{ew}	**huis**	hur^{ew}ss
uw	like the sound described in u 2), followed by a weak oo sound	ew^{oo}	**duw**	dew^{oo}

Finnish

Basic expressions *Perusilmaisut*

Yes/No.	**Kyllä/Ei.**	kewllæ/ayⁱ
Please.	**Olkaa hyvä.**	oalkaa hewvæ
Thank you.	**Kiitos.**	keetoass
I beg your pardon?	**Anteeksi?**	ahntāyksi

Introductions *Esittely*

Good morning.	**(Hyvää) huomenta.**	(hewvææ) h°amayntah
Good afternoon.	**(Hyvää) päivää.**	(hewvææ) pæⁱvææ
Good night.	**Hyvää yötä.**	hewvææ ᵉʷurtæ
Good-bye.	**Näkemiin.**	nækaymeen
Hello/Hi!	**Hei/Terve!**	hayⁱ/tayrvay
My name is...	**Nimeni on...**	nimmayni oan
What's your name?	**Mikä teidän nimenne on?**	mikkæ tayⁱdæn nimmaynnay oan
Pleased to meet you.	**Hauska tutustua.**	hah°°skah tootoostooah
How are you?	**Mitä kuuluu?**	mittæ kōōlōō
Very well, thanks. And you?	**Kiitos, hyvää. Entä sinulle?**	keetoass hewvææ. ayntæ sinnoollay
Where do you come from?	**Mistä päin tulette?**	mistæ pæⁱn toolayttay
I'm from...	**Olen...-sta/...-lta**	oalayn...-stah/...-ltah
Australia	**Australia**	ah°°straaliah
Canada	**Kanada**	kahnahdah
Great Britain	**Iso-Britannia**	isoa-britahnniah
United States	**USA (Yhdysvallat)**	ōōæssaa (ewhdewsvahllaht)
I'm with my...	**Minulla on mukana...**	minnoollah oan mookahnah
wife	**vaimo**	vahⁱmoa
husband	**aviomies**	ahvioamⁱays
family	**perhe**	payrhay
boyfriend	**poikaystävä**	poaⁱkahewstævæ
girlfriend	**tyttöystävä**	tewtturewstævæ
I'm here on business/ vacation.	**Olen täällä liike/ lomalla.**	oalayn tǣllæ leekay/ loamahllah

GUIDE TO PRONUNCIATION/EMERGENCIES, see page 47

Suomi

Questions *Kysymyksiä*

When?/How?	**Milloin?/Kuinka?**	milloa'n/koo'nkah
What?/Why?	**Mitä?/Miksi?**	mittæ/miksi
Who?	**Kuka?**	kookah
Which?	**Mikä?/Kumpi?**	mikkæ/koompi
Where is/are...?	**Missä on/ovat...?**	missæ oan/oavaht
Where can I find/get...?	**Mistä löydän...?**	mistæ lur^{ew}dæn
How far?	**Kuinka kaukana?**	koo'nkah kah^{oo}kanah
How long (time)?	**Kuinka kauan?**	koo'nkah kah^{oo}ahn
How much/many?	**Kuinka paljon/monta?**	koo'nkah pahlyoan/moantah
Can I have...?	**Saanko...?**	saahnkoa
Can you help me?	**Voitteko auttaa minua?**	voa'ttaykoa ah^{oo}ttaa minnooah
What does this/that mean?	**Mitä tämä/tuo tarkoittaa?**	mittæ tæmæ/t^{oo}oa tahrkoa'ttaa
I understand.	**Ymmärrän.**	ewmmærræn
I don't understand.	**En ymmärrä.**	ayn ewmmærræ
Can you translate this for us?	**Voitteko kääntää tämän meille?**	voa'ttaykoa kæntæ tæmæn may'llay
Do you speak English?	**Puhutteko englantia?**	poohoottaykoa aynglahntiah
I don't speak (much) Finnish.	**En puhu (paljon) suomea.**	ayn poohoo (pahlyoan) s^{oo}oamayah

A few more useful words *Muutama hyödyllinen sana lisää*

better/worse	**parempi/huonompi**	pahraympi/h^{oo}oanoampi
big/small	**suuri/pieni**	soori/p'ayni
cheap/expensive	**halpa/kallis**	hahlpah/kahlliss
early/late	**aikainen/myöhäinen**	ah'ka'nayn/m^{ew}urhæ'nayn
good/bad	**hyvä/huono**	hewvæ/h^{oo}oanoa
hot/cold	**kuuma/kylmä**	kōomah/kewlmæ
near/far	**lähellä/kaukana**	læhayllæ/kah^{oo}kahnah
right/wrong	**oikea/väärä**	oa'kaya/væræ
vacant/occupied	**vapaa/varattu**	vahpaa/vahrahttoo

Hotel—Accommodation *Hotelli*

I have a reservation.	**Minulla on varaus.**	minnoollah oan **vahra**°°s
We've reserved 2 rooms.	**Olemme varanneet kaksi huonetta.**	oalaymmay **vah**rahnnayt **kahk**si h°°oanayttah
Do you have any vacancies?	**Onko teillä vapaita huoneita?**	**oan**koa tay'llæ vahpah'tah h°°oanay'tah
I'd like a...	**Haluaisin...**	**hah**looah'sin
single room	**yhden hengen huoneen**	**ewh**dayn **hayn**gayn h°°oan**ayn**
double room	**kahden hengen huoneen**	**kahh**dayn **hayn**gayn h°°oan**ayn**
with twin beds	**jossa on kaksi vuodetta**	**yaos**sah oan **kahk**si v°°oadayttah
with a double bed	**jossa on kaksoisvuode**	**yaos**sah oan **kahk**soa'sv°°oaday
with a bath	**jossa on kylpyhuone**	**yaos**sah oan **kewl**pewh°°oanay
with a shower	**jossa on suihku**	**yaos**sah oan **soo'h**koo
We'll be staying...	**Viivymme...**	**vee**vewmmay
overnight only	**vain yhden yön**	vah'n **ewh**dayn ᵉʷurn
a few days	**muutamia päiviä**	**mōō**tahmiah pæ'viæ
a week	**viikon**	**vee**koan
Is there a camp site near here?	**Onko lähellä leirin-täaluetta?**	**oan**koa læhayllæ lay'rintæahlooayttah

Decision *Päätös*

May I see the room?	**Saanko nähdä huoneen?**	**saan**koa **næh**dæ h°°oan**ayn**
That's fine. I'll take it.	**Tämä on hyvä. Otan sen.**	**tæ**mæ oan **hew**væ. **oa**tahn sayn
No. I don't like it.	**Ei. En pidä siitä.**	ay' ayn **pi**dæ **see**ttæ
It's too... dark/small	**Se on liian... pimeä/pieni**	say oan **lee**ahn **pimm**ᵉʸæ/p'ay**ni**
Do you have anything...?	**Onko teillä mitään...?**	**oan**koa tay'llæ mittæn
better	**parempaa**	**pah**raympaa
bigger	**suurempaa**	**sōō**raympaa
cheaper	**halvempaa**	**hahl**vaympaa
quieter	**rauhallisempaa**	rah°°**hahl**lissaympaa
May I have my bill?	**Saisinko laskuni?**	**sah'**sinkoa **lahs**kooni
It's been a very enjoyable stay.	**Olen viihtynyt erinomaisesti.**	**oa**layn **veeh**tewnewt ayrinoamah'saysti

NUMBERS, see page 46

Eating out *Ravintolat*

I'd like to reserve a table for 4. — **Varaisin pöydän neljälle.** — vahrahisin p^{w}ewdæn nayljællay

We'll come at 8. — **Tulemme kello 8.** — toolaymmay kaylloa kahhdayksahn

I'd like breakfast/lunch/dinner. — **Saisinko aamiai-sen/lounas/päiväl-linen.** — sah^{i}sinkoa aamiah^{i}ssayn/loa^{oo}nahss/pæ^{i}vællinnayn

What do you recommend? — **Mitä suositteli-sitte?** — mittæ s^{oo}oasittaylissittay

Do you have any vegetarian dishes? — **Onko teillä kas-vissyöjän annok-sia?** — oankoa tay^{i}llæ kahsvissew^{ur}yæn ahnnoaksiah

Breakfast *Aamiainen*

I'd like... — **Saisinko...** — sah^{i}sinkoa

bread/butter — **leipää/voita** — lay^{i}pää/voa^{i}tah

cheese — **juustoa** — y^{oo}stoaah

eggs — **munia** — mooniah

ham and eggs — **kinkkua ja munia** — kinkkooah yah mooniah

jam/rolls — **hilloa/sämpylöitä** — hilloah/sæampewlur^{i}tæ

Starters (Appetizers) *Alkuruokia*

kaviaaria	kahv^{i}aariah	caviar
leikkeleitä	lay^{i}kkaylaytæ	cold meats
lohta	loahtah	salmon
mätiä	mætiæ	roe
parsaa	pahrsaa	asparagus
poronkieltä	poaroank^{i}ayltæ	reindeer tongue
silakoita	sillahkoa^{i}tah	Baltic herring

baked	**uunissa paistettu**	ōōnissah pah^{i}stayttoo
boiled	**keitetty**	kay^{i}tayttew
fried/grilled	**paistettu/grillattu**	pah^{i}stayttoo/grillahttoo
roast	**paahdettu**	paahdayttoo
stewed	**muhennokseksi keitetty**	moohaynnoaksayksi kay^{i}tayttew
underdone (rare)	**puolikypsä**	p^{oo}oalikewpsæ
medium	**keski-kypsä**	kayski-kewpsæ
well-done	**hyvin/kypsäksi paistettu**	hewvin/kewpsæksi pah^{i}stayttoo

Meat *Liharuokia*

beef	**naudanlihaa**	nah°°dahnlihaa
chicken/duck	**kana/ankka**	kahna/ahnkkah
lamb	**lammasta**	lahmmahstah
pork	**porsaanlihaa**	poarsaanlihaa
veal	**vasikanlihaa**	vahsikkahnlihaa
hirvenliha	hirvaynlihah	elk
karhunpaisti	kahrhoonpah'sti	bear steak
palapaisti	pahlahpah'sti	beef ragout
piparjuuriliha	pippahyōōrilihah	boiled beef with horse-radish sauce
poronkäristys	poaronkæristewss	sautéed reindeer stew
poronliha	poaroanlihah	reindeer meat

Vegetables and salads *Vihanneksia ja salaatteja*

beans	**pavut**	pahvoot
cabbage	**kaali**	kaali
carrots	**porkkanat**	poarkkahnaht
cauliflower	**kukkakaali**	kookkahkaali
lettuce	**lehtisalaatti**	layhtisahlaatti
mushrooms	**sieni**	ŝayni
onions	**sipulit**	sippoolit
peas	**herneit**	hayrnāyt
potatoes	**perunat**	payroonaht
tomatoes	**tomaattit**	toamaattit
hapankaalisalaatti	hahpahnkaalisahlaatti	sauerkraut salad
perunalaatikko	payroonahlaatikkoa	potato bake
pinaattiohukaiset	pinnaattioahookah'sayt	spinach pancakes
porkkanaohukaiset	poarkkahnahoa-hookah'sayt	carrot pancakes
rosolli	roasoalli	beetroot salad with salt herring

Fruit and desserts *Hedelmiä ja jälkiruokia*

apple	**omena**	oamaynah
banana	**banaani**	bahnaani
cherries	**kirsikat**	keersikkaht
lemon	**sitruuna**	sitrōōnah
orange	**appelsiini**	ahppaylseeni
peach	**persikka**	payrsikkah
pear	**päärynä**	pǣrewnæ
plums	**luumut**	lōōmoot
strawberries	**mansikat**	mahnsikkaht

jäätelö	yæetaylur	ice-cream
marengit	mahrayngit	meringues
mustikkapiirakka	moostikkahpeerahkkah	bilberry pie
omenapiirakka	oamaynahpeerahkah	apple pie
suklaakakku	sooklaakahkkoo	chocolate cake
vohvelit	voahvaylit	waffles

Drinks *Juomia*

beer	olut	oaloot
(hot) chocolate	kaakao	kaahkahoa
coffee	kahvi	kahhvi
black	mustana	moostahnah
with milk	maidon kanssa	mahˈdoan kahnssah
fruit juice	hedelmämehu	haydaylmæmayhoo
milk	maito	mahˈto
mineral water	mineraalivesi	minnayraalivaysi
sugar	sokeria	soakayriah
tea	tee	tāy
wine	viini	veeni
red/white	puna/valko	poonah/vahlkoa

Complaints—Bill (check) *Valituksia—Lasku*

This is too ...	Tämä on liian ...	tæmæ oan leeahn
bitter/salty	kitkerää/suolaista	kitkayrǣ/sᵒᵒalahˈstah
sweet	makeaa	mahkayaa
That's not what I ordered.	Tämä ei ole sitä, mitä tilasin.	tæmæ ayˈ oalay sittæ mittæ tillahsin
I'd like to pay.	Haluaisin maksaa.	hahlooahˈsin mahksaa
I think there's a mistake in this bill.	Tässä laskussa taitaa olla virhe.	tæssæ lahskoossah tahˈtaa oallah veerhay
Is everything included?	Sisältyykö siihen kaikki?	sissæltēwkur seehayn kahˈkki
Can I pay with this credit card?	Voinko maksaa tällä luottokortilla?	voaˈnkoa mahksaa tællæ lᵒᵒattoakoartilla
We enjoyed it, thank you.	Kiitos, pidimme siitä kovasti.	keetoass piddimmay seetæ koavahsti

NUMBERS, see page 46

Travelling around *Kulkuneuvot*

Plane *Lento*

Is there a flight to Ivalo?	**Onko lentoa Ivaloon?**	oankoa layntoah ivvahlo͞an
What time should I check in?	**Mihin aikaan minun on ilmoit-tauduttava?**	mihin ah'kaahn minnoon oan ilmoa'ttah°°doottahvah
I'd like to... my reservation.	**Haluaisin... varaukseni.**	hahlooa'siin... vahrahooksayn
cancel	**peruuttaa**	payro͞ottaa
change	**muuttaa**	mo͞ottaa
confirm	**vahvistaa**	vahhvistaa

Train *Juna*

I'd like a ticket to Pori.	**Saisinko lipun Poriin.**	sah'sinkoa lippoon poareen
single (one-way)	**menolippu**	maynoalippoon
return (round trip)	**menopaluu**	maynoapahlo͞o
first/second class	**ensimmäinen/ toinen luokka**	aynsimmæ'nayn/toanayn l°°oakkah
How long does the journey (trip) take?	**Kuinka kauan matka kestää?**	koo'nkah kah°°ahn mahtkah kaystǣ
When is the... train to Tampere?	**Milloin Tampe-reelle lähtee... juna?**	milloa'n tampayrǣyllay læhtǣy... yoonah
first	**ensimmäinen**	aynsimmæ'nayn
last/next	**viimeinen/seuraava**	veemay'nayn/say°°raavah
Is this the right train to Tampere?	**Onko tämä Tampe-reen juna?**	oankoa tæmæ tahmpayrǣyn yoonah

Bus—Tram (streetcar) *Bussi—Raitiovaunu*

Which tram (streetcar) goes to the town centre?	**Mikä raitiovaunu menee kaupungin keskustaan?**	mikkæ rah'tioavah°°noo maynǣy kah°°poongin kayskoostaan
How much is the fare to...?	**Mitä on maksu ...-n/...-lle?**	mittæ oan mahksoo ...-n/...-llay
Will you tell me when to get off?	**Sanoisitteko, kun minun täytyy nousta pois?**	sahnoa'sittaykoa koon minnoon tæ°ᵂtēw noa°°stah poais

TELLING THE TIME, see page 45

Taxi *Taksi*

What's the fare to...?	... – Mitä maksaa ajaa sinne?	mittæ mahksaa ahyaa sinnay
Take me to this address.	Viekää minut tähän osoitteeseen.	v¹aykǣ minnoot tæhæn oasoa¹ttǣyssǣyn
Please stop here.	Pysähtykää tässä.	pewssæhtewkǣ tæssæ
Could you wait for me?	Voitteko odottaa?	voa¹ttaykoa oadoattaa

Car hire (rental) *Auton vuokraus*

I'd like to hire (rent) a car.	Haluaisin vuokrata auton.	hahlooah¹sin v°°oakrahtah ah°°toan
I'd like it for a day/a week.	Haluaisin sen päiväksi/viikoksi.	hahl°°ah¹sin sayn pæ¹væksi/veekoaksi
Where's the nearest filling station?	Missä on lähin bensiiniasema?	missæ oan læhin baynseeniahsaymah
Fill it up, please.	Tankki täyteen, kiitos.	tahnkki tæ°ᵉʷtǣyn keetoass
Give me... litres of petrol (gasoline).	Saanko... litraa bensiiniä.	saankoa... litraa baynseeniæ
How do I get to...?	Miten pääsen...-n/...-lle?	mitayn pǣsayn...-n/...-llay
I've had a break-down at...	Autoni meni epä-kuntoon...-n koh-dalla.	a°°toani mayni aypækoontōan...-n koahdahllah
Can you send a mechanic?	Voitteko lähettää korjaajan?	voa¹ttaykoa læhayttǣ koaryaayahn
Can you mend this puncture (fix this flat)?	Voitteko korjata tämän renkaan?	voa¹ttaykoa koaryahtah tæmæn raynkaahn

---

Olette väärällä tiellä.	You're on the wrong road.
Ajakaa suoraan eteenpäin.	Go straight ahead.
Se on tuolla vasemmalla/oikealla.	It's down there on the left/right.
Vastapäätä (...-a/...-ta/...-tta)/ ...-n takana	opposite/behind...
...-n vieressä/...-n jälkeen	next to/after...
pohjoisessa/etelässä	north/south
idässä/lännessä	east/west

Sightseeing *Kiertoajelu*

Where's the tourist office?	**Missä on matkatoimisto?**	missæ oan...mahtkahtoa'mistoa
Is there an English-speaking guide?	**Onko siellä englantia puhuva opas?**	oankoa s'ayllæ aynglahntiah poohoovah oapahss
Where is/are the...?	**Missä on/ovat...?**	missæ oan/oavaht
botanical gardens	**kasvitieteellinen puutarha**	kahsvit'aytayllinnayn pōōtahrhah
castle	**linna**	linnah
cathedral	**tuomiokirkko**	t°°amioakeerkkoa
city centre/downtown	**keskusta**	kayskoostah
exhibition	**näyttely**	næ°ʷttaylew
harbour	**satama**	sahtahmah
market	**(kauppa)tori**	(kah°°ppah)toari
museum	**museo**	moossayoa
shopping area	**ostoskeskus**	oastoaskayskooss
square	**tori**	toari
tower	**torni**	toarni
zoo	**eläintarha**	aylæ'ntahrhah
What are the opening hours?	**Mitkä ovat aukioloajat?**	mitkæ oavaht ah°°kioaloaahyaht
When does it close?	**Milloin se suljetaan?**	milloa'n say soolyaytaan
How much is the entrance fee?	**Mikä on pääsymaksu?**	mikkæ oan pæēsewmahksoo

Relaxing *Virkistyminen*

What's playing at the ... Theatre?	**Mitä ... -teatterissa esitetään?**	mittæ ... tayahttayrissah ayssittaytǣn
Are there any seats for tonight?	**Onko täksi illaksi paikkoja?**	oankoa tæksi illahksi pah'kkoayah
Would you like to go out with me tonight?	**Lähtisit(te)kö kansani ulos tänä iltana?**	læhtissit(tay)kur kahnssahni ooloass tænæ iltahnah
Is there a discotheque in town?	**Onko tässä kaupungissa diskoa?**	oankoa tæssæ kah°°poongissah diskoaah
Would you like to dance?	**Haluaisitteko tanssia?**	hahlooah'sittaykoa tahnssiah
Thank you, it's been a wonderful evening.	**Kiitos, on ollut ihana ilta.**	keetoass oan oalloot ihhahnah iltah

TELLING THE TIME, see page 45

Shops, stores and services *Myymälät ja palvelut*

Where's the nearest...?	Missä on lähin...?	missæ oan læhin
baker's	leipomo	laypoamoa
bookshop	kirjakauppa	keeryuaka°°uppah
butcher's	lihakauppa	lihahka°°uppah
chemist's/drugstore	apteekki	ahptaykki
dentist	hammaslääkäri	hahmmahslækæri
department store	tavaratalo	tahvahrahtaloa
grocer's	sekatavarakauppa	saykahtahvahrahka°°uppah
hairdresser's/barber's	kampaaja/parturi	kahmpaayah/pahrtoori
market	tori	toari
newsstand	lehtikioski	layhtikioaski
post office	posti	poasti
supermarket	valintamyymälä	vahlintahmēwmælæ

General expressions *Yleisiä ilmauksia*

Where's the main shopping area?	Missä on tärkein ostosalue?	missæ oan tærkay'n oastoasahlooay
Do you have any...?	Onko teillä...-a?	oankoa tay'llæ...-a
Don't you have anything...?	Eikö teillä olisi jotain...?	aykur tay'llæ oalissi yoatah'n
cheaper	halvempaa	hahlvaympaa
better	parempaa	pahraympaa
larger	suurempaa	sōoraympaa
smaller	pienempää	p'aynaympǣ
Can I try it on?	Voinko sovittaa sitä?	voa'nkoa soavittaa sittæ
Where's the fitting room?	Missä on sovituskoppi?	missæ oan soavittooskoappi
How much is this?	Paljonko tämä maksaa?	pahl'yoankoa tæmæ mahksaa
Please write it down.	Voisitteko kirjoittaa.	voa'sittayko keeryoattaa
I don't want to spend more than... marks.	En halua maksaa enempää kuin... markkaa.	ayn hahlooah mahksaa aynaympǣ koo'n... mahrkkaa
No, I don't like it.	Ei, en pidä siitä.	ay' ayn piddæ seetæ
I'll take it.	Otan sen.	oatahn sayn
Do you accept credit cards?	Hyväksyttekö luottokortteja?	hewvæksewttaykur l°°oattoakoarttayyah
Can you order it for me?	Voitteko tilata sen minulle?	voa'ttaykoa tillahtah sayn minnoollay

NUMBERS, see page 46

black	mustaa	moostaa
blue	sinistä	sinnistæ
brown	ruskeata	rooskayahtah
green	vihreää	vihrayǣ
grey	harmaata	hahrmaahtah
orange	oranssia	oarahnssiah
red	punaista	poonah'stah
white	valkoista	vahlkoa'stah
yellow	keltaista	kayltah'stah
light...	vaalean...	vaalayahn
dark...	tumman...	toommahn

I'd like a/an/ some...	Haluaisin ...-n/-a	hahlooah'sin ...-n/-a
aspirin	aspiriinia	aahspireeniah
battery	pariston	pahristoan
bottle opener	pullonavaaja	poolloanahvaayah
bread	leipää	lay'pǣ
newspaper	sanomalehden	sahnoamahlayhdayn
American/English	amerikkalaisen/	ahmayrikkahlah'sayn/
	englantilaisen	aynglantillah'sen
postcard	postikortin	poastikoartin
shampoo	shampoota	shahmpoatah
soap	saippuaa	sa'ppooaa
sun-tan cream	aurinkovoidetta	ah°°rinkoavoa'dayttah
toothpaste	hammastahnaa	hahmmahstahhnaa
half-kilo of	puoli kiloa	p°°oali killoah
tomatoes	tomaatteja	toamaattayyah
a litre of milk	litran maitoa	litrahn mah'toah
I'd like a film for this camera.	Haluaisin filmin tähän kameraan.	hahlooah'sin filmin tæhæn kahmayraan
black and white	mustavalkoista	moostahvahlkoa'stah
colour	värillistä	værillistæ
I'd like a haircut, please.	Saisinko tukanleik-kuun.	sah'sinkoa tookahnlay'kk°°ōn

Souvenirs *Muistoesineitä*

candles	kyntillät	kewnttilæt
furs	turkikset	toorkiksayt
glass	lasi	lahsi
handicrafts	käsityöt	kæsit°ʷurt
reindeer hide	porontalja	poaroantahlyah
table linen	pöytä-ja lautaslii	pur°ʷtæ-yah
	nat	lah°°tahsleenaht

At the bank *Pankissa*

Where's the nearest bank/currency exchange office?	**Missä on lähin pankki/valuutan-vaihtopaikka?**	missæ oan læhin pahnkki/vahlōōtahnvah'h-toapaihkkah
I want to change some dollars/pounds.	**Haluaisin vaihtaa dollareita/puntia.**	hahlooah'sin vah'htaa doallahray'tah/poontiah
I want to cash a traveller's cheque.	**Haluaisin muuttaa matkasekin rahaksi.**	hahlooah'sin mōōttaa mahtkahshaykin rahhaahksi
What's the exchange rate?	**Mikä on vaihto-kurssi?**	mikkæ oan vah'htoakoorssi

At the post office *Posti*

I'd like to send this (by)...	**Lähettäisin tämän...**	læhayttæisin tæmæn
airmail express	**lentopostissa pikana**	layntoapoastissah pikkahnah
A... penni stamp, please.	**Saisinko... pennin postimerkin.**	sah'sinkoa... paynnin poastimayrkin
What's the postage for a postcard to Los Angeles?	**Mitä maksaa posti-kortti Los Angele-siin?**	mittæ mahksaa poastikoartti loas ahngaylaysseen
Is there any post (mail) for me? My name is...	**Onko minulle pos-tia? Nimeni on...**	oankoa minnoollay poastiah. nimmayni oan

Telephoning *Puhelut*

Where's the nearest telephone booth?	**Missä on lähin puhelinkioski?**	missæ oan læhin poohaylink'oaski
May I use your phone?	**Voinko käyttää puhelintanne?**	voa'nnkoa kæ⁰ʷttæ poohaylintahnnay
Hello. This is...	**Hei. Täällä...**	hay' tællæ
I'd like to speak to...	**Onko... tavatta-vissa.**	oankoa... tahvahttahvissah
When will he/she be back?	**Milloin hän palaa?**	milloa'n hæn pahlaa
Will you tell him/her I called?	**Kertoisitteko hänelle, että soitin.**	kayrtoa'sittaykoa hænayllaay ayttæ soa'tin

NUMBERS, see page 46

Time and date *Päivät ja päivämäärät*

It's...	Se on...	say oan
five past one	viittä yli yksi	veettæ ewli ewksi
a quarter past three	neljännestä/vartin yli kolme	naylyænnaystæ/vahrtin ewli koalmay
twenty past four	kahtakymmentä yli neljä	kahhtahkewmmayntæ ewli naylyæ
half past six	puoli seitsemän	p°°oali say'tsaymæn
twenty-five to seven	kahtakym- mentäviittä vaille seitsemän	kahhtahkewm- mayntæveettæ vah'llay say'tsaymæn
a quarter to nine	viisitoista minuttia vaille yhdeksän	veesitoa'stah minoottiah vah'llay ewhhdayksæn
ten to ten	kymmentä vaille kymmenen	kewmmayntæ va'llay kewmmaynayn
twelve o'clock	kaksitoista	kahksitoa'stah
in the morning	aamulla	aamoollah
in the afternoon/ evening	päivällä/illalla	pæ'vællæ/illahllah
during the day	päivällä	pæ'vællæ
at night	yöllä	ew'''llæ
yesterday/today	eilen/tänään	ay'layn/yænæn
tomorrow	huomenna	h°°oamaynnah
spring/summer	kevät/kesä	kayvæt/kayssæ
autumn/winter	syksy/talvi	sewksew/tahlvi

Sunday	sunnuntai	soonnoontah'
Monday	maanantai	maanahtah'
Tuesday	tiistai	teestah'
Wednesday	keskiviikko	kayskiveekkoa
Thursday	torstai	toarstah'
Friday	perjantai	payryahntah'
Saturday	lauantai	lah°°ahntah'
January	tammikuu	tahmmikk̄oo
February	helmikuu	haylmikōo
March	maaliskuu	maalisskōo
April	huhtikuu	hoohtikk̄oo
May	toukokuu	toa°°koak̄oo
June	kesäkuu	kayssæk̄oo
July	heinäkuu	hay'næk̄oo
August	elokuu	ayloak̄oo
September	syyskuu	sēwsk̄oo
October	lokakuu	loakahk̄oo
November	marraskuu	mahrrahsk̄oo
December	joulukuu	yoa°°look̄oo

NUMBERS, see page 46

Numbers *Luvut*

0	**nolla**	noallah
1	**yksi**	ewksi
2	**kaksi**	kahksi
3	**kolme**	koalmay
4	**neljä**	naylyæ
5	**viisi**	veessi
6	**kuusi**	kōōssi
7	**seitsemän**	say'tsaymæn
8	**kahdeksan**	kahhdayksahn
9	**yhdeksän**	ewhdayksæn
10	**kymmenen**	kewmmaynayn
11	**yksitoista**	ewksitoa'stah
12	**kaksitoista**	kahksitoa'stah
13	**kolmetoista**	koalmaytoa'stah
14	**neljätoista**	naylyætoa'stah
15	**viisitoista**	veessitoa'stah
16	**kuusitoista**	kōōssitoa'stah
17	**seitsemäntoista**	say'tsaymæntoa'stah
18	**kahdeksantoista**	kahhdayksahntoa'stah
19	**yhdeksäntoista**	ewhdayksæntoa'stah
20	**kaksikymmentä**	kahksikewmmayntæ
21	**kaksikym-** **mentäyksi**	kahksikewmmayntæewksi
30	**kolmekymmentä**	koalmaykewmmayntæ
40	**neljäkymmentä**	naylyækewmmayntæ
50	**viisikymmentä**	veessikewmmayntæ
60	**kuusikymmentä**	kōōssikewmmayntæ
70	**seitsemänkym-** **mentä**	say'tsaymænkewm- mayntæ
80	**kahdeksankym-** **mentä**	kahhdayksahnkewm- mayntæ
90	**yhdeksänkym-** **mentä**	ewhdayksænkewm- mayntæ
100	**sata**	sahtah
1000	**tuhat**	toohaht
1,000,000	**miljoona**	milyōōnah
1,000,000,000	**miljardi**	milyahrdi
first	**ensimmäinen**	aynsimmæinayn
second	**toinen**	toa'nayn
third	**kolmas**	koalmahss
once	**kerran**	kayrrahn
twice	**kahdesti**	kahhdaysti
a half	**puolikas**	p°°oalikkahs
a quarter	**neljäsosa**	naylyæsoassah
a third	**kolmasosa**	koalmahsoassah

TELEPHONING, see page 44

Emergency *Hätätilanne*

Call the police	**Kutsukaa poliisi**	kootsookaa **poa**leessi
Get a doctor	**Hakekaa lääkäri**	hahkaykaa **læ**kæri
Go away	**Menkää tiehenne**	maynkǣ t'aynaynnay
HELP	**APUA**	ahpooah
I'm ill	**Olen sairas**	oalayn sah'rahs
I'm lost	**Olen eksynyt**	oalayn ayksewnewt
Leave me alone	**Jättäkää minut rauhaan**	yættækǣ minnoot rah°°haan
LOOK OUT	**VAROKAA**	vahroakaa
STOP THIEF	**OTTAKAA VARAS KIINNI**	oattahkaa **vah**rahs **keen**ni
My... has been stolen.	**...-ni on varastettu**	-ni oan **vah**rahstayttoo
I've lost my...	**Olen kadottanut ...-ni.**	oalayn kahdoattahnoot ...-ni
handbag	**käsilaukku**	kæssilah°°kkooni
passport	**passi**	pahssi
wallet	**lompakko**	loampahkkoa
Where can I finid a doctor who speaks English?	**Mistä loytyisi lääkäri, joka puhuu englantia?**	mistæ lur°ʷtew'si lǣkæri yoakah poohōō aynglahntiah

Guide to Finnish pronunciation *Ääntäminen*

Consonants

Letter	Approximate pronunciation	Symbol	Example	
k, m, n, t, v	as in English			
d	as in rea**d**y, but sometimes very weak	d	**taide**	tah'day
g	in words of Finnish origin, only found after n; **ng** is pronounced as in si**ng**er	ng	**sangen**	sahngayn
h	as in **h**ot, whatever its position in the word	h	**lahti**	lahhti
j	like **y** in **y**ou	y	**ja**	yah
l	as in **l**et	l	**talo**	tahloa
r	always rolled	r	**raha**	rahhah

TELEPHONING, see page 44

| s | always as in set (never as in present) | s/ss | sillä kiitos | sillæ keetoass |

To make doubly sure that the Finnish s receives its correct pronunciation as s in English set, and not as a z sound in present, ss is often used in our phonetic transcriptions. Similarly, a double consonant is sometimes employed after i to ensure this is pronounced like i in pin, and not like i in kite. In these cases you can quickly check with the Finnish spelling whether you should pronounce a single or a double consonant.

Vowels

a	like a in car; short or long	ah aa	matala iltaa	mahtahlah iltaa
e	like a in late; but a pure vowel, not a diphthong; short or long	ay	kolme teevati	koalmay tāyvati
i	like i in pin (short) or ee in see (long); ir + consonant like i in pin (short)	i ee eer	takki siitä kirkko	tahkki seetæ keerkoa
o	a sound between aw in law and oa in coat; short or long	oa ōā	olla kookas	oallah kōākahss
u	like oo in pool; short or long	oo ōō	hupsu uuni	hoopsoo ōōni
y	like u in French sur or ü in German über; say ee as in see, and round your lips while still trying to pronounce ee; it can be short or long	ew ēw	yksi syy	ewksi sēw
ä	like a in hat; short or long	æ ǣ	äkkiä hyvää	ækkiæ hewvǣ
ö	like ur in fur, but without any r sound, and with the lips rounded; short or long	ur ūr	tyttö likööri	tewttur likkūrri

Dipthongs

In Finnish, dipthongs occur only in the first syllable of a word, except those ending in -i, where they can occur anywhere. They should be pronounced as a combination of the two vowel sounds. The phonetic transcription indicates which vowel should be pronounced louder.

French

Basic expressions *Expressions courantes*

Yes/No.	**Oui/Non.**	wee/nawng
Please.	**S'il vous plaît.**	seel voo pleh
Thank you.	**Merci.**	mehrsee
I beg your pardon?	**Pardon?**	pahrdawng

Introductions *Présentations*

Good morning.	**Bonjour.**	bawngzhoor
Good afternoon.	**Bonjour.**	bawngzhoor
Good night.	**Bonne nuit.**	bon nwee
Good-bye.	**Au revoir.**	oa rervwahr
My name is...	**Je m'appelle...**	zher mahpehl
Pleased to meet you.	**Enchanté(e).**	ahngshahngtay
What's your name?	**Comment vous appelez-vous?**	kommahng voo zahperlay voo
How are you?	**Comment allez-vous?**	kommahng tahlay voo
Fine thanks.	**Très bien, merci.**	treh byang mehrsee
And you?	**Et vous?**	ay voo
Where do you come from?	**D'où êtes-vous?**	doo eht voo
I'm from...	**Je viens...**	zher vyang
Australia	**de l'Australie**	der loastrahlee
Canada	**du Canada**	dew kahnahdah
Great Britain	**de la Grande-Bretagne**	der lah grahngd brertañ
United States	**des Etats-Unis**	day zaytah zewnee
I'm with my...	**Je suis avec...**	zher swee ahvehk
wife	**ma femme**	mah fahm
husband	**mon mari**	mawng mahree
family	**ma famille**	mah fahmeey
boyfriend	**mon ami**	mawng nahmee
girlfriend	**mon amie**	mawng nahmee
I'm here on business.	**Je suis en voyage d'affaires.**	zher swee zahng vwahyahzh dahfehr
I'm here on holiday (vacation).	**Je suis en vacances.**	zher swee zahng vahkahngss

GUIDE TO PRONUNCIATION, see page 63/EMERGENCIES, page 62

Questions *Questions*

When?	**Quand?**	kahng
How?	**Comment?**	kommahng
What?/Why?	**Quoi?/Pourquoi?**	kwah/poorkwah
Who?	**Qui?**	kee
Which?	**Lequel/Laquelle?**	lerkehl/lahkehl
Where is...?	**Où est/Où se trouve...?**	oo eh/oo ser troov
Where are...?	**Où sont/Où se trouvent...?**	oo sawng/oo ser troov
Where can I find/ get...?	**Où puis-je trouver...?**	oo pweezh troovay
How far?	**A quelle distance?**	ah kehl deestahngss
How long?	**Combien de temps?**	kawngbyang der tahng
How much/many?	**Combien?**	kawngbyang
Can I have...?	**Puis-je avoir...?**	pweezh ahvwahr
Can you help me?	**Pouvez-vous m'aider?**	poovay voo mehday
What does this/that mean?	**Que veut dire ceci/ cela?**	ker vur deer serssee/ serlah
I understand.	**Je comprends.**	zher kawngprahng
I don't understand.	**Je ne comprends pas.**	zher ner kangprahng pah
Can you translate this for me?	**Pouvez-vous me traduire ceci?**	poovay voo mer trahdweer serssee
Do you speak English?	**Parlez-vous anglais?**	pahrlay voo ahnggleh
I don't speak (much) French.	**Je ne parle pas (bien) français.**	zher ner pahrl pah (byang) frahngsseh

A few more useful words *Autres mots utiles*

better/worse	**meilleur/pire**	mehyurr/peer
big/small	**grand/petit**	grahng/pertee
cheap/expensive	**bon marché/cher**	bawng mahrshay/sherhr
early/late	**tôt/tard**	toa/tahr
good/bad	**bon/mauvais**	bawng/moaveh
hot/cold	**chaud/froid**	shoa/frwah
near/far	**près/loin**	preh/lwang
old/new	**ancien/nouveau**	ahngssyang/noovoa
right/wrong	**juste/faux**	zhewst/foa
vacant/occupied	**libre/occupé**	leebr/okkewpay

Hotel–Accommodation *Hôtel*

I have a reservation.	**J'ai fait réserver.**	zhay feh rayzehrvay
We've reserved 2 rooms.	**Nous avons réservé deux chambres.**	noo zahvawng rayzehrvay dur shahngbr
Do you have any vacancies?	**Avez-vous de chambres disponibles?**	ahvay voo day shahngbr deesponeebl
I'd like a... room	**Je voudrais une chambre...**	zher voodreh ewn shahngbr
single	**pour une personne**	poor ewn pehrson
double room	**pour deux personnes**	poor dur pehrson
with twin beds	**avec des lits jumeaux**	ahvehk day lee zhewmoa
with a double bed	**avec un grand lit**	ahvehk ang grahng lee
with a bath/shower	**avec salle de bains/douche**	ahvehk sahl der bang/doosh
We'll be staying...	**Nous resterons...**	noo rehsterrawng
overnight only	**juste cette nuit**	zhewst seht nwee
a few days	**quelques jours**	kehlker zhoor
a week	**une semaine**	ewn sermehn
Is there a camp site near here?	**Y a-t-il un camping près d'ici?**	ee ahteel ang kahngpeeng preh deessee

Decision *Décision*

May I see the room?	**Puis-je voir la chambre?**	pweezh vwahr lah shahngbr
That's fine. I'll take it.	**D'accord. Je la prends.**	dahkor. zher lah prahng
No. I don't like it.	**Non, elle ne me plaît pas.**	nawng ehl ner mer pleh pah
Do you have anything...?	**Avez-vous quelque chose...?**	ahvay voo kehlker shoaz
bigger	**de plus grand**	der plew grahng
cheaper	**de meilleur marché**	de mehyurr mahrshay
quieter	**de plus tranquille**	der plew trahngkeel
May I have my bill, please?	**Puis-je avoir ma note, s'il vous plaît?**	pweezh ahvwahr mah not seel voo pleh
It's been a very enjoyable stay.	**Le séjour a été très agréable.**	ler sayzhoor ah aytay treh zahgrayahbl

NUMBERS, see page 62

Eating out *Restaurant*

I'd like to reserve a table for 4.	**Je voudrais réserver une table pour 4 personnes.**	zher voodreh rayzehrvay ewn tahbl poor 4 pehrson
We'll come at 8.	**Nous viendrons à 8 heures.**	noo vyangdrawng ah 8 urr
I'd like ...	**Je voudrais ...**	zher voodreh
breakfast	**le petit déjeuner**	ler pertee dayzhurnay
lunch	**le déjeuner**	ler dayzhurnay
dinner	**le dîner**	ler deenay
What do you recommend?	**Que me recommandez-vous?**	ker mer rerkommahngday voo
Do you have any vegetarian dishes?	**Avez-vous des plats végétariens?**	ahvay voo day plah vayzhaytahryang

Breakfast *Petit déjeuner*

May I have some ...	**Pourrais-je avoir ...?**	poorehzh ahvwahr
bread	**du pain**	dew pang
butter	**du beurre**	dew burr
cheese	**du fromage**	dew fromahzh
ham and eggs	**des œufs au jambon**	day zur oa zhahngbawng
jam	**de la confiture**	der lah kawngfeetewr
rolls	**des petit pains**	da pertee pang

Starters *Hors-d'œuvre*

assiette anglaise	ahssyeht ahngglehz	assorted cold cuts
bouchée à la reine	boohsay ah lah rehn	pastry shell filled with sweetbreads
œufs à la diable	ur ah lah dyahbl	devilled eggs
pâté	pahtay	liver purée blended with other meats

Soups *Potages et soupes*

bisque	beesk	seafood chowder
consommé	kawngssommay	consommé
crème	krehm	cream
d'asperges	dahspehrzh	of asparagus
potage	potahzh	soup
au cresson	oa krehssawng	watercress
julienne	zhewlyehn	shredded vegetables
soupe à l'oignon	soop ah lonyawng	French onion soup

NUMBERS, see page 62

Fish and seafood *Poissons et fruits de mer*

cod	**morue**	morew
crab	**crabe**	krahb
frog's legs	**cuissses de grenouilles**	kweess der grernooy
mussels	**moules**	mool
oysters	**huîtres**	weetr
salmon	**saumon**	soamawng
snails	**escargots**	ehskahrgoa

baked	**au four**	oa foor
boiled	**bouilli**	booyee
fried	**frit**	free
grilled	**grillé**	greeyay
roast	**rôti**	roatee
stewed	**à l'étouffée**	ah laytoofay
underdone (rare)	**saignant**	sehñahng
medium	**à point**	ah pwang
well-done	**bien cuit**	byang kwee

Meat *Viande*

I'd like some...	**Je voudrais...**	zher voodreh
beef	**du boeuf**	dew burf
chicken/duck	**du poulet/canard**	dew pooleh/kahnahr
lamb	**de l'agneau**	der lahñoa
pork/veal	**du porc/veau**	dew por/voa
boeuf bourguignon	burf boorgeeñawng	rich beef stew with red burgundy wine
carbon(n)ade flamande	kahrbonnahd flahmahngd	beef slices with onions braised in beer
coq au vin	kok oa vang	chicken stewed in red wine

Vegetables *Légumes*

beans (French green)	**haricots verts**	ahreekoa vehr
carrots	**carottes**	kahrot
mushrooms	**champignons**	sshahngpeeñawng
onions	**oignons**	oñawng
peas	**petits pois**	pertee pwah
potatoes	**pommes (de terre)**	pom (der tehr)
truffles	**truffes**	trewf

Fruit and dessert *Fruits et desserts*

| apple | **pomme** | pom |
| cherries | **cerises** | serreez |

lemon	**citron**	seetrawng
orange	**orange**	orahngzh
pear	**poire**	pwahr
plums	**prunes**	prewn
strawberries	**fraises**	frehz
crêpe suzette	krehp sewzeht	thin pancakes in orange juice
gâteau au chocolat	gahtoa oa shokolah	chocolate cake
glace aux fraises/à la vanille	glahss oa frehz/ah lah vahneey	strawberry/vanilla ice-cream
tarte aux pommes	tahrt oa pom	apple tart (pie)

Drinks *Boissons*

beer	**une bière**	ewn byehr
(hot) chocolate	**un chocolat (chaud)**	ang shokolah (shoa)
coffee	**un café**	ang kahfay
black	**noir**	nwahr
with cream	**crème**	krehm
fruit juice	**un jus de fruits**	ang zhew der frwee
milk	**un lait**	ang leh
mineral water	**de l'eau minérale**	der loa meenayrahl
tea	**un thé**	ang tay
wine	**de vin**	der vang
red/white	**rouge/blanc**	roozh/blahng
a bottle	**une bouteille**	ewn bootehy
a glass	**un verre**	ang vehr

Complaints and paying *Réclamations et l'addition*

This is too...	**C'est trop...**	seh troa
bitter/sweet	**amer/sucré**	ahmehr/sewkray
salty	**salé**	sahlay
That's not what I ordered.	**Ce n'est pas ce que j'ai commandé.**	ser neh pah ser ker zhay kommahngday
I'd like to pay.	**L'addition, s'il vous plaît.**	lahdeessyawng seel voo pleh
I think there's a mistake in this bill.	**Je crois qu'il y a une erreur dans l'addition.**	zher krwah keel ee ah ewn ehrurr dahng lahdeessyawng
Can I pay with this credit card?	**Puis-je payer avec cette carte de crédit?**	pweezh pehyay ahvehk seht kahrt der kraydee
We enjoyed it, thank you.	**C'était très bon, merci.**	sayteh treh bawng mehrsee

NUMBERS, see page 62

Travelling around *Excursions*

Plane *Avion*

Is there a flight to...?	**Y a-t-il un vol pour...?**	ee ahteel ang vol poor
What time should I check in?	**A quelle heure est l'enregistrement?**	ah kehl urr eh lahng-rerzheestrermahng
I'd like to... my reservation.	**Je voudrais... ma réservation.**	zher voodreh... mah rayzehrvahssyawng
cancel	**annuler**	ahnnewlay
change	**changer**	shahnzhay
confirm	**confirmer**	kawngfeermay

Train *Train*

I'd like a ticket to...	**Je voudrais un billet pour...**	zher voodreh ang beeyeh poor
single (one-way)	**aller**	ahlay
return (round trip)	**aller-retour**	ahlay rertoor
first/second class	**première/deuxième classe**	prermyehr/durzyehm klahss
How long does the journey (trip) take?	**Combien de temps dure le trajet?**	kawnbyang der tahng dewr ler trahzheh
When is the... train to...?	**Quand part le... train pour...?**	kahng pahr ler... trang poor
first	**premier**	prermyay
next	**prochain**	proshang
last	**dernier**	dehrnyay
Is this the train to...?	**C'est bien le train pour..., n'est-ce pas?**	seh byang ler trang poor ... nehss pah

Bus–Tram (streetcar) *Bus–Tram*

Which tram goes to the town centre?	**Quel bus va au centre-ville?**	kehl boos vah oh sahngtr veel
How much is the fare to...?	**Quel est le prix du trajet jusqu'à...?**	kehl eh ler pree dew trahzheh zhewskah
Will you tell me when to get off?	**Pourriez-vous me dire quand je dois descendre?**	pooryay voo mer deer kahng zher dwah dehssahngdr

TELLING THE TIME, see page 61

Taxi *Taxi*

How much is the fare to...?	**Quel est le tarif pour...?**	kehl eh ler tahreef poor
Take me to this address.	**Conduisez-moi à cette adresse.**	kawngdweezay mwah ah seht ahdrehss
Please stop here.	**Arrêtez-vous ici, s'il vous plaît.**	ahrehtay voo eessee seel voo pleh
Could you wait for me?	**Pourriez-vous m'attendre?**	pooryay voo mahtahngdr

Car hire (rental) *Location de voitures*

I'd like to hire (rent) a car.	**Je voudrais une voiture.**	zher voodreh looay ewn vwahtewr
I'd like it for...	**Je l'utiliserai...**	zher lewteeleezerray
a day	**un jour**	ang zhoor
a week	**une semaine**	ewn sermehn
Where's the nearest filling station?	**Où est la station-service la plus proche?**	oo eh lah sstahssyawng sehrveess lah plew prosh
Full tank, please.	**Le plein, s'il vous plaît.**	ler plang seel voo pleh
Give me... litres of petrol (gasoline).	**Donnez-moi... litres d'essence.**	donnay mwah... leetr dehssahngss
How do I get to...?	**Comment-puis-je aller à...?**	kommahng pweezh ahlay ah
I've had a break-down at...	**Je suis tombé en panne à...**	zher swee tawngbay ahng pahn ah
Can you send a mechanic?	**Pouvez-vous envoyer un mécan-icien?**	poovay voo ahngvwahyay ang maykahneessyyang
Can you mend this puncture (fix this flat)?	**Pourriez-vous réparer ce pneu?**	pooryay voo raypahray ser pnur

---

Vous êtes sur la mauvaise route.	You're on the wrong road.
Allez tout droit.	Go straight ahead.
C'est là-bas à...	It's down there on the...
gauche/droite	left/right
à côté de/au-delà de...	next to/after...
nord/sud/est/ouest	north/south/east/west

EMERGENCIES, see page 62

Sightseeing *Visites touristiques*

Is there an English-speaking guide?	**Y a-t-il un guide qui parle anglais?**	ee ahteel ang geed kee pahrl ahnggleh
Where is...?	**Où se trouve...?**	oo ser troov
Where are...?	**Où se trouvent...?**	oo ser troov
botanical garden	**le jardin botanique**	ler zhahrdang bottahneek
castle	**le château**	ler shahtoa
cathedral	**la cathédrale**	lah kahtaydrahl
church	**l'église**	laygleez
city centre	**le centre (de la ville)**	ler sahngtr (der lah veel)
exhibition	**l'exposition**	lehxpozeessyawng
harbour	**le port**	ler por
market	**le marché**	ler mahrshay
museum	**le musée**	ler mewzay
shopping area	**le quartier commerçant**	ler kahrtyay kommehrssahng
square	**la place**	lah plahss
tower	**la tour**	lah toor
When does it open?	**A partir de quelle heure est-ce ouvert?**	ah pahrteer der kehl urr ehss oovehr
When does it close?	**Quelle est l'heure de fermeture?**	kehl eh lurr der fermertewr
How much is the entrance fee?	**Combien coûte l'entrée?**	kawngbyang koot lahngtray

Relaxing *Divertissements*

What's playing at the... Theatre?	**Que joue-t-on au théâtre...?**	ker zhootawng oa tayahtr
Are there any seats for tonight?	**Y a-t-il des place pour ce soir?**	ee ahteel day plahss poor ser swahr
How much are the seats?	**Combien coûtent les places?**	kawngbyang koot lay plahss
Would you like to go out with me tonight?	**Voulez-vous sortir avec moi ce soir?**	voolay voo sorteer ahvehk mwah ser swahr
Is there a discotheque in town?	**Y a-t-il une discothèque en ville?**	ee ahteel ewn deeskotehk ahng veel
Would you like to dance?	**Voulez-vous danser?**	voolay voo dahngssay
Thank you, it's been a wonderful evening.	**Merci, j'ai passé une merveilleusse soirée.**	mehrsee zhay pahssay ewn mehrvehyurz swahray

DAYS OF THE WEEK, see page 61/NUMBERS, see page 62

Shops, stores and services *Magasins et services*

Where's the nearest...?	**Où est... le/la plus proche?**	oo eh... ler/lah plew prosh
bakery	**la boulangerie**	lah boolahngzherree
bookshop	**la librairie**	lah leebrehree
butcher's	**la boucherie**	lah boosherree
chemist/drugstore	**la pharmacie**	lah fahrmahssee
dentist	**le dentiste**	ler dahngteest
department store	**le grand magasin**	ler grahng mahgahzang
grocery	**l'épicerie**	laypeesserree
hairdresser	**le coiffeur**	ler kwahfurr
newsagent	**le marchand de journaux**	ler mahrshahng de zhoornoa
post office	**le bureau de poste**	ler bewroa de post
supermarket	**le supermarché**	ler sewphrmahrshay
toilets	**les toilettes**	lay twahleht

General expressions *Expressions générales*

Do you have any...?	**Avez-vous...?**	ahvay voo
Can you show me this/that?	**Pouvez-vous me montrer ceci/cela?**	poovay voo mer mawngtray sersee/serlah
Haven't you anything...?	**N'auriez-vous pas quelque chose de...?**	noaryay voo pah kehlker shoaz der
cheaper	**meilleur marché**	mahyurr mahrshay
better	**mieux**	myur
larger	**plus grand**	plew grahng
smaller	**plus petit**	plew pertee
Can I try it on?	**Puis-je l'essayer?**	pweezh lehssehyay
How much is this?	**Combien coûte ceci?**	kawngbyang koot serssee
Please write it down.	**Pourriez-vous l'écrire, s'il vous plaît.**	pooryay voo laykreer seel voo pleh
I don't want to spend more than... francs.	**Je ne veux pas dépenser plus de ... francs.**	zher ner vur pah daypahngssay plew der ...frahng
No, I don't like it.	**Non, cela ne me plaît pas.**	nawng serlah ner mer pleh pah
I'll take it.	**Je le prends.**	zher ler prahng
Do you accept credit-cards?	**Acceptez-vous les cartes de crédit?**	ahksehptay voo lay kahrt der kraydee

NUMBERS, see page 62

black	**noir**	nwahr
blue	**bleu**	blur
brown	**brun**	brang
green	**vert**	vehr
orange	**orange**	orahngzh
red	**rouge**	roozh
yellow	**jaune**	zhoan
white	**blanc**	blahng
light...	**... clair**	klehr
dark...	**... foncé**	fawngssay

I want to buy a/an/some...	**Je voudrais acheter...**	zher voodreh ahshertay
aspirin	**de l'aspirine**	der lahspeereen
bottle-opener	**un ouvre-bouteilles**	ahng noovr bootehy
bread	**du pain**	dew pang
newspaper American/English	**un journal américain/ anglais**	ang zhoornahl amayreekang/ahnggleh
postcard	**une carte postale**	ewn kahrt postahl
shampoo	**du shampooing**	dew shahngpwang
soap	**du savon**	dew sahvawng
sun-tan cream	**de l'huile solaire**	der lweel solehr
toothpaste	**du dentifrice**	dew dahngteefreess
a half kilo of tomatoes	**un demi-kilo/une livre de tomates**	ang dermee keeloa/ewn leevr der tomaht
a litre of milk	**un litre de lait**	ang leetr der leh
I'd like a film for this camera.	**Je voudrais un film pour cet appareil.**	zher voodreh ang feelm poor seht ahpahrehy
black and white	**en noir et blanc**	ang nwahr ay blahng
colour	**en couleurs**	ang koolurr
I'd like a hair-cut, please.	**Un coup de cheveaux, s'il vous plaît.**	ewn koop de shervur seel voo pleh

Souvenirs *Souvenirs*

chocolate	**le chocolat**	ler shocolat
cuckoo clock	**le coucou**	ler kookoo
crystal	**le cristal**	ler kreestahl
lace	**les dentelles**	lay dahngtehl
perfume	**le parfum**	le pahrfang
tapestry	**la tapisserie**	lah tahpeesserree
women's top fashion	**la haute couture**	lah oat kootewr

At the bank A la banque

Where's the nearest bank/currency exchange office?	**Où est la banque/ bureau de change la plus proche?**	oo eh lah bahngk/ bewroa der shahngzh lah plew prosh
I want to change some dollars/pounds.	**Je voudrais chan- ger des dollars/ livres.**	zher voodreh shahngzhay day dollahr/leevr
What's the exchange rate?	**Quel est le cours du change?**	kehl eh ler koor dew shahngzh
I want to cash a traveller's cheque.	**Je désire toucher ce chèque de voyage.**	zher dayzeer tooshay ser shehk der vwahyahzh

At the post office A la poste

I want to send this by...	**Je voudrais envoyer ceci...**	zher voodreh ahngvwahyay sersee
airmail express	**par avion par exprès**	pahr ahvyawng pahr ehxprehss
I want... ...-centime stamps.	**Je voudrais...tim- bres à...centimes.**	zher voodreh...tangbr ah...sahngteem
What's the postage for a postcard/letter to United States?	**Quel est le tarif d'une carte pos- tale/lettre pour les Etats-Unis?**	kehl eh ler tahreef dewn kahrt postahl/lettre poor lay zaytah zewnee
Is there any post/mail for me? My name is...	**Y a-t-il du courrier pour moi? Je m'appelle...**	ee ahteel dew kooryay poor mwah. zher mahpehl

Telephoning Pour téléphoner

Where is the nearest telephone?	**Où se trouve le téléphone le plus proche?**	oo ser troov ler taylayfon ler plew prosh
May I use your phone?	**Puis-je utiliser votre téléphone?**	pweezh ewteeleezay votr taylayfon
Hello. This is...	**Allo. C'est...**	ahloa. seh
I'd like to speak to...	**Je désire parler à...**	zher dayzeer pahrlay ah
When will he/she be back?	**Quand sera-t-il/elle de retour?**	kahng serrah teel/tehl der rertoor
Will you tell him/her I called?	**Veuillez lui dire que j'ai appelé.**	vuryay lwee deer ker zhay ahperlay

Time and date *L'heure et date*

It's...	Il est...	eel eh
five past one	une heure cinq	ewn urr sangk
quarter past three	trois heures un quart	trwah zuur ang kahr
twenty past four	quatre heures vingt	kahtr urr vang
half past six	six heures et demie	see zurr ay dermee
twenty-five to seven	sept heures moins vingt-cinq	seht urr mwang vangt sangk
ten to ten	dix heures moins dix	dee zurr mwang deess
noon/midnight	midi/minuit	meedee/meenwee
in the morning	du matin	dew mahtang
in the afternoon	de l'après-midi	der lahpreh meedee
in the evening	du soir	dew swahr
during the day	pendant la journée	pahngdahng lah zhoornay
at night	la nuit	lah nwee
yesterday	hier	yehr
today	aujourd'hui	oazhoorwee
tomorrow	demain	dermang
spring/summer	le printemps/l'été	le prangtahng/laytay
autumn/winter	l'automne/l'hiver	loaton/leevehr

Sunday	dimanche	deemahngsh
Monday	lundi	langdee
Tuesday	mardi	mahrdee
Wednesday	mercredi	mehrkrerdee
Thursday	jeudi	zhurdee
Friday	vendredi	vahngdredee
Saturday	samedi	sahmdee
January	janvier	zhahngvyay
February	février	fayvreeyay
March	mars	mahrs
April	avril	ahvreel
May	mai	may
June	juin	zhwang
July	juillet	zhweeyeh
August	août	oot
September	septembre	sehptahngbr
October	octobre	oktobr
November	novembre	novahngbr
December	décembre	dayssahngbr

NUMBERS, see page 62

Numbers *Nombres*

0	**zéro**	zayroa
1	**un, une**	ang ewn
2	**deux**	dur
3	**trois**	trwah
4	**quatre**	kahtr
5	**cinq**	sangk
6	**six**	seess
7	**sept**	seht
8	**huit**	weet
9	**neuf**	nurf
10	**dix**	deess
11	**onze**	owngz
12	**douze**	dooz
13	**treize**	trehz
14	**quatorze**	kahtorz
15	**quinze**	kangz
16	**seize**	sehz
17	**dix-sept**	deess seht
18	**dix-huit**	deez weet
19	**dix-neuf**	deez nurf
20	**vingt**	vang
21	**vingt et un**	vang tay ang
30	**trente**	trahngt
40	**quarante**	kahrahngt
50	**cinquante**	sangkahngt
60	**soixante**	swahssahngt
70	**soixante-dix**	swahssahngt deess
80	**quatre-vingt**	kahtrer vang
90	**quatre-vingt-dix**	kahtrer vang deess
100	**cent**	sahng
1000	**mille**	meel
first	**premier (1er)**	prermyay
second	**deuxième (2e)**	durzyehm
once/twice	**une fois/deux fois**	ewn fwah/dur fwah
a half	**une moitié**	ewn mwahtyay

Emergency *Urgences*

Call the police	**Appelez la police**	ahperlay lah poleess
Get a doctor	**Appelez un méde-cin**	ahperlay ang maydssang
Go away	**Allez-vous-en**	ahlay voo zahng
HELP	**AU SECOURS**	oa serkoor
I'm ill	**Je suis malade**	zher swee mahlahd

TELEPHONING, see page 60

I'm lost	**Je me suis perdu(e)**	zher mer swee pehrdew
Leave me alone	**Laissez-moi tranquille**	lehssay mwah trahngkeel
LOOK OUT	**ATTENTION**	ahtahngssyawng
STOP THIEF	**AU VOLEUR**	oa volurr
My ... has been stolen.	**On m'a volé ...**	awng mah volay
I've lost my ...	**J'ai perdu ...**	zhay pehrdew
handbag	**mon sac à main**	mawng sahk ah mang
wallet	**mon portefeuille**	mawng portfury
passport	**mon passeport**	mawng pahsspor
luggage	**mes bagages**	may bahgahzh
Where can I find a doctor who speaks English?	**Où puis-je trouver un mèdecin qui parle anglais?**	oo pweezh troovay ang maydssang kee pahrl ahnggleh

Guide to French pronunciation *Prononciation*

Consonants

Letter	Approximate pronunciation	Symbol	Example	
b, c, d, f, k, l, m, n, p, s, t, v, x, z	as in English			
ch	like sh in shut	sh	**chercher**	shershay
ç	like s in sit	s	**ça**	sah
g	1) before e, i, y, like s in pleasure	zh	**manger**	mahngzhay
	2) before a, o, u, like g in go	g	**garçon**	gahrsawng
gn	like ni in onion	ñ	**ligne**	leeñ
h	always silent		**homme**	om
j	like s in pleasure	zh	**jamais**	zhahmeh
qu	like k in kill	k	**qui**	kee
r	rolled in the back of the mouth	r	**rouge**	roozh
w	usually like v in voice	v	**wagon**	vahgawng

Vowels

a, à, â	between the **a** in h**a**t and the **a** in f**a**ther	ah	**mari**	mahree
é, er, ez	like **a** in l**a**te	ay	**été**	aytay
è, ê, e	like **e** in g**e**t	eh	**même**	mehm
e	sometimes like **er** in oth**er** (quite short)	er	**je**	zher
i	like **ee** in m**ee**t	ee	**il**	eel
o	generally like **o** in h**o**t	o	**donner**	donner
	but sometimes as in wr**o**te	oa	**rose**	roaz
ô	like **o** in wr**o**te	oa	**Rhône**	roan
u	no equivalent in English. Round your lips and try to say **ee**	ew	**cru**	krew

Sounds spelt with two or more letters

ai, ay, ey	can be pronounced as **a** in l**a**te	ay	**j'ai**	zhay
aient, ais	like **e** in g**e**t	eh	**chaîne**	shehn
ait, aï, ei	like **e** in g**e**t	eh	**peine**	pehn
eu, eû, œu	like **ur** in f**ur**, but with lips rounded, not spread	ur*	**peu**	pur
oi, oy	like **w** followed by the **a** in h**a**t	wah	**moi**	mwah
ou, oû	like **oo** in l**oo**k	oo	**nouveau**	noovoa
ui	approximately like **wee** in bet**wee**n	wee	**traduire**	trahdweer

Nasal sounds

am, an, em, en	something like **arn** in t**arn**ish	ahng	**tante**	tahngt
ien	like **yan** in **yan**k	yang	**bien**	byang
im, in, aim, ain, eim, ein	like **ang** in r**ang**	ang	**instant**	angstahng
om, on	like **ong** in s**ong**	awng	**maison**	mayzawng
um, un	like **ang** in r**ang**	ang	**brun**	brang

---

*The **r** should not be pronounced when reading this transcription.

German

Basic expressions *Die ersten Worte*

Yes/No.	**Ja/Nein.**	yaa/nighn
Please.	**Bitte.**	**bit**ter
Thank you.	**Danke.**	**dahn**ker
I beg your pardon?	**Wie bitte?**	vee **bit**ter

Introductions *Vorstellen*

Good morning.	**Guten Morgen.**	**goo**tern **mor**gern
Good afternoon.	**Guten Tag.**	**goo**tern taag
Good night.	**Guten Abend.**	**goo**tern **aa**bernt
Good-bye.	**Auf Wiedersehen.**	owf **vee**derrzayern
My name is...	**Ich heiße...**	ikh **high**sser
Pleased to meet you.	**Sehr erfreut.**	zayr ehr**froyt**
What's your name?	**Wie heißen Sie?**	vee **high**ssern zee
How are you?	**Wie geht es Ihnen?**	vee gayt ehss **ee**nern
Fine thanks.	**Danke, gut.**	**dahn**ker goot
And you?	**Und Ihnen?**	unt **ee**nern
Where do you come from?	**Woher kommen Sie?**	voa**hayr kom**mern zee
I'm from...	**Ich bin aus...**	ikh bin owss
Australia	**Australien**	ow**straa**liern
Canada	**Kanada**	**kah**nahdah
Great Britain	**Großbritannien**	**groas**brittahniern
United States	**den Vereinigten Staaten**	dayn feh**righ**nigtern **shtaa**tern
I'm with my...	**Ich bin mit... hier.**	ikh bin mit... heer
wife	**meiner Frau**	**migh**nerr frow
husband	**meinem Mann**	**migh**nerm mahn
family	**meiner Familie**	**migh**nerr fah**mee**lier
boyfriend	**meinem Freund**	**migh**nerm froynt
girlfriend	**meiner Freundin**	**migh**nerr **froyn**din
I'm on my own.	**Ich bin allein hier.**	ikh bin ah**lign** heer
I'm here on business/vacation.	**Ich bin geschäftlich/auf Urlaub hier.**	ikh bin ger**shehft**likh/owf **oor**lowp heer

GUIDE TO PRONUNCIATION, see page 79/EMERGENCIES, page 78

Questions *Fragen*

When?	**Wann?**	vahn
How?	**Wie?**	vee
What?/Why?	**Was?/Warum?**	vahss/vah**rum**
Who?	**Wer?**	vayr
Which?	**Welcher/Welche/** **Welches?**	**vehl**kherr/**vehl**kher/ **vehl**kherss
Where is/are...?	**Wo ist/sind...?**	voa ist/zint
Where can I find/ get...?	**Wo finde/** **bekomme ich...?**	voa **fin**der/ber**kom**mer ikh
How far?	**Wie weit?**	vee vight
How long?	**Wie lange?**	vee **lahn**ger
How much?	**Wieviel?**	vee**feel**
How many?	**Wie viele?**	vee **fee**ler
Can I have...?	**Kann ich... haben?**	kahn ikh... **haa**bern
Can you help me?	**Können Sie mir** **helfen?**	**kur**nern zee meer **hehl**fern
What does that mean?	**Was bedeutet das?**	vahss ber**doy**tert dahss
I understand.	**Ich verstehe.**	ikh fer**shtay**er
I don't understand.	**Ich verstehe nicht.**	ikh fer**shtay**er nikht
Can you translate this for me?	**Könnten Sie mir** **das übersetzen?**	**kurn**tern zee meer dahss ewberr**zeht**sern
Do you speak English?	**Sprechen Sie** **Englisch?**	**shpreh**khern see **ehng**lish
I don't speak much German.	**Ich spreche kaum** **Deutsch.**	ikh **shpreh**kher kowm doych

A few more useful words *Weitere nützliche Wörter*

better/worse	**besser/schlechter**	**behs**serr/**shlehkh**terr
big/small	**groß/klein**	groass/klighn
cheap/expensive	**billig/teuer**	**bil**likh/**toy**err
early/late	**früh/spät**	frew/shpait
good/bad	**gut/schlecht**	goot/shlehkht
hot/cold	**heiß/kalt**	highss/kahlt
near/far	**nah/weit**	naa/vight
old/new	**alt/neu**	ahlt/noy
right/wrong	**richtig//falsch**	**rikh**tikh/fahlsh
vacant/occupied	**frei/besetzt**	frigh/ber**zehtst**

Hotel—Accommodation *Hotel*

I have a reservation.	**Ich habe reservieren lassen.**	ikh **haab**er rehzerr**vee**rern lahssern
We've reserved 2 rooms.	**Wir haben zwei Zimmer reservieren lassen.**	veer **haa**bern tsvigh **tsimm**err rehzerr**vee**rern **lah**ssern
Do you have any vacancies?	**Haben Sie noch freie Zimmer?**	**haa**bern zee nokh **frigh**er **tsimm**er
I'd like a...	**Ich hätte gern ein...**	ikh **heh**ter gehrn ighn
single room	**Einzelzmmer**	**ighn**tserltsimmerr
double room	**Doppelzimmer**	**dopp**erltsimmerr
with twin beds	**mit zwei Einzelbetten**	mit tsvigh **ighn**tserlbehtern
with a double bed	**mit einem Doppelbett**	mit **ighn**erm **dopp**erlbeht
with a bath/shower	**mit Bad/Dusche**	mit baat/**du**sher
We'll be staying...	**Wir bleiben...**	veer **bligh**bern
overnight only	**nur eine Nacht**	noor **igh**ner nakht
a few days	**einige Tage**	**igh**nigger **taa**ger
a week	**eine Woche**	**igh**ner **vo**kher
Is there a camp site near here?	**Gibt es hier in der Nähe einen Campingplatz?**	gipt ehss heer in derr **nai**er **igh**nern **kehm**pingplahts

Decision *Entscheidung*

May I see the room?	**Kann ich das Zimmer sehen?**	kahn ikh dahss **tsimm**er **zay**ern
That's fine. I'll take it.	**Gut, ich nehme es.**	goot ikh **nay**mer ehss
No. I don't like it.	**Nein, es gefällt mir nicht.**	nighn ehss ger**fehlt** meer nikht
It's too...	**Es ist zu...**	ehss ist tsu
dark/small	**dunkel/klein**	**dun**kerl/**klighn**
Do you have anything...?	**Haben Sie etwas...?**	**haa**bern see **eht**vahss
better/bigger	**Besseres/Größeres**	**beh**sserrerrs/**grurss**errerrs
cheaper	**Billiges**	**billig**errerrs
quieter	**Ruhiges**	**roo**iggerrerrs
May I have my bill, please?	**Kann ich bitte die Rechnung haben?**	kahn ikh **bitter** dee **rehkh**nung **haa**bern
It's been a very enjoyable stay.	**Es war ein sehr angenehmer Aufenthalt.**	ehss vaar ighn zayr **ahn**gernaymerr **owf**ehnthahlt

NUMBERS, see page 78

Eating out *Gaststätten*

I'd like to reserve a table for 4.	**Ich möchte einen Tisch für 4 Personen reservieren lassen.**	ikh murkhter ighnern tish fewr 4 pehrzoanern rehzehrveeerern lahssern
We'll come at 8.	**Wir kommen um 8 Uhr.**	veer kommern um 8 oor
I'd like...	**Ich hätte gern...**	ikh hehter gehrn
breakfast	**das Frühstück**	dahss frewshtewk
lunch	**das Mittagessen**	dahss mittahgehssern
dinner	**das Abendessen**	dahss aaberntehssern
What do you recommend?	**Was würden Sie mir empfehlen?**	vahss vewrdern zee meer ehmpfaylern
Do you have any vegetarian dishes?	**Haben Sie vegetarische Gerichte?**	haabern zee vehgehtaarisher gerrikhter

Breakfast *Frühstück*

May I have some...	**Kann ich... haben?**	kahn ikh... haabern
bread	**Brot**	broat
butter	**Butter**	butterr
cheese	**Käse**	kaizer
ham and eggs	**Spiegeleier mit Schinken**	shpeegerligherr mit shinkern
jam	**Marmelade**	mahrmehlaader
rolls	**Brötchen**	brurtkhern

Starters *Vorspeisen*

Appetithäppchen	ahpehteethehpkhern	canapés
Bismarckhering	bismahrkhayring	soused herring with onion
Hoppel-Poppel	hopperl-popperl	scrambled eggs with sausage or bacon
Käsehäppchen	kaizerhehpkhern	cheese sticks
Russische Eier	russisher igherr	boiled eggs with mayonnaise

Soups *Suppen*

Bauernsuppe	bowernzupper	cabbage and frankfurter soup
Fischsuppe	fishzuppper	fish soup
Hühnerbrühe	hewnerrbrewer	chicken broth
Labskaus	laapskowss	thick stew
Linsensuppe	linzernzupper	lentil soup
Schildkrötensuppe	shiltkrurternzupper	turtle soup

NUMBERS, see page 78

Fish and seafood *Fissch und Meeresfrüchte*

cod	**Kabeljau**	kaaberlow
lobster	**Hummer**	hummerr
mussels	**Muscheln**	musherln
oysters	**Austern**	owsterrn
plaice	**Scholle**	sholler
shrimp	**Garnelen**	gahrnaylern

baked	**gebacken**	gerbahkern
boiled	**gekocht**	gerkokht
fried	**gebraten**	gerbraatern
grilled	**gegrillt**	gergrilt
roasted	**gebraten**	gerbraatern
stewed	**gedämpft**	gerdehmpft
underdone (rare)	**blutig**	blootikh
medium	**mittel**	mitterl
well-done	**gut durchgebraten**	goot doorchgerbraatern

Meat *Fleisch*

I'd like some...	**Ich hätte gern ...**	ikh hehter gehrn
beef	**Rindfleisch**	rintflighsh
chicken/duck	**Huhn/Ente**	hoon/ehnter
lamb	**Lammfleisch**	lahmflighsh
pork	**Schweinefleisch**	shvighnerflighsh
veal	**Kalbfleisch**	kahlpflighsh

Bauernschmaus (bowernshmowsr)	saurkraut, bacon, sausage, dumplings and potatoes
Kohlroulade (koalroolaader)	cabbage leaves stuffed with minced meat

Würste	voorster	sausages
Bierwurst	beervoorst	smoked pork/beef
Bratwurst	braatvoorst	fried pork
Weißwurst	vighsvoorst	veal and bacon

Vegetables *Gemüse*

beans	**Bohnen**	boanern
cabbage	**Kohl**	koal
carrots	**Karotten**	kahrottern
mushrooms	**Pilze**	piltser
onions	**Zwiebeln**	tsveeberln
peas	**Erbsen**	ehrpsern
potatoes	**Kartoffeln**	kahrtofferln
tomatoes	**Tomaten**	tommaatern

Fruit and dessert *Obst und Nachtisch*

apple	**Apfel**	**ah**pferl
cherries	**Kirschen**	**keer**shern
lemon	**Zitrone**	tsi**troan**er
orange	**Aprikosen**	ahprek**koa**zern
pear	**Birne**	**beer**ner
strawberries	**Erdbeeren**	**ehrt**bayrern
-eis, -glace	-ighss -glahsser	ice-cream
Schwarzwälder-kirschtorte	**schvarts**vehlder-**keersh** torter	Black Forest gateau

Apfelstrudel
(**ah**pferlshtrooderl) — pastry filled with apple, nuts, raisins and jam

Hefekranz
(**hay**ferkrahnts) — ring shaped cake with almonds or candied fruit

Drinks *Getränke*

I'd like...	**Ich hätte gern...**	ikh **heh**ter gehrn
beer	**ein Bier**	ighn beer
(hot) chocolate	**eine (heiße) Schokolade**	**igh**ner (**high**sser) shokko**llaa**der
coffee	**einen Kaffee**	**igh**nern kah**fay**
with cream	**mit Sahne**	mit **zaa**ner
fruit juice	**einen Fruchtsaft**	**igh**nern frukh**t**zahft
(glass of) milk	**(ein Glas) Milch**	(ighn glaass) milkh
mineral water	**ein Mineralwasser**	ighn minner**raal**vahsserr
red/white wine	**Rotwein/Weißwein**	**roat**vighn/**vighs**vighn
tea	**einen Tee**	**igh**nern tay

Complaints and paying *Reklamationen und die Rechnung*

This is too...	**Das ist zu...**	dahss ist tsu
bitter/sweet	**bitter/süß**	**bitt**er/zewss
salty	**salzig**	**zahl**tsikh
That's not what I ordered.	**Das habe ich nicht bestellt.**	dahss **haa**ber ikh nikht ber**stehlt**
I'd like to pay.	**Ich möchte zahlen.**	ikh **murkh**ter **tsaa**lern
I think there's a mistake in this bill.	**Ich glaube, Sie haben sich verrechnet.**	ikh **glow**ber zee **haa**bern zikh fehr**rehkh**nert
Can I pay with this credit card?	**Kann ich mit dieser Kreditkarte bezahlen?**	kahn ikh mit **dee**zer kray**dit**kahrter ber**tsaa**lern
That was a very good meal.	**Das Essen war sehr gut.**	dahss **ehs**sern vaar zayr goot

NUMBERS, see page 78

Travelling around *Reisen im Lande*

Plane *Flugzeug*

Is there a flight to...?	**Gibt es einen Flug nach...?**	gipt ehss **igh**nern floog naakh
What time should I check in?	**Wann muß ich einchecken?**	vahn muss ikh **ighn**shehkern
I'd like to... my reservation.	**Ich möchte meine Reservierung...**	ikh **murkh**ter **migh**ner rehzer**vee**rung
cancel	**annullieren**	ahnul**lee**rern
change	**umbuchen**	**um**bookhern
confirm	**bestätigen**	ber**shtait**iggern

Train *Eisenbahn*

I'd like a ticket to...	**Ich möchte eine Fahrkarte nach...**	ikh **murkh**ter **igh**ner **faar**kahrter naakh
single (one-way)	**einfach**	**ighn**fahkh
return (round trip)	**hin und zurück**	hin unt stoo**rewk**
first/second class	**erste/zweite Klasse**	**ehr**ster/**tsvigh**ter **klah**sser
How long does the journey (trip) take?	**Wie lange dauert die Fahrt?**	vee **lahng**er **dow**errt dee faart
When is the... train to..?	**Wann fährt der... Zug nach...?**	vahn fairt derr... tsoog naakh
first/next	**erste/nächste**	**ehr**ster/**naikh**ster
last	**letzte**	**leht**ster
Is this the right train to...?	**Ist das der Zug nach...?**	ist dahss derr tsoog naakh

Bus–Tram (streetcar) *Bus–Straßenbahn*

Which tram goes to the town centre?	**Welche Straßenbahn fährt ins Stadtzentrum?**	**vehl**kher **shtraa**ssern-baan fairt ins **shtaht**tsehntrum
How much is the fare to...?	**Was kostet es nach...?**	vahss **ko**stert ehss naakh
Will you tell me when to get off?	**Könne Sie mir bitte sagen, wann ich aussteigen muß?**	**kur**nern zee meer **bit**ter **zaa**gern vahn ikh **ows**shtighgern muss

Taxi *Taxi*

What's the fare to...?	**Was kostet es bis...?**	vahss **ko**stert ehss biss

TELLING THE TIME, see page 77

GERMAN

Take me to this address.	Bringen Sie mich zu dieser Adresse.	bringern zee mikh tsoo deezer ahdrehsser
Please stop here.	Halten Sie hier, bitte.	hahltern zee heer bitter
Will you wait for me?	Würden Sie bitte auf mich warten?	vewrdern zee bitter owf mikh vahrtern

Car hire (rental) *Autoverleih*

I'd like to hire (rent) a car.	Ich möchte ein Auto mieten.	ikh murkhter ighn owto meetern
I'd like it for a a day/a week.	Ich möchte es für einen Tag/eine Woche.	ikh murkhter ehss fewr ighnern taag/ighner vokher
Where's the nearest filling station?	Wo ist die nächste Tankstelle?	voa ist dee naikhster tahnkshtehler
Fill it up, please.	Volltanken, bitte.	voltahnkern bitter
Give me... litres of petrol (gasoline).	Geben Sie mir... Liter Benzin.	gaybern zee mir... leeterr behntseen
Where can I find this address/place?	Wie komme ich zu dieser Adresse/ diesem Ort?	vee kommer ikh tsoo deezerr ahdrehsser/ deezerm ort
I've had a breakdown.	Ich habe eine Panne.	ikh haaber ighner pahner
Can you send a mechanic?	Können Sie einen Mechaniker schicken?	kurnern zee ighnern mehkhahnikkerr shikkern
Can you mend this puncture (fix this flat)?	Können Sie diesen Reifen flicken?	kurnern zee deezern righfern flikkern

---

Sie sind auf der falschen Straße.	You're on the wrong road.
Fahren Sie geradeaus.	Go straight ahead.
Es ist dort vorne ...	It's down there on the...
links/rechts	left/right
neben/nach ...	next to/after...
Nord/Süd/Ost/West	north/south/east/west

Deutsch

EMERGENCIES, see page 78

Sightseeing *Besichtigungen*

Is there an English-speaking guide?	**Gibt es einen englischsprechenden Fremdenführer?**	gipt ehss **igh**nern **ehng**lishshprehkherndern **frehm**dernfewrerr
Where is/are the...?	**Wo ist/Wo sind...?**	voa ist/voa zint
art gallery	**die Kunstgalerie**	derr **kunst**gahlehree
cathedral	**die Kathedrale/der Dom**	dee kahteh**draa**ler/derr doam
church	**die Kirche**	dee **keer**kher
city centre/downtown	**die Innenstadt**	dee **innern**shtaht
exhibition	**die Ausstellung**	dee **owss**shtehlung
market	**der Markt**	derr mahrkt
museum	**das Museum**	dahss mu**zay**um
shopping area	**das Geschäftsviertel**	dahss ger**shehfts**feerterl
square	**der Platz**	derr plahts
tower	**der Turm**	der toorm
zoo	**der Zoo**	derr tsoa
What are the opening hours?	**Welches sind die Öffnungszeiten?**	**vehl**kherss zint dee **urf**nungstsightern
When does it close?	**Wann schließt es?**	vahn shleest ehss
How much is the entrance fee?	**Was kostet der Eintritt?**	vahss **kost**ert derr **ighn**trit

Relaxing *Unterhaltung*

What's playing at the... Theatre?	**Was wird im ... Theater gegeben?**	vahss veert im ... tay**aa**terr ger**gay**bern
Are there any tickets for tonight?	**Gibt es noch Karten für heute abend?**	gipt ehss nokh **kahr**tern fewr **hoy**ter **aa**bernt
How much are the tickets?	**Wie teuer sind die Karten?**	vee **toy**terr zint dee **kahr**tern
Would you like to go out with me tonight?	**Möchten Sie heute abend mit mir ausgehen?**	**murkh**tern zee **hoy**ter **aa**bernt mit meer **ows**gayern
Is there a discoteque in town?	**Gibt es hier eine Diskothek?**	gipt ehss heer **igh**ner disko**tayk**
Would you like to dance?	**Möchten Sie tanzen?**	**murk**htern zee **tahn**tsern
Thank you, it's been a wonderful evening.	**Danke, es war ein wunderbarer Abend.**	**dahn**ker ehss vaar ighn **voon**derrbaarerr **aa**bernt

TELLING THE TIME, see page 77

Shops, stores and services *Geschäfte, Läden usw.*

Where's the nearest...?	**Wo is der/die/das nächste...?**	voa ist derr/dee/dahss naikhster
bakery	**die Bäckerei**	dee behkerrigh
bookshop	**die Buchhandlung**	dee bukhhahndlung
butcher's	**die Fleischerei/ Metzgerei**	dee flighsherrigh/ mehtsgerrigh
chemist's/drugstore	**die Apotheke**	dee ahpottayker
dentist	**der Zahnarzt**	derr tsaanahrtst
department store	**das Warenhaus**	dahss vaarernhowss
grocery	**das Lebensmittel- geschäft**	dahss laybernsmitterl- gershehft
hairdresser (ladies/ men)	**der Damenfriseur/ Herrenfriseur**	derr daamernfrizurr/ hehrernfrizurr
newsagent	**der Zeitungs- händler**	derr tsightungshehndlerr
post office	**das Postamt**	dahss postahmt
souvenir shop	**der Andenkenladen**	derr ahndehnkernlaadern
supermarket	**der Supermarkt**	derr zooperrmahrkt
toilets	**die Toilette**	dee toahlehter

General expressions *Allgemeine Redewendungen*

Where's the main shopping area?	**Wo ist das Geschäftsviertel?**	voa ist dahss gershehftsfeerterl
Do you have any...?	**Haben Sie...?**	haabern zee
Can you show me...?	**Können Sie mir... zeigen?**	kurnern zee meer... tsighgern
that/those	**das da/die dort**	dahss daa/dee dort
Haven't you anything...?	**Haben Sie nichts...?**	haabern zee nikhts
cheaper/better	**Billigeres/Besseres**	billiggerrerss/behsserrerss
larger/smaller	**Größeres/Kleineres**	grursserrerss/klighnerrerss
Can I try it on?	**Kann ich es anprobieren?**	kahn ikh ehss ahnprobbeeern
How much is this?	**Wieviel kostet das?**	veefeel kostert dahss
Please write it down.	**Schreiben Sie es bitte auf.**	shrighbern zee ehss bitter owf
I don't want to spend more than... marks.	**Ich möchte nicht mehr als... Mark ausgeben.**	ikh murkhter nikht mayr ahlss... mahrk owsgaybern
No, I don't like it.	**Nein, das gefällt mir nicht.**	nighn dahss gerfehlt meer nikht
I'll take it.	**Ich nehme es.**	ikh naymer ehss

NUMBERS, see page 78

Do you accept credit cards?	**Nehmen Sie Kreditkarten?**	naymern zee kray**dit**kahrtern

black	**schwarz**	shvahrts
blue	**blau**	blow
brown	**braun**	brown
green	**grün**	grewn
orange	**orange**	or**rahng**zher
red	**rot**	roat
yellow	**gelb**	gehlp
white	**weiß**	vighss
light...	**hell...**	hehl
dark...	**dunkel...**	**du**nkerl

I'd like a/an/some...	**Ich hätte gern...**	ikh **heh**ter gehrn
aspirin	**Aspirin**	ahspi**reen**
battery	**eine Batterie**	**igh**ner bahter**ree**
newspaper	**eine Zeitung**	**igh**ner **tsigh**tung
American	**amerikanische**	ahmehrik**kaa**nisher
English	**englische**	**ehng**lisher
postcard	**eine Postkarte**	**igh**ner **post**kahrter
shampoo	**ein Haarwaschmittel**	ighn **haar**vahshmitterl
soap	**eine Seife**	**igh**ner **zigh**fer
sun-tan cream	**Sonnencreme**	**zon**nernkraym
toothpaste	**Zahnpasta**	**tsaan**pahstah
half-kilo of tomatoes	**ein halbes Kilo Tomaten**	ighn **hahl**bers **kee**lo tom**maa**tern
litre of milk	**einen Liter Milch**	**igh**nern **lee**terr milkh
I'd like a ... film for this camera.	**Ich hätte gern einen Film für diese Kamera.**	ikh **heh**ter gehrn **igh**nern film fewr **dee**zer **kah**mehraa
black and white	**Schwarzweißfilm**	shvahrts**vighs**film
colour	**Farbfilm**	**fahrp**film
I'd like a hair-cut, please.	**Haare schneiden, bitte.**	**haa**rer **shnigh**dern **bit**ter

Souvenirs *Andenken*

I'd like a/an/some...	**Ich hätte gern...**	ikh **heh**ter gehrn
beer stein	**der Bierkrug**	derr **beer**kroog
chocolate	**die Schokolade**	dee shokkol**laa**der
leather goods	**die Lederwaren**	dee **lay**derrvaarern
ski equipment	**dei Skiausrüstung**	dee **shee**owsrewstung
wood carving	**die Holzschnitzarbeit**	dee **holts**shnitsahrbight

At the bank *Bank*

Where's the nearest bank/currency exchange office?	**Wo ist die nächste Bank/Wechsel- stube?**	voa ist dee **naikh**ster bahnk/**vehk**serlshtoober
I want to change some dollars/pounds.	**Ich möchte Dollar/ Pfund wechseln.**	ikh **murkh**ter **doll**ahr/ pfunt **vehk**serln
What's the exchange rate?	**Wie ist der Wechselkurs?**	vee ist derr **vehk**serlkoorss
I want to cash a traveller's cheque.	**Ich möchte einen Reisescheck ein- lösen.**	ikh **murkh**ter **ighn**ern **righ**zershehk **ighn**lurzern

At the post office *Post*

I'd like to send this by...	**Ich möchte dies... senden.**	ikh **murkh**ter deess... **zehn**dern
airmail	**per Luftpost**	pehr **luft**post
express	**per Expreß**	pehr ehk**sprehss**
A...-pfennig stamp please.	**Eine Briefmarke zu ... Pfennig, bitte.**	**ighn**er **breef**maarker tsoo ... **pfehn**nikh **bitt**er
What's the postage for a letter/postcard to Los Angeles?	**Was kostet ein Brief/eine Post- karte nach Los Angeles?**	vahss **kost**et ighn breef/ **ighn**er **post**kaarter naakh los **ehnd**zehrlerss
Is there any post/mail for me?	**Ist Post für mich da?**	ist post few mikh daa

Telephoning *Telefonieren*

Where's the nearest telephone booth?	**Wo ist die nächste Telefonzelle?**	voa ist dee **naikh**ster taylay**foant**sehler
May I use your phone?	**Darf ich Ihr Telefon benutzen?**	dahrf ikh eer taylay**foan** ber**nut**sern
Hello. This is... speaking.	**Hallo. Hier spricht...**	**hahl**oa. heer shprikht ...
I'd like to speak to...	**Ich möchte... sprechen.**	ikh **murkh**ter... **shpreh**khern
When will he/she be back?	**Wann ist er/sie zurück?**	vahn ist err/zee tsoo**rewk**
Will you tell him/her that I called?	**Würden Sie ihm/ihr sagen, daß ich angerufen habe?**	**vewr**dern zee eem/eer **zaa**gern dahss ikh **ahn**gerroofern **haa**ber

Days and date *Tage und Datum*

It's...	**Es ist...**	ehss ist
five past one	**fünf nach eins**	fewnf nakh ighns
quarter past three	**viertel nach drei**	feerterl nahkh drigh
twenty past four	**zwanzig nach vier**	tsvahntsikh nahkh feer
half-past six	**halb sieben**	hahlp zeebern
twenty-five to seven	**fünf nach halb sieben**	fewnf nakh hahlp zeebern
ten to ten	**zehn vor zehn**	tsayn foar tsayn
noon/midnight	**Mittag/Mitternacht**	mittaag/mitterrnahkht
in the morning	**morgens**	morgerns
in the afternoon	**nachmittags**	nahkhmittaags
in the evening	**abends**	aaberrnds
during the day	**tagsüber**	taagsewberr
at night	**nachts**	nahkhts
yesterday	**gestern**	gehsterrn
today	**heute**	hoyter
tomorrow	**morgen**	morgern
spring	**der Frühling**	derr frewling
summer	**der Sommer**	derr zommerr
autumn	**der Harbst**	derr hehrpst
winter	**der Winter**	derr vinterr

Sunday	**Sonntag**	zontaag
Monday	**Montag**	moantaag
Tuesday	**Dienstag**	deenstaag
Wednesday	**Mittwoch**	mitvokh
Thursday	**Donnerstag**	donnerrstaag
Friday	**Freitag**	frightaag
Saturday	**Samstag/Sonnabend**	zahmstaag/zonnaabernt
January	**Januar**	yahnuarr
February	**Februar**	faybruaar
March	**März**	mehrts
April	**April**	ahpril
May	**Mai**	migh
June	**Juni**	yooni
July	**Juli**	yooli
August	**August**	owgust
September	**September**	sehptehmberr
October	**Oktober**	oktoaberr
November	**November**	novvehmberr
December	**Dezember**	daytsehmberr

NUMBERS, see page 78

Numbers *Zahlen*

0	**null**	nul
1	**eins**	ighns
2	**zwei**	tsvigh
3	**drei**	drigh
4	**vier**	feer
5	**fünf**	fewnf
6	**sechs**	zehks
7	**sieben**	**zee**bern
8	**acht**	ahkht
9	**neun**	noyn
10	**zehn**	tsayn
11	**elf**	ehlf
12	**zwölf**	tsvurlf
13	**dreizehn**	**drigh**tsayn
14	**vierzehn**	**feer**tsayn
15	**fünfzehn**	**fewnf**tsayn
16	**sechzehn**	**zehkh**tsayn
17	**siebzehn**	**zeep**tsayn
18	**achtzehn**	**ahkh**tsayn
19	**neunzehn**	**noyn**tsayn
20	**zwanzig**	**tsvahn**tsikh
30	**dreißig**	**drigh**ssikh
40	**vierzig**	**feer**tsikh
50	**fünfzig**	**fewnf**tsikh
60	**sechzig**	**zehkh**tsikh
70	**siebzig**	**zeep**tsikh
80	**achtzig**	**ahkh**tsikh
90	**neunzig**	**noyn**tsikh
100	**(ein)hundert**	(ighn)**hund**errt
1,000	**(ein)tausend**	(ighn)**tow**zernt
first/second	**erste/zweite**	**ehr**ster/**tsvigh**ter
once/twice	**einmal/dreimal**	**ighn**mal/**tsvigh**maal
a half	**eine Hälfte**	**ighn**er **hehlf**ter

Emergency *Notfall*

Call the police	**Rufen sie die Polizei**	**roo**fern zee dee polli**tsigh**
Get a doctor	**Holen Sie einen Arzt**	**hoa**lern zee **igh**nern ahrtst
Go away	**Gehen Sie weg**	**gay**ern zee vehk
HELP	**HILFE**	**hil**fer
I'm ill	**Ich bin krank**	ikh bin krahnk
I'm lost	**Ich habe mich verirrt**	ikh **haa**ber mikh fe**hreert**
STOP THIEF	**HALTET DEN DIEB**	**hahl**tert dayn deep

TELEPHONING, see page 76

My ... has been stolen.	**Mein(e) ... ist mir gestohlen worden.**	mighn(er) ... ist meer gershtoalern voardern
I've lost my ...	**Ich habe meine ... verloren.**	ikh **haaber mighner** ... fehrloarern
handbag	**Handtasche**	**hahnt**tahsher
wallet	**Brieftasche**	**breeftahsher**
passport	**Paß**	pahss
luggage	**Gepäck**	ger**pehk**
Where is there a doctor who speaks English?	**Wo gibt es einen Arzt, der Englisch spricht?**	voa gipt ehss **igh**nern ahrtst derr **ehng**lish shprikht

Guide to German pronunciation *Aussprache*

Consonants

Letter	Approximate pronunciation	Symbol	Example	
f, h, k, l, m, n, p, t, x	as in English			
b	1) at the end of a word like **p** in u**p**	p	**ab**	ahp
	2) as in English	b	**bis**	biss
c	1) before **e, i, ö** and **ä**, like **ts** in hi**ts**	ts	**Celsius**	**tsehlz**iuss
	2) like **c** in **cat**	k	**Café**	kah**fay**
ch	1) like **ch** in Scottish lo**ch**, otherwise more like **h** in **huge**	kh	**doch**	dokh
	2) sometimes like **k** in **kit**	k	**Wachs**	vahks
d	1) at the end of a word like **t** in ea**t**	t	**Rad**	raat
	2) elsewhere, like **d** in **do**	d	**durstig**	**doors**tikh
g	1) always hard as in **go** but at the end of a word like **ck** in ta**ck**	g	**gehen**	**gay**ern
		k	**weg**	vehk
	2) when preceded by **i** at the end of a word like **ch** in Scottish lo**ch**	kh	**billig**	**bill**ikh
j	like **y** in **yes**			
qu	like **k** followed by **v** as in **vat**	kv	**Quark**	kvark
r	generally rolled in the back of the mouth	r	**warum**	vah**rum**

s	1) like z in zoo	z	**sie**	zee
	2) like sh in shut	sh	**spät**	shpait
	3) like s in sit	s/ss	**es ist**	ehss ist
ß	always like s in sit	s/ss	**heiß**	highss
sch	like sh in shut	sh	**schnell**	shnehl
tsch	like ch in chip	ch	**deutsch**	doych
tz	like ts in hits	ts	**Platz**	plahts
v	1) like f in for	f	**vier**	feer
	2) like v in vice	v	**Vase**	vaazer
w	like v in vice	v	**wie**	vee
z	like ts in hits	ts	**zeigen**	tsighgern

Vowels

a	1) short like u in cut	ah	**lassen**	lahssern
	2) long like a in car	aa	**Abend**	aabernt
ä	1) short like e in let	eh	**Lärm**	lehrm
	2) long like ai in hair	ai	**spät**	shpait
e	1) short like e in let	eh	**sprechen**	shprehkhern
	2) long like a in late, but pronounced without moving tongue or lips	ay	**geben**	gaybern
	3) unstressed, like er in other	er*	**bitte**	bitter
i	1) short like i in hit	i	**billig**	billikh
	2) long like ee in meet	ee	**ihm**	eem
ie	like ee in bee	ee	**hier**	heer
o	1) short like o in got	o	**voll**	fol
	2) long like o in note, but pronounced without moving tongue or lips	oa	**ohne**	oaner
ö	like ur in fur	ur*	**können**	kurnern
u	1) short like oo in foot	u	**Nuß**	nuss
	2) long like oo in moon	oo	**gut**	goot
ü	like French u in une; round your lips and try to say ea as in mean	ew	**über**	ewber
y	like German ü	ew	**typisch**	tewpish

Diphthongs

ai, ay, ei, ey	like igh in high	igh	**mein**	mighn
au	like ow in now	ow	**auf**	owf
äu, eu	like oy in boy	oy	**new**	noy

* The r should not be pronounced when reading this transcription.

Greek

Basic expressions *Μερικές βασικές εκφράσεις*

Yes/No.	Ναι/Όχι.	neh/okhee
Please.	Παρακαλώ.	pahrahkahlo
Thank you.	Ευχαριστώ.	ehfkhahreesto
Sorry!	Συγγνώμη!	seenghnommee

Introductions *Συστάσεις*

Good morning.	Καλημέρα.	kahleemehrah
Good afternoon.	Καλησπέρα.	kahleespehrah
Good night.	Καληνύχτα.	kahleeneektah
Good-bye.	Αντίο.	ahndeeo
My name is...	Λέγομαι...	lehghommeh
Pleased to meet you.	Χαίρομαι που σας γνωρίζω!	khehrommeh poo sahss ghnorreezo
What's your name?	Πώς λέγεστε;	poss lehyehsteh
How are you?	Πώς είστε;	poss eesteh
Fine thanks.	Πολύ καλά,	pollee kahlah
And you?	ευχαριστώ. Εσείς;	ehfkhahreesto. ehseess
Where do you come from?	Από πού είστε;	ahpo poo eesteh
I'm from...	Είμαι από το/την...	eemeh ahpo to/teen
Australia	Αυστραλία	ahfstrahleeah
Canada	Καναδά	kahnahdhah
Great Britain	Μεγάλη Βρετανία	mehghahlee vrahtahneeah
United States	Ηνωμένες Πολιτείες	eenommehnnehss polleeteeehss
I'm with my...	Είμαι με... μου.	eemeh meh... moo
wife	την γυναίκα	teen yeenehkah
husband	τον άνδρα	tonn ahndrah
family	την οικογένεια	teen eekoyehneeah
boyfriend/girlfriend	τον φίλο/την φίλη	tonn feelo/teen feelee
I'm here on vacation.	Είμαι εδώ για διακοπές.	eemeh ehdho yeeah dheeahkoppehss
I'm here on business.	Είμαι εδώ για δουλειά.	emeh ehdho yeeah dhooleeah

GUIDE TO PRONUNCIATION/EMERGENCIES, see page 95

Questions *Ερωτήσεις*

When?	**Πότε;**	**pot**teh
How?	**Πώς;**	poss
What?/Why?	**Τί;/Γιατί;**	tee/yeeah**tee**
Who?/Which?	**Ποιός;**	pee**oss**
Where is/are...?	**Πού είναι...;**	poo **ee**neh
Where can I find/ get...?	**Πού μπορώ να βρω/αγοράσω...;**	poo bo**rro** nah vro/ agho**rasso**
How far?	**Πόσο μακρυά;**	**po**sso mahkree**ah**
How long?	**Πόση ώρα;**	**po**ssi **o**ra
How much/many?	**Πόσο/Πόσα;**	**po**sso/**po**ssah
May I?	**Μπορώ...;**	bo**rro**
Can I have...?	**Μπορώ να έχω...;**	bo**rro** nah **eh**kho
Can you help me?	**Μπορείτε να με βοηθήσετε;**	bo**ree**teh nah meh voee**thee**sehteh
What does this mean?	**Τι σημαίνει αυτό;**	tee see**meh**nee ah**f**to
I understand.	**Καταλαβαίνω.**	kahtahlah**veh**no
I don't understand.	**Δεν καταλαβαίνω.**	dehn kahtahlah**veh**no
Can you translate this for me?	**Μπορείτε να μου το μεταφράσετε;**	bo**ree**teh nah moo to mehtah**frah**ssehteh
Do you speak English?	**Μιλάτε Αγγλικά;**	mee**lah**teh ahnggleekah
I don't speak (much) Greek.	**Δεν μιλώ (καλά) Ελληνικά.**	dehn mee**lo** (kah**lah**) ehleenee**kah**

A few more useful words *Περισσότερες χρήσιμες λξεις*

better/worse	**καλύτερος/ χειρότερος**	kah**lee**tehross/ khee**ro**ttehross
big/small	**μεγάλος/μικρός**	mehgh**ah**loss/mee**kross**
cheap/expensive	**φθηνός/ακριβός**	ftee**noss**/ahkree**voss**
early/late	**νωρίς/αργά**	nor**reess**/ahr**ghah**
good/bad	**καλός/κακός**	kah**loss**/kah**koss**
hot/cold	**ζεστός/κρύος**	zah**stoss**/**kree**oss
old/new	**παλιός/καινούργιος**	pahlee**oss**/kehn**oo**ryeeoss
right/wrong	**σωστός/λάθος**	sos**toss**/**la**thoss
vacant/occupied	**ελεύθερος/ κατειλημμένος**	eh**leh**fthehross/ kahteeleem**meh**noss

Hotel—Accommodation   Ξενοδοχείο

I have a reservation.	Έχω κάνει κράτηση.	ehkho kahnee krahteessee
We've reserved two rooms.	Έχουμε κλείσει δύο δωμάτια.	ehkhoommeh kleessee dheeo dhommahtteeah
Do you have any vacancies?	Υπάρχουν άδεια δωμάτια;	eepahrkoon ahdheeah dhommahteeah
I'd like a... room.	Θα ήθελα ένα... δωμάτιο.	thah eethehlah ehnah... dhommahtteeo
single/double	μονό/διπλό	monno/dheeplo
with twin beds	με δύο κρεββάτια	meh dheeo krehvahteeah
with a double bed	με διπλό κρεββάτι	meh dheeplo krevahtee
with a bath/shower	με μπάνιο/ντους	meh bahneeo/dooss
We'll be staying...	Θα μείνουμε...	thah meenoomeh
overnight only	μόνο μια νύχτα	monno meeah neektah
a few days	λίγες μέρες	leeyehss mehrehss
a week	μια εβδομάδα	meeah ehvdhommahdhah
Is there a campsite near here?	Υπάρχει μέρος για κάμπινγκ εδώ κοντά;	eepahrkhee mehross yeeah "camping" ehdho kondah

Decision   Απόφαση

May I see the room?	Μπορώ να δω το δωμάτιο;	borro nah dho to dhommahtteo
That's fine. I'll take it.	Είναι εντάξει. Θα το πάρω.	eeneh ehndahksee. thah to pahro
No. I don't like it.	Όχι. Δεν μου αρέσει.	okhee. dhehn moo ahrehssee
It's too...	Είναι πολύ...	eeneh pollee
dark/small	σκοτεινό/μικρό	skotteeno/meekro
It's too noisy.	Έχει πολύ θόρυβο.	ehkhee pollee thorreevo
Do you have anything...?	Έχετε κάτι...;	ehkhehteh kahtee
better	καλύτερο	kahleetehro
bigger	μεγαλύτερο	mehghahleetehro
cheaper	φθηνότερο	fteenottehro
quieter	πιο ήσυχο	peeo eesseekho
May I have my bill, please?	Μπορώ να έχω τον λογαριασμό, παρακαλώ;	borro nah ehkho tonn loghahreeahzmo pahrahkahlo
It's been a very enjoyable stay.	Η διαμονή ήταν πολύ ευχάριστη.	ee dheeahmonnee eetahn pollee ehfkhahreestee

Eating out Εστιατόριο–Φαγητά

I'd like to reserve a table for four.	Θα ήθελα να κλείσω ένα τραπέζι για 4.	thah **ee**thehlah nah **klee**sso **eh**nah trah**peh**zee yeeah 4
We'll come at 8.	Θα έλθουμε στις 8.	thah **ehl**thoomeh steess 8
I'd like...	Θα ήθελα...	thah **ee**thehlah
breakfast	πρωινό	proyeh**no**
lunch	μεσημεριανό	mehseemehreeah**no**
dinner	δείπνο	dheep**no**
What do you recommend?	Τι μας συστήνετε;	tee mahss see**stee**nehteh
Do you have any vegetarian dishes?	Έχετε πιάτα για χορτοφάγους;	**eh**khehteh pee**ah**tah yeeah khorto**fah**ghooss

Breakfast Πρωινό

May I have some...	Μπορώ να έχω...;	borro nah **eh**kho
bread	λίγο ψωμί	**lee**gho pso**mmee**
butter	λίγο βούτυρο	**lee**gho **voo**teero
cereal	δημητριακά	dheemeetreeah**kah**
ham and eggs	αυγά με ζαμπόν	ahv**ghah** meh zahm**bonn**
jam	μαρμελάδα	mahrmeh**lah**dhah
rolls	λίγα ψωμάκια	**lee**ghah pso**mmah**keeah

Starters (Appetizers) Ορεκτικά

αγγινάρες	ahnggeenahgrehss	artichokes
ελιές (γεμιστές)	ehleeehss (yehmee**stehss**)	(stuffed) olives
ντολμαδάκια	dolmahdhakeeah	stuffed vine leaves
ταραμοσαλάτα	tahrahmossahlahtah	fish roe paté
τυροπιττάκια	teeroppeetahkeeah	cheese filled pastries

Fish and seafood Ψάρι και θαλασσινά

crab	καβούρι	kah**voo**ree
mullet	κέφαλος	**keh**fahlos
prawns (shrimps)	γαρίδες	ghah**ree**dhehss
sardines	σαρδέλλα	sahr**deh**lah
swordfish	ξιφίας	ksee**fee**ahss
trout	πέστροφα	**peh**stroffah
tuna	τόννος	**to**nnos
χταπόδι κρασάτο	khtah**po**dhee krah**ssah**to	octopus in wine sauce

NUMBERS, see page 94

baked	του φούρνου	too **foor**noo
boiled	βραστό	vrah**sto**
fried	τηγανητό	teeghahnee**to**
grilled	της σχάρας	teess **skhah**rahss
roast	ψητό	psee**to**
underdone (rare)	λίγο ψμένο	leegho psee**meh**no
medium	μέτρια ψημένο	**meh**treeah psee**meh**no
well-done	καλοψημένο	kahlopsee**meh**no

Meat Κρέας

I'd like some...	Θα ήθελα...	thah **ee**thehlah
bacon	μπέικον	**bee**konn
beef	βοδινό	vodhee**no**
chicken	κοτόπουλο	kotto**pool**lo
duck	πάπια	**pah**peeah
ham	ζαμπόν	zahm**bonn**
lamb	αρνί	ahr**nee**
pork	χοιρινό	kheeree**no**
veal	μοσχάρι	mo**skhah**ree

παπουτσάκια (pahpoo**tsah**keeah)
baked vegetable marrow (zucchini) stuffed with rice and/or meat, onions and white sauce

σουβλάκι (soo**vlah**kee)
chunks of meat marinated in olive oil and lemon juice, and grilled on a skewer

λαγός στιφάδο (lah**ghoss** stee**fah**dho)
hare cooked with spring onions, wine or tomatoes

Vegetables Λαχανικά

beans (green)	φασόλια	fah**ssol**leeah
carrots	καρότα	kah**rot**tah
mushrooms	μανιτάρια	mahnee**tah**reah
onions	κρεμμύδια	kreh**mee**dheeah
peas	μπιζέλια	bee**zeh**leeah
potatoes	πατάτες	pah**tah**tehss
spinach	σπανάκι	spah**nah**kee
tomatoes	ντομάτες	dom**mah**tehss

μουσακάς χωρίς κρέας (moossah**kahss** kho**rees** kreh**ahss**)
vegetarian moussaka made of aubergines, tomatoes, onions and cheese, with a béchamel sauce

χωριάτικη σαλάτα (khorreea**hteekee** sah**lah**tah)
salad made of olives, tomatoes, onions, cucumber, green pepper and *feta* (goat cheese)

Fruits and dessert Φρούτα και Επιδόρπια

apples	μήλα	meela
banana	μπανάνα	bahnahnah
cherries	κεράσια	kehrahssah
lemon	λεμόνι	lehmonnee
orange	πορτοκάλι	portokkahlee
pear	αχλάδι	ahkhlahdhee
strawberries	φράουλες	frahoolah
λουκούμι	lookoomee	Turkish delight
μηλόπιτα	meeloppeetah	apple pie
παγωτό	pahghotto	ice cream
πάστα	pahstah	tart
ρυζόγαλο	reezoghahlo	rice pudding

Drinks Ποτάν

beer	μπύρα	beerah
(hot) chocolate	μια (ζεστή) σοκολάτα	meeah (zehstee) sokkollahtah
coffee	έναν καφέ	ehnan kahfeh
black	σκέτο	skehto
with milk	με γάλα	meh ghahlah
fruit juice	ένα χυμό φρούτων	ehnah kheemo frootonn
milk	ένα γάλα	ehnah ghahlah
mineral water	ένα μεταλλικό νερό	ehnah mehtahleeko nahro
tea	ένα τσάι	ehnah tsahee
wine	κρασί	krahssee
red/white	κόκκινο/άσπρο	kokkeeno/ahspro

Complaints and paying Παράπονα – λογαριασμός

This is too...	Αυτό είναι πολύ...	ahfto eeneh pollee
bitter/sweet/salty	πικρό/αλμυρό/ γλυκό	peekro/ahlmeero/ ghleeko
That's not what I ordered.	Δεν είναι αυτό που παράγγειλα.	dhehn eeneh ahfto poo pahrahnggeelah
I'd like to pay.	Θα ήθελα να πληρώσω.	thah eethehlah nah pleerosso
I think there's a mistake in this bill.	Νομίζω έχει γίνει λάθος στον λογαριασμό.	nommeezo ekhee yeenee lahthoss stonn loghahreeahzmo
Can I pay with this credit card?	Μπορώ να πληρώσω με αυτή την πιστ- ωτική κάρτα;	borro nah pleerosso meh ahftee teen peestoteekee kahrtah
We enjoyed it, thank you.	Το απολαύσαμε, ευχαριστούμε.	to ahpollahfsahmeh ehfkhahreestoomeh

Travelling around *Ταξιδεύοντας*

Plane *Αεροπλάνο*

Is there a flight to Athens?	Υπάρχει πτήση για την Αθήνα;	eepahrkhee pteessee yeeah teen ahtheenah
What time should I check in?	Τι ώρα πρέπει να είμαι στο αεροδρόμιο;	tee orrah prehpee nah eemeh sto ahehrodhrommeeo
I'd like to... my reservation.	Θα ήθελα να... την κράτησή μου.	thah eethehlah nah... teen krahteessee moo
cancel	ακυρώσω	ahkeerosso
change	αλλάξω	ahlahkso
confirm	επιβεβαιώσω	ehpeevehvehosso

Train *Τραίνο*

I'd like a ticket to Patras.	Θα ήθελα ένα εισιτήριο για Πάτρα.	thah eethehlah ehnah eessseeteereeo yeeah pahtrah
single (one-way)	απλό	ahplo
return (roundtrip)	με επιστροφή	meh ehpeestroffee
first/second class	πρώτη/δεύτερη θέση	prottee/dhehftehree thehssee
How long does the journey (trip) take?	Πόση ώρα διαρκεί το ταξίδι;	possee orrah dheeahrkee to tahkseedhee
When is the... train to Patras?	Πότε είναι το... τραίνο για την Πάτρα;	potteh eeneh to... trehno yeeah teen pahtrah
first/next/last	πρώτο/τελευταίο/ επόμενο	protto/tehlehfteho/ ehpommehno
Is this the right train to Tripolis?	Είναι αυτό το τραίνο για Τρίπολη;	eeneh ahfto to trehno yeeah treepollee

Bus *Λεωφορείο*

Which bus goes to the town centre?	Ποιό λεωφορείο πηγαίνει στο κέντρο της πόλης;	peeo lehofforreeo peeyehnee sto kehndro teess polleess
How much is the fare to...?	Πόσο κάνει το εισιτήριο για...;	posso kahnee to essee-teereeo yeeah
Will you tell me when to get off?	Θα μου πείτε πότε να κατέβω;	thah moo peeteh potteh nah kahtehvo

TELLING THE TIME, see page 93/NUMBERS, see page 94

Taxi Ταξί

How much is the fare to...?	Ποιά είναι η τιμή για...;	peeah eeneh ee teemee yeeah
Take me to this address.	Πηγαίνω σε αυτή τη διεύθυνση.	peeyehneh seh ahftee tee dheeehftheensee
Please stop here.	Παρακαλώ σταματήστε εδώ.	pahrahkahlo stahmah-teesteh ehdho

Car hire (rental) Ενοικίαση αυτοκινήτων

I'd like to hire (rent) a car.	Θα ήθελα να νοικιάσω ένα αυτοκίνητο.	thah eethehlah nah neekeeahsso ehnah ahftokkeeneeto
I'd like it for...	Θα το ήθελα για...	thah to eethehlah yeeah
a day/week	μια μέρα/βδομάδα	meeah mehrah/ vdhommahdhah
Where's the nearest filling station?	Πού είναι το κοντι-νότερο πρατήριο βενζίνης;	poo eeneh to kondee-nottehro prahteereeo vehnzeeneess
Full tank, please.	Γεμίστε το, παρακαλώ.	yehmeezmah pahrah-kahlo
Give me... litres of petrol (gasoline).	Θα ήθελα... λίτρα βενζίνα.	thah eethehlah... leetrah vehnzeenee
How do I get to...?	Πώς μπορώ να πάω στο..;	poss borro nah paho sto
I've broken down at...	Έπαθα βλάβη στο...	ehpahthah vlahvee sto
Can you send a mechanic?	Μπορείτε να στείλετε έναν μηχανικό;	borreeteh nah steelehteh ehnan meekhahneeko
Can you mend this puncture (fix this flat)?	Το λάστιχο έχει τρυπήσει. Μπορείτε να το φτιάξετε;	to lahsteekho ehkhee treepeessee. borreeteh nah to dheeortho-ssehteh •

Έχετε πάρει λάθος δρόμο.	You're on the wrong road.
Να πάτε ίσια.	Go straight ahead.
Είναι εκεί κάτω...	It's down there on the...
αριστερά/δεξιά	left/right
δίπλα σε/μετά...	next to/after...
βόρεια/νότια/ανατολικά/δυτικά	north/south/east/west

NUMBERS, see page 94

Αγγλικά

Sightseeing Αξιοθέατα

Where's the tourist office?	Πού είναι το γραφείο τουρισμού;	poo **ee**neh to ghrah**fee**o tooreez**moo**
Is there an English-speaking guide?	Υπάρχει ξεναγός που να μιλάει Αγγλικά;	ee**pahr**khee ksehnah-**ghoss** poo nah mee**lah**ee ahnggleek**ah**
Where is/are ...?	Πού είναι...;	poo **ee**neh
art gallery	η γκαλερί (τέχνης)	ee gahleh**ree** (**tehkh**neess)
botanical garden	ο βοτανικός κήπος	o vottahnee**koss kee**poss
cathedral	η μητρόπολη	ee meet**rop**pollee
church	η εκκλησία	ee ehklees**see**ah
city centre/downtown	το κέντρο της πόλης	to **kehn**dro teess **pol**leess
exhibition	η έκθεση	ee **ehk**thehssee
harbour	το λιμάνι	to lee**mah**nee
market	η αγορά	ee agho**rah**
museum	το μουσείο	to moos**see**o
square	η πλατεία	ee plah**tee**ah
temple	ο ναός	o nah**oss**
tower	ο πύργος	o **peer**ghoss
zoo	ο ζωολογικός κήπος	o zo-olloyee**koss kee**poss
What are the opening hours?	Ποιές είναι οι ώρες λειτουργίας;	peee**hss ee**neh ee **or**rehss leetooryee**ahss**
When does it close?	Πότε κλείνει;	**pot**teh **klee**nee
How much is the entrance fee?	Πόσο κοστίζει η είσοδος;	**pos**so kos**tee**zee ee **ees**sodhoss

Relaxing Ξεκούραση

What's playing at the ... Theatre?	Τι παίζουν στο Θέατρο...;	tee **peh**zoon sto **the**hahtro
Are there any seats for tonight?	Υπάρχουν θέσεις για απόψε;	ee**pahr**khoon **theh**sseess yeeah ah**pop**seh
How much are the seats?	Πόσο κοστίζει η είσοδος;	**pos**so kos**tee**zee ee **ees**sodhoss
Would you like to go out with me tonight?	Θα θέλατε να βγούμε έξω μαζί απόψε;	thah **theh**lahteh nah **vghoo**meh **ehk**so mah**zee** ah**pop**seh
Is there a disco-theque in town?	Υπάρχει ντισκοτέκ στην πόλη;	ee**pahr**khee dheesko-**theek** steen **pol**lee
Would you like to dance?	Θα θέλατε να χορέψουμε;	thah **theh**lahteh nah khor**rehp**soomeh
Thank you, it's been a wonderful evening.	Ευχαριστώ, ήταν μια υπέροχη βραδυά.	ehfkhahree**sto ee**tahn meeah ee**peh**rokhee vrahdhee**ah**

DAYS OF THE WEEK, see page 93

Shops, stores and services *Μαγαζιά και εξυπηρέτηση*

Where's the nearest...?	Πού είναι ο κοντινότερο...;	poo **ee**neh to kondee**not**tehro
bakery	το αρτοποιείο (ο φούρνος)	to ahrtoppee**ee**o (o **foorn**noss)
bookshop/store	το βιβλιοπωλείο	to veevleeoppol**lee**o
butcher's	το κρεοπωλείο	to krehoppol**lee**o
chemist/drugstore	το φαρμακείο	to fahrmah**kee**o
dentist	ο οδοντίατρος	o odhond**dee**ahtross
department store	το πολυκατάστημα	to poleekah**tahs**teemah
grocery	το παντοπωλείο	to pahndoppol**lee**o
hairdresser (ladies/men)	το κομμωτήριο/ κουρείο	to kommot**tee**reeo/ koor**ee**o
news-stand	το περίπτερο	to pehr**eep**tehro
post office	το ταχυδρομείο	to tahkheedhrom**mee**o
supermarket	σουπερμάρκετ	"supermarket"
toilets/restrooms	οι τουαλέττες	ee tooah**leh**tehss

General expressions *Γενικές εκφράσεις*

Where's the main shopping area?	Πού είναι το εμπορικό κέντρο;	poo **ee**neh to **ehm**boreeko **kehn**dro
Do you have any...?	Έχετε μερικά...;	**eh**kheteh mehree**kah**
Can you show me this/that?	Μπορείτε να μου δείξετε αυτό/εκείνο;	borr**ee**teh nah moo **dhee**ksehteh ahf**to**/eh**kee**no
Haven't you anything...?	Δεν έχετε τίποτε..;	dhehn **eh**khehteh **tee**poteh
cheaper/better	φθηνότερο/καλύτερο	ftee**not**tehro/kah**lee**tehro
larger	μεγαλύτερο	mehghah**lee**tehro
smaller	μικρότερο	mee**krot**tehro
Can I try it on?	Μπορώ να το δοκιμάσω;	borr**o** nah to dhokkee**mah**sso
How much is this?	Πόσο κάνει αυτό;	**posso kah**nee ahf**to**
Please write it down.	Γράψτε το, παρακαλώ.	**ghrahps**teh to pahrahkah**lo**
I don't want to spend more than... drachmas.	Δεν θέλω να ξοδέψω περισσότερα από... δραχμές.	dhehn **theh**lo nah kso**dheh**pso pehree**sso**ttehrah ahpo ... dhrah**khmehss**
No, I don't like it.	Όχι, δεν μου αρέσει.	**okhee** dhehn moo ah**reh**ssee
I'll take it.	Θα το πάρω.	thah to **pah**ro
Do you accept credit cards?	Δέχεστε πιστωτικές κάρτες;	**dheh**khehsteh peestottee**kehss kahr**tehss

NUMBERS, see page 94

black	μαύρο	mahvro
blue	μπλε	bleh
brown	καφέ	kahfeh
green	πράσινο	prahsseeno
orange	πορτοκαλί	portokkahlee
red	κόκκινο	kokkeeno
white	άσπρο	ahspro
yellow	κίτρινο	keetreeno
light...	ανοιχτό...	ahneekhto
dark...	σκούρο...	skooro

I want to buy a/an/some...	Θέλω να αγοράσω...	thehlo nah ahghorrahzo
aspirin	ασπιρίνες	ahspeereenehss
newspaper	μια εφημερίδα	meeah ehfeemehreedhah
American	Αμερικανική	ahmehreekahneekee
English	Αγγλική	ahnggleekee
postcard	μια καρτ-ποστάλ	meeah kahrt postahl
shampoo	ένα σαμπουάν	ehnah sahmbooahn
soap	ένα σαπούνι	ehnah sahpoonee
sun-tan cream	μια κρέμα για τον ήλιο	meeah krehmah yeeah tonn eeleeo
toothpaste	μια οδοντόπαστα	meeah odhondopahstah
a half kilo of tomatoes	μισό κιλό τομάτες	meesso keelo dommahtehss
a litre of milk	ένα λίτρο γάλα	ehnah leetro ghahlah
I'd like a film for this camera.	Θα ήθελα ένα φιλμ γι' αυτή τη μηχανή.	thah eethehla ehnah feelm yeeahftee tee meekhahnee
black and white	ασπρόμαυρο	ahsprommahvro
colour	έγχρωμο	ehngkhrommo
I'd like a hair-cut, please.	Θέλω να με κουρψετε, παρακαλώ.	thehlo nah meh koorehpsehteh pahrahkahlo

Souvenirs Σουβενίρ (Ενθύμια)

ceramics	κεραμικά	kehrahmeekah
embroidery	κέντημα	kehndeemah
hand-knotted carpet	κιλίμι	keeleemee
icon	εικόνα	eekonnah
olive oil	ελαιόλαδο	ehlehollahdho
pottery	είδη αγγειο-πλαστικής	eedhee ahnggeeoplahsteekeess
woollen rug	φλοκάτη	flokkahtee

At the bank *Τράπεζα*

Where's the nearest currency exchange office?	Πού είναι το κοντινότερο γραφείο συναλλάγματος;	poo **ee**neh to kondee**no**ttehro ghrah**fee**o seenahl**lahgh**mahtoss
Where's the nearest bank?	Πού είναι η κοντινότερη τράπεζα;	poo **ee**neh ee kondee**no**ttehree trah**peh**zah
I want to change some dollars/pounds.	Θέλω ν' αλλάξω μερικά δολάρια/ λίρες.	**theh**lo nahl**lah**kso mah**ree**kah dhol**lahr**reah/ **lee**rehs
I want to cash a traveller's cheque.	Θέλω να εξαργυρώσω ένα τράβελερς τσεκ.	**theh**lo nah ehksahryee-**ros**so **eh**nah "traveller's" tshehk

At the post office *Ταχυδρομείο*

I want to send this by...	Θέλω να στείλω αυτό...	**theh**lo nah **stee**lo ahf**to**
air mail	αεροπορικώς	ahehroppor**ree**koss
express	εξπρές	"express"
A... drachma stamp, please.	Γραμματόσημα των ... δραχμών, παρακαλώ.	ghrahmah**tos**seeman tonn... dhrah**khmonn** pahrahkah**lo**
What's the postage for a letter to the United States?	Πόσο κοστίζει ένα γράμμα για Ηνωμένες Πολιτείες;	**pos**so kos**tee**zee **eh**nah **ghrah**mah **yeeah** eeno-**mmeh**nehss polleet**eee**hss
Is there any post/mail for me?	Υπάρχουν γράμματα για μένα;	ee**pahr**khoon **grah**mmahtah **yee**ah **meh**nah

Telephoning *Τηλεφωνώντας*

Where is the nearest telephone booth?	Πού είναι ο κοντινό-τερος τηλεφωνικός θάλαμος;	pee **ee**neh o kondee**no**tehross teelehfonnee**koss thah**lahmoss
May I use your phone?	Μπορώ να χρησιμοποιήσω το τηλέφωνό σας;	bo**rro** nah khreessee-mopp**eee**esso to teel**eh**fonno sahss
Hello. This is... speaking.	Γειά σας. Είμαι ο/η...	yee**ah**ssahss. **ee**meh o/ee
I'd like to speak to...	Θα ήθελα να μιλήσω με...	thah **ee**thehlah nah mee**lee**sso meh
When will he/she be back?	Πότε θα επιστρέψει;	**pot**teh thah ehpee-**streh**psee

Time and date Ώρα και Ημερομηνία

It's...	Είναι...	eeneh
five past one	μία και πέντε	**mee**ah keh **pehn**deh
quarter past three	τρεις και τέταρτο	treess keh **teh**tahrto
twenty past four	τέσσερις και είκοσι	**tehs**sehreess keh **ee**kossee
half past six	έξι και μισή	**ehk**see keh mee**ss**ee
twenty-five to seven	επτά παρά εικοσιπέντε	ehp**tah** pah**rah** eekossee**pehn**deh
ten to ten	δέκα παρά δέκα	**dheh**kah pah**rah** **dheh**kah
twelve o'clock	δώδεκα	**dho**dhehkah
in the morning/ afternoon/evening	το πρωί/απόγευμα/ βράδυ	to pro**ee**/ah**po**yehvmah/ **vrah**dhee
during the day	στη διάρκεια της ημέρας	stee dheeahrkeeah teess **meh**rahss
at night	τη νύχτα	tee **neek**tah
yesterday	χθές	khthehss
today	σήμερα	**see**mehrah
tomorrow	αύριο	**ahv**reeo
spring/summer	άνοιξη/καλοκαίρι	**ah**neeksee/kahlo**kkeh**ree
autumn (fall)	φθινόπωρο	ftheen**op**porro
winter	χειμώνας	khee**mon**nahss

Sunday	Κυριακή	keereeah**kee**
Monday	Δευτέρα	dhehf**teh**rah
Tuesday	Τρίτη	**tree**tee
Wednesday	Τετάρτη	teh**tahr**tee
Thursday	Πέμπτη	**pehmp**tee
Friday	Παρασκευή	pahrahskeh**vee**
Saturday	Σάββατο	**sah**vahto
January	Ιανουάριος	eeahnoo**ah**reeoss
February	Φεβρουάριος	fehvroo**ah**reeoss
March	Μάρτιος	**mahr**teeoss
April	Απρίλιος	ah**pree**leeoss
May	Μάιος	**mah**eeoss
June	Ιούνιος	ee**oo**neeoss
July	Ιούλιος	ee**oo**leeoss
August	Αύγουστος	**ahv**ghoostoss
September	Σεπτέμβριος	sehp**tehm**vreeoss
October	Οκτώβριος	ok**to**vreeoss
November	Νοέμβριος	no**ehm**vreeoss
December	Δεκέμβριος	dheh**kehm**vreeoss

NUMBERS, see page 94

Αγγλικά

Numbers *Αριθμοί*

0	μηδέν	**mee**dhehn
1	ένα	**eh**nah
2	δύο	**dhee**o
3	τρία	**tree**ah
4	τέσσερα	**teh**ssehrah
5	πέντε	**peh**ndeh
6	έξι	**eh**ksee
7	επτά	ehp**tah**
8	οκτώ	ok**to**
9	εννιά	ehnee**ah**
10	δέκα	**dheh**kah
11	έντεκα	**ehn**dehkah
12	δώδεκα	**dho**dhehkah
13	δεκατρία	dhehkah**tree**ah
14	δεκατέσσερα	dhehkah**teh**ssehrah
15	δεκαπέντε	dhehkah**peh**ndeh
16	δεκαέξι	dhehkah**eh**ksee
17	δεκαεπτά	dhehkahehp**tah**
18	δεκαοκτώ	dhehkahok**to**
19	δεκαεννιά	dhehkahehnee**ah**
20	είκοσι	**ee**kossee
21	είκοσι ένα	**ee**kossee **eh**nah
30	τριάντα	tree**ah**ndah
40	σαράντα	sah**rah**ndah
50	πενήντα	peh**nee**ndah
60	εξήντα	ehk**see**ndah
70	εβδομήντα	ehvdho**mee**ndah
80	ογδόντα	ogh**dho**ndah
90	ενενήντα	ehneh**nee**ndah
100	εκατό	ehkah**to**
1,000	χίλια	**khee**leeah
100,000	εκατό χιλιάδες	ehkah**to** kheelee**ah**dehss
1,000,000	ένα εκατομμύριο	**eh**nah ehkahtom**mee**reeo
first	πρώτος	**prot**toss
second	δεύτερος	**dhehf**tehross
third	τρίτος	**tree**toss
once	μια φορά	**mee**ah for**rah**
twice	δύο φορές	**dhee**o for**rehss**
a half	μισό	mee**sso**
a quarter	ένα τέταρτο	**eh**nah **teh**tahrto
a third	ένα τρίτο	**eh**nah **tree**to

Emergency Ἔκτακτες–Ἀνάγκες

Call the police!	Καλέστε την αστυνομία	kahlehsteh teen ahsteenomeeah
Get a doctor	Καλέστε ένα γιατρό	kahlehsteh ehnah yeeahtro
Go away	Απομακρυνθείτε	ahpomahkreentheeteh
HELP	ΒΟΗΘΕΙΑ	voeetheeah
I'm ill	Είμαι άρρωστος (-η)	eemeh ahrostoss (-ee)
I'm lost	Έχω χαθεί	eehkho khahthee
Leave me alone	Αφήστε με ήσυχο (-η)	ahfeesteh meh eesseekho (-ee)
LOOK OUT	ΠΡΟΣΟΧΗ	prossokhee
STOP THIEF	ΣΤΑΜΑΤΗΣΤΕ ΤΟΝ ΚΛΕΦΤΗ	stahmahteesteh tonn klehftee
My ... has been stolen.	Εκλάπη το... μου.	ehklahpee to ... moo
I've lost my ...	Έχασα... μου.	ehkhahssah ... moo
handbag	την τσάντα	teen tsahndah
passport	το διαβατήριο	to dheeahvahteereeo
wallet	το πορτοφόλι	to portoffollee
Where can I find a doctor who speaks English?	Πού μπορώ να βρω ένα γιατρό να μιλά Αγγλικά;	poo borro nah vro ehnah eeahtro nah meelahee ahnggleekah

Guide to Greek pronunciation Προφορά

Vowels

Letter	Approximate pronunciation	Symbol	Example	
α	like the vowel in car, but pronounced further forward in the mouth	ah	άρομα	ahrommah
ε	like e in sell	eh	μέρα	mehrah
η, ι, υ	like ee in meet	ee	κύριος	keereeoss
o, ω	like o in got	o	παρακαλώ	pahrahkahlo

TELEPHONING, see page 92

96

Consonants

β	like **v** in **v**ine	v	βιβλίο	vee**vlee**o
γ	1) a voiced version of the **ch** sound in Scottish lo**ch**	gh	μεγάλος	meh**ghah**loss
	2) like **y** in **y**et	y	γεμάτος	yeh**mah**toss
δ	like **th** in **th**is	dh	δεν	dhehn
ζ	like **z** in **z**oo	z	ζεστός	zeh**stoss**
θ	like **th** in **th**ing	th	θα	thah
κ	like **k** in **k**it	k	καλός	kah**loss**
λ	like **l** in **l**emon	l	λάθος	**lah**thoss
μ	like **m** in **m**an	m	μέσα	**meh**ssah
ν	like **n** in **n**ew	n	νέος	**neh**oss
ξ	like **x** in si**x**	ks	έξω	**ehk**so
π	like **p** in **p**ot	p	προς	pross
ρ	like **r** in **r**ed	r	πριν	preen
σ, ς	1) like **z** in **z**oo	z	κόσμος	**koz**moss
	2) like **s** in **s**ee	s/ss	Πόσσο στο	**pos**so sto
τ	like **t** in **t**ea	t	τότε	**tot**teh
φ	like **f** in **f**ive	f	φέρτε	**fehr**teh
χ	like **ch** in Scottish lo**ch**	kh	άσχημος	**ahs**khee-moss
ψ	like **ps** in dro**ps**y	ps	διψώ	dhee**pso**

Groups of letters

αι	like **e** in g**e**t	eh	είναι	**ee**neh
ει, οι	like **ee** in s**ee**	ee	ρείτε	**pee**teh
ου	like **oo** in r**oo**t	oo	μου	moo
αυ	1) like **uff** in p**uff**	ahf	αυτό	ahf**to**
	2) similar to **ave** in h**ave**	ahv	αυγό	ahv**gho**
ευ	1) like **ef** in l**ef**t	ehf	ευχή	ehf**khee**
	2) like **ev** in l**ev**el	ehv	ευμενής	ehvmeh**neess**
γγ	like **ng** in li**ng**er	ngg	Αγγλία	ahng**glee**ah
γκ	1) like **g** in **g**o	g	γκαμήλα	gah**meelah**
	2) like **ng** in li**ng**er	ngg	άγκυρα	**ahng**geerah
γξ	like **nks** in li**nks**	ngks	φάλαγξ	**fah**lahngks
γχ	like **ng** followed by the **ch** of Scottish lo**ch**	ngkh	μελαγχολία	mehlahng-**kholleeah**
μπ	1) like **b** in **b**eer	b	μπορείτε	bor**reeteh**
	2) like **mb** in lu**mb**er	mb	Όλυμπος	ol**leemboss**
ντ	1) like **d** in **d**ear	d	ντμάτα	dom**mahtah**
	2) like **nd** in u**nd**er	nd	κένσρο	**kehn**dro
τ	like **ds** in see**ds**	dz	τζάκι	**dzah**kee

Italian

Basic expressions *Espressioni correnti*

Yes/No.	**Sì/No.**	see/no
Please.	**Per favore.**	pair fah**voa**ray
Thank you.	**Grazie.**	**graat**seeay
I beg your pardon?	**Prego?**	**pray**goa

Introductions *Presentazioni*

Good morning.	**Buon giorno.**	bwon **joar**noa
Good afternoon.	**Buon giorno.**	bwon **joar**noa
Good night.	**Buona notte.**	**bwo**nah **not**tay
Good-bye.	**Arrivederci.**	ahrreevay**dair**chee
So long.	**Ciao!**	**chaa**oa
My name is…	**Mi chiamo…**	mee kee**aa**moa
Pleased to meet you.	**Piacere.**	peeah**chay**ray
What's your name?	**Come si chiama?**	**koa**may see kee**aa**mah
How are you?	**Come sta?**	**koa**may stah
Fine thanks. And you?	**Bene grazie. E lei?**	**bai**nay **graat**seeay. ay **lai**ee
Where do you come from?	**Da dove viene?**	dah **doa**vay vee**ay**nay
I'm from…	**Sono…**	**soa**noa
Australia	**di l'Australia**	dee low**straa**leeah
Canada	**di Canada**	dee kah**nah**dah
Great Britain	**di Gran Bretagna**	dee grahn bray**taa**ñah
United States	**degli Stati Uniti**	**day**lee **staa**tee oo**nee**tee
I'm with my…	**Sono con…**	**soa**noa kon
wife	**mia moglie**	**mee**ah **moa**lyay
husband	**mio marito**	**mee**oa mah**ree**toa
family	**la mia famiglia**	lah **mee**ah fah**mee**lyah
boyfriend	**il mio ragazzo**	eel **mee**oa rah**gaht**tsoa
girlfriend	**la mia ragazza**	lah **mee**ah rah**gaht**tsah
I'm here on business/ on vacation.	**Sono qui per affari/ in vacanza.**	**soa**noa **koo**ee pair ah**ffaa**ree/een vah**kah**ntsah

GUIDE TO PRONUNCIATION/EMERGENCIES, see page 111

Questions *Domande*

When?	**Quando?**	kwahndoa
How?	**Come?**	koamay
What?	**Che cosa/Che?**	kay kawsah/kay
Why?	**Perchè?**	pehrkay
Who?/Which?	**Chi?/Quale?**	kee/kwaalay
Where is...?	**Dov'è/Dove si trova...?**	doavai/doavay see trawvah
Where are...?	**Dove sono/Dove si trovano...?**	doavay soanoa/doavay see trawvahnoa
Where can I find/get...?	**Dove posso trovare...?**	doavay possoa trovaaray
How far?	**Quanto dista?**	kwahntoa deestah
How long?	**Quanto tempo?**	kwahntoa tehmpoa
How much/many?	**Quanto/Quanti?**	kwahntoa/kwahntee
Can I have...?	**Posso avere...?**	possoa ahvayray
Can you help me?	**Può aiutarmi?**	pwo aheeootaarmee
What does this mean?	**Che cosa significa questo?**	kay kawsah seeñeefeekah kooaystoa
I understand.	**Capisco.**	kahpeeskoa
I don't understand.	**Non capisco.**	noan kahpeeskoa
Can you translate this for me?	**Può tradurmi questo?**	pwo trahdoormee kooaystoa
Do you speak English?	**Parla inglese?**	pahrlah eengglaysay
I don't speak (much) Italian.	**Non parlo (bene) l'italiano.**	noan pahrloa (bainay) leetahleeaanoa

A few more useful words *Qualche altra parola utile*

better/worse	**migliore/peggiore**	meelyoaray/paydjoaray
big/small	**grande/piccolo**	grahnday/peekkoaloa
cheap/expensive	**buon mercato/caro**	bwawn mayrkahtoa/kaaroa
early/late	**presto/tardi**	prehstoa/tahrdee
good/bad	**buono/cattivo**	bwawnoa/kahtteevoa
hot/cold	**caldo/freddo**	kahldoa/frayddoa
near/far	**vicino/lontano**	veecheenoa/lontaanoa
old/new	**vecchio/nuovo**	vehkkeeoa/nwawvoa
right/wrong	**giusto/sbagliato**	joostoa/zbahlyaatoa
vacant/occupied	**libero/occupato**	leebayroa/okkoopaatoa

Hotel–Accommodation *Albergo*

I have a reservation.	**Ho fatto una prenotazione.**	oa **fahttoa** oonah praynoatahtseeoanay
We've reserved 2 rooms.	**Abbiamo prenotato due camere.**	ahbbeeaamoa praynoatah-toa dooay kaamayray
Do you have any vacancies?	**Avete camere libere?**	ahvaytay kaamayray leebayray
I'd like a...room...	**Vorrei una camera...**	vorraiee oonah kaamarah
single	**singola**	**seeng**goalah
double	**doppia**	**doap**peeah
with twin beds	**con due letti**	kon **dooay leht**tee
with a double bed	**con un letto matrimoniale**	kon oon **leht**toa matreemoaneeaalay
with a bath/shower	**con bagno/doccia**	kon **baañoa/dot**chah
We'll be staying...	**Resteremo...**	raystayraymoa
overnight only	**una notte**	oonah **not**tay
a few days	**qualche giorno**	**kwahl**kay joarnoa
a week	**un settimana**	oonah saytteemaanah
Is there a camp site near here?	**C'è un campeggio qui vicino?**	chai oon kahm**payd**joa kooee veecheenoa

Decision *Decisione*

May I see the room?	**Posso vedere la camera?**	**pos**soa vay**day**ray lah **kaa**mayrah
That's fine. I'll take it.	**Va bene, la prendo.**	vah **bai**nay lah **prehn**doa
No. I don't like it.	**No, non mi piace.**	noa noan mee pee**ah**chay
It's too...	**È troppo...**	ai **trop**poa
dark/small	**buia/piccola**	**booee**ah/**peek**koalah
noisy	**rumorosa**	roomoa**roa**zah
Do you have anything...?	**Ha qualcosa...?**	ah kwahl**kaw**sah
better	**migliore**	meel**yoa**ray
bigger	**più grande**	peeoo **grahn**day
cheaper	**meno caro**	mainoa **kaa**roa
quieter	**più tranquillo**	peeoo trahngkooeelloa
May I have my bill, please?	**Posso avere il conto, per favore?**	**pos**soa ah**vay**ray eel **koan**toa pair fah**voa**ray
It's been a very enjoyable stay.	**È stato un soggiorno molto piacevole.**	ai **staa**toa oon soad**joar**noa **moal**toa peeh**chay**voalay

NUMBERS, see page 110

Eating out *Ristorante*

I'd like to reserve a table for 4.	**Vorrei riservare un tavolo per 4.**	vorraiee reesehrvaaray oon taavoala pair 4
We'll come at 8.	**Verremo alle 8.**	vayrraymoa ahllay 8
I'd like…	**Vorrei…**	vorraiee
breakfast	**la colazione**	lah kolahtseeoanay
lunch	**il pranzo**	eel prahndzoa
dinner	**la cena**	lah chaynah
What do you recommend?	**Cosa consiglia?**	kawsah akonseelyah
Do you have any vegetarian dishes?	**Avete dei piatti vegetariani?**	ahvaytay daiee peeahtte vajyaytahreeaanee

Breakfast *Colazione*

May I have some…	**Posso avere…**	possoa ahvayray
bread	**del pane**	dayl paanay
butter	**del burro**	dayl boorroa
cheese	**del formaggio**	dayl foarmahdjoa
ham and eggs	**uova e prosciutto**	wawvah ay proashoottoa
jam	**della marmellata**	dayllah mahrmayllaatah
rolls	**dei panini**	daiee pahneenee

Appetizers *Antipasti*

carciofini sottolio	kahrchofeenee soattolyoa	artichoke hearts in olive oil
frutti di mare	froottee ee maaray	mixed seafood
insalata di pollo	eensahlaatah dee poalloa	chicken salad
sardine all'olio	sahrdeenay ahllolyoa	sardines in oil

Pasta and sauces *Pasta e salse*

agnolotti (ahñoalottee)	round parcels filled with meat, vegetables and cheese
amatriciana (ahmahtreechaanah)	sauce of tomatoes, red peppers, bacon, onion garlic and wine
cappelletti (kahppayllayttee)	small ravioli filled with meat, herbs, ham and cheese
carrettiera (kahrraytteeayrah)	sauce of tuna, mushrooms, tomato purée and pepper
puttanesca (poottahnayskah)	sauce of capers, olives, parsley, garlic, olive oil and black pepper

Fish and seafood *Pesci e frutti di mare*

carp	**carpa**	kahrpah
cod	**merluzzo**	mayrloottsoa
crab	**granchi**	grahngkee
lobster	**aragosta**	ahrahgoastah
mussels	**cozze**	koatsay
oysters	**ostriche**	ostreekay
scallops	**arselle**	ahrsehllay
swordfish	**pesce spada**	payshay spaadah

Meat *Carne*

I'd like some...	**Vorrei...**	vorraiee
beef	**del manzo**	dayl mahndzoa
chicken	**del pollo**	dayl poalloa
lamb	**dell'agnello**	dayllahñehlloa
pork	**del maiale**	dayl maaeeaalay
veal	**del vitello**	dal veetehlloa
abbacchio	ahbbahkkeeoa	roast lamb with ancho-vies
pollo alla diavola	poalloa ahllah deeaavoalah	highly spiced grilled chicken
spezzatino	spaytsahteenoa	meat or poultry stew

baked	**al forno**	ahl fornoa
boiled	**lesso**	layssoa
fried/roast	**fritto/arrosto**	freettoa/ahrroastoa
grilled	**ai ferri**	ahee fehrree
stewed	**in umido**	een oomeedoa
underdone (rare)	**al sangue**	ahl sahnggooay
medium	**a puntino**	al poonteenoa
well-done	**ben cotto**	bain kottoa

Vegetables *Verdure*

beans (French)	**fagiolini**	fahjoaleenee
cabbage	**cavolo**	kaavoaloa
carrots	**carote**	kahrawtay
mushrooms	**funghi**	foonggee
onions	**cipolle**	cheepollay
peas	**piselli**	peesehllee
potatoes	**patate**	paytaatay
tomatoes	**pomodoro**	poamoadawroa

Fruit and dessert *Frutta e dolce*

apple	**mela**	**may**lah
cherries	**ciliege**	cheeleee**ay**jay
lemon	**limone**	lee**mo**anay
orange	**arancia**	ah**rahn**chah
pear	**pera**	**pay**rah
plums	**susina**	soo**zee**nah
strawberries	**fragole**	**fraa**goalay
budino	boo**dee**noa	pudding
gelato	jay**laa**toa	ice-cream
zabaglione	dzahbahl**yo**anay	eggyolks, sugar and Marsala wine

Drinks *Bevande*

I'd like...	**Vorrei...**	vor**rai**ee
beer	**una birra**	**oo**nah **beer**rah
(hot) chocolate	**un cioccolato**	oon choakkoa**laa**toa
coffee	**un caffè**	oon kahf**fai**
with cream	**con panna**	kon **pahn**nah
fruit juice	**un succo di frutta**	oon **sook**koa dee **froot**tah
milk	**del latte**	dayl **laht**tay
mineral water	**dell'acqua minerale**	dayll**ahk**kwah meenay**raa**lay
tea	**un tè**	oon tai
wine	**di vino**	dee **vee**noa
a bottle	**una bottiglia**	**oo**nah bot**teel**yah
a glass	**un bicchiere**	oon beek**kee**airay
red/white	**rosso/bianco**	**roas**soa/bee**ahng**koa

Complaints and paying *Reclami e il conto*

This is too bitter/ sweet.	**Questo è troppo amaro/dolce.**	**kooays**toa ai **trop**poa ah**maa**roa/**doal**chay
That's not what I ordered.	**Non è ciò che avevo ordinato.**	noan ai cho kay ah**vay**voa oarkee**naa**toa
I'd like to pay.	**Vorrei pagare.**	vor**rai**ee pah**gaa**ray
I think there's a mistake in this bill.	**Penso che abbiate fatto un errore nel conto.**	**pehn**soa kay ahb**bee**aatay **faht**toa oon ayr**roa**ray nayl **koan**toa
Can I pay with this credit card?	**Posso pagare con questa carta di credito?**	**pos**soa pah**gaa**ray kon **kooays**tah **kahr**tah dee **kray**deetoa
We enjoyed it, thank you.	**Ci è piaciuto, grazie.**	chee ai peeah**choo**toa **graat**seeay

NUMBERS, see page 110

Travelling around *Escursioni*

Plane *Aereo*

Is there a flight to ...?	C'è un volo per ...	chai oon **voa**loa pair
What time should I check in?	A che ora devo presentarmi?	ah kay **oa**rah **day**voa prayzehn**taar**mee
I'd like to ... my reservation.	Vorrei ... la mia prenotazione.	vor**rai**ee ... lah **mee**ah praynoatahtseeoanay
cancel	annullare	ahnnool**laa**ray
change	cambiare	kahmbee**aa**ray
confirm	confermare	koanfayr**maa**ray

Train *Treno*

I'd like a ticket to ...	Desidero un biglietto per ...	day**zee**dayroa oon bee-**lyay**ttoa pair
single (one-way)	andata	ahn**daa**tah
return (round trip)	andata e ritorno	ahn**daa**tah ay ree**tor**noa
first/second class	prima/secondo classe	**pree**mah/say**koan**dah **klahs**say
How long does the journey (trip) take?	Quanto tempo dura il percorso?	**kwahn**toa **tehm**poa **doo**rah eel payr**koar**soa
When is the ... train to ...?	Quando parte ... treno per ...?	**kwahn**doa **pahr**tay ... **tray**noa pair
first	il primo	eel **pree**moa
next	il prossimo	eel **pros**seemoa
last	l'ultimo	**lool**teemoa
Is this the right train to ...?	È il treno guisto per ...?	ai eel **tray**noa **joos**toa pair

Bus–Tram (streetcar) *Autobus –Tram*

Which bus do I take for the Colosseum?	Quale autobus devo prendere per andare al Colosseo?	**kwaa**lay **ow**toabooss **day**voa **prehn**dayray pair ahn**daa**ray ahl koaloas**sai**oa
How much is the fare to ...?	Quanto costa il biglietto per ...?	**kwahn**toa **kos**tah eel bee**lyay**ttoa pair
Will you tell me when to get off?	Può dirmi quando devo scendere?	pwo **deer**mee **kwahn**doa **day**voa **shayn**dayray

Taxi *Taxi*

What's the fare to ...?	Qual è il prezzo della corsa fino a ...?	kwahl ai eel **preht**tsoa **day**llah **kor**ssah **fee**noa ah

TELLING THE TIME, see page 109

Take me to this address.	**Mi conduca a questo indirizzo.**	mee koandookah ah kooaystoa eendeereettsoa
Please stop here.	**Per favore, si fermi qui.**	pair fahvoaray see fayrmee kooee
Could you wait for me?	**Può aspettarmi?**	pwo ahspehttaarmee

Car hire (rental) *Autonoleggio*

I'd like to hire (rent) a car.	**Vorrei noleggiare una macchina.**	vorraiee noalaydjaaray oonah mahkkeenah
I'd like it for...	**La vorrei per...**	lah vorraiee pair
a day	**un giorno**	oon joarnoa
a week	**una settimana**	oonah saytteemaanah
Where's the nearest filling station?	**Dov'è la stazione di rifornimento più vicina?**	doavai lah stahtseeoanay dee reeforneemayntoa peeoo veecheenah
Fill it up, please.	**Il pieno, per favore.**	eel peeainoa pair fahvoaray
Give me... litres of petrol (gasoline).	**Mi dia... litri di benzina.**	mee deeah... leetree dee bayndzeenah
How do I get to...?	**Come si va a...?**	koamay see vah ah
I've had a break-down at...	**Ho avuto un guasto a...**	oa ahvootoa oon gwaastoa ah
Can you send a mechanic?	**Può mandare un meccanico?**	pwo mahndaaray oon maykkaaneekoa
Can you mend this puncture (fix this flat)?	**Può riparare questa foratura?**	pwo reepahraaray kooaystah forahtoorah

---

Lei è sulla strada sbagliata.	You're on the wrong road.
Vada diritto.	Go straight ahead.
È laggiù a...	It's down there on the...
sinistra/destra	left/right
di fronte/dietro...	opposite/behind...
accanto a/dopo...	next to/after...
nord/sud/est/ovest	north/south/east/west

NUMBERS, see page 110

Sightseeing *Visite turistiche*

Where's the tourist office?	Dov'è l'ufficio turistico?	doavai looffeechoa tooreesteekoa
Is there an English-speaking guide?	C'è una guida che parla inglese?	chai oonah gooeedahkay pahrlah eengglaysay
Where is...?	Dove si trova...?	doavay see trawvah
Where are...?	Dove si trovano...?	doavay see trawvahnoa
abbey	l'abbazia	lahbbahtseeah
castle	il castello	eel kahstehlloa
cathedral	la cattedrale	lah kahttaydraalay
church	la chiesa	lah keeayzah
city centre	il centro città	eel chayntroa cheettah
exhibition	l'esposizione	layspozeetseeoanay
harbour	il porto	eel portoa
market	il mercato	eel mayrkaatoa
museum	il museo	eel moozaioa
shopping area	la zona dei negozi	lah dzonah daiee naygotsee
square	la piazza	lah peeahtsah
tower	la torre	lah toarray
When does it open?	Quando apre?	kwahndoa aapray
When does it close?	Quando chiude?	kwahndoa keeeooday
How much is the entrance fee?	Quanto costa l'entrata?	kwahntoa kostah layntraatah

Relaxing *Divertimenti*

What's playing at the... Theatre?	Che spettacolo c'è al teatro...?	kay spayttaakoaloa chai ahl tayaatroa
Are there any seats for tonight?	Ci sono posti per questa sera?	chee soanoa postee pair kooaysstah sayrah
How much are the seats?	Quanto costano i posti?	kwahntoa kostahnoa ee postee
Would you like to go out with me tonight?	Uscirebbe con me stasera?	oosheerehbbay kon mai stahsayrah
Is there a disco-theque in town?	C'è una discoteca in città?	chai oonah deeskoataykah een cheettah
Would you like to dance?	Vuole ballare?	vwolay bahllaaray
Thank you, it's been a wonderful evening.	Grazie, è stata una magnifica serata.	graatseeay ai staatah oonah mahñeefeekah sayraatah

TELLING THE TIME, see page 109

Shops, stores and services *Negozi e servizi*

Where's the nearest...?	Dove si trova... più vicino(a)?	doavay see trawvah... peeoo veecheenoa(ah)
bakery	la panetteria	lah pahnehttayreeah
bookshop	la libreria	lah leebrayreeah
butcher's	la macelleria	lah mahchayllayreeah
chemist/drugstore	la farmacia	lah fahrmahacheeah
delicatessen	la salumeria	lah sahloomayreeah
department store	il grande magaz-zino	eel grahnday mahgahdzeenoa
grocery	il megozio di ali-mentari	eel maygotseeoa dee ahleemayntaaree
hairdresser	il parrucchiere	eel pahrrookkeeayray
newsagent	il giornalaio	eel joarnahlaaeeoa
post office	l'ufficio postale	looffeechoa poastaalay
supermarket	il supermercato	eel soopairmayrkaatoa
toilets	i gabinetti	ee gahbeenayttee

General expressions *Espressioni generali*

Where's the main shopping area?	Dov'è la zona prin-ciple dei negozi?	doavai lah dzoanah preencheepaalay daieenaygotsee
Do you have any...?	Ha dei...?	ah daiee
Can you show me this/that?	Mi può mostrare questo/quello?	mee pwo moastraaray kooaystoa/kooaylloa
Haven't you anything...?	Non ha qual-cosa...?	noan ah kwahlkawsah
cheaper	meno caro	maynoa kaaroa
better	migliore	meelyoaray
larger/smaller	più grande	peeoo grahnday
Can I try it on?	Posso provarlo?	possoa provahrloa
How much is this?	Quanto costa questo?	kwahntoa kostah kooaystoa
Please write it down.	Per favore, me lo scriva.	pair fahvoaray may loa skreevah
I don't want to spend more than... lire.	Non voglio spen-dere più di... lire.	noan volyoa spehndayray peeoo dee... leeray
No, I don't like it.	No, non mi piace.	noa noan mee peeaachay
I'll take it.	Lo prendo.	loa prayndoa
Do you accept credit-cards?	Accettate carte di credito?	ahtchehttaatay kahrtay dee kraydeetoa
Can you order it for me?	Può ordinarmelo?	pwo oardeenaarmayloa

NUMBERS, see page 110

black	**nero**	nayroa
blue	**blu**	bloo
brown	**marrone**	mahrroanay
green	**verde**	vayrday
grey	**grigio**	greejoa
orange	**arancio**	ahrahnchoa
red	**rosso**	roassoa
yellow	**giallo**	jahlloa
white	**bianco**	beeahngkoa
light...	**... chiaro**	keeaaroa
dark...	**... scuro**	skooroa

I'd like a/an/some...	**Desidero...**	dayzeedayroa
aspirin	**delle aspirine**	dayllay ahspeereenay
bottle-opener	**un apribottiglia**	oon ahpreebotteelyah
bread	**del pane**	dayl paanay
newspaper	**un giornale**	oon joarnaalay
postcard	**una cartolina**	oonah kahrtoaleenah
shampoo	**dello shampoo**	daylloa shahmpoa
soap	**una saponetta**	oonah sahpoanayttah
sun-tan cream	**una crema solare**	oonah kraimah soalaaray
toothpaste	**un dentifricio**	oon daynteefreechoa
a half kilo of tomatoes	**mezzo chillo di pomodori**	mehdzoa keeloa dee pomodawree
a litre of milk	**un litro di latte**	oon leetroa dee lahttay
I'd like a film for this camera.	**Vorrei una pellicola per questa macchina fotografica.**	vorraiee oonah pehlleekoalah pair kooaystah mahkkeenah foatoagraafeekah
black and white	**in bianco e nero**	een beeahngkoa ay nayroa
colour	**a colori**	ah koaloaree
I'd like a hair-cut, please.	**Voglio il taglio dei capelli, per favore.**	volyoa eel taalyoa daiee kahpehllee pair fahvoaray

Souvenirs *Oggetti ricordo*

antiques	**l'antichità**	lahteekeetah
chocolate	**il cioccolato**	eel choakkoalaatoa
flask of Chianti	**il fiasco di Chianti**	eel feeaaskoa dee keeahntee
leather work	**la pelletteria**	lah paylleyttayreeah
porcelain	**la porcellana**	lah poarchallaanah
silk	**la seta**	lah saitah

At the bank *In banca*

Where's the nearest bank/currency exchange office?	**Dov'è la banca/ l'ufficio cambio più vicina?**	doavai lah bahngkah looffeechoa kahmbeeoa peeoo veecheenah
I want to change some dollars/pounds.	**Desidero cambiare dei dollari/delle sterline.**	dayzeedayroa kahmbeeaaray daiee dollahree/dayllay stayrleenay
What's the exchange rate?	**Qual è il corso del cambio?**	kwahl ai ee koarsoa dayl kahmbeeoa
I want to cash a traveller's cheque.	**Voglio incassare un traveller's cheque**	voloa eengkahssaaray oon "traveller's cheque"

At the post office *Ufficio postale*

I want to send this by...	**Desidero inviare questo per...**	dayzeedayroa eenveeaaray kooaystoa pair
airmail	**via aerea**	veeah ahayrayah
express	**espresso**	aysprehssoa
I want... ...-lire stamps.	**Vorrei... franco- bolli da... lire.**	vorraiee... frahngkoa- boallee dah... leeray
What's the postage for a postcard/letter to United States?	**Qual è l'affranca- tura per una cartolina/lettera per gli Stati Uniti?**	kwahl ai lahffrahngkahtoo- rah pair oonah kahrtoa- leenah/lehttayrah pair lyee staatee ooneetee
Is there any post/mail for me?	**C'è dela posta per me?**	chai dayllah postah pair may?

Telephoning *Per telefonare*

Where is the nearest telephone booth?	**Dov'è la cabina te- lefonica più vicina?**	doavai lah kahbeenah tay- layfoneekah peeoo veecheenah
I'd like a telephone token.	**Vorrei un gettone (telefonico).**	vorraiee oon jayttoanay (taylayfoneekoa)
May I use your phone?	**Posso usare i suo tekefono?**	possoa oozaaray eel soooa taylayfoanoa
Hello. This is... speaking.	**Pronto. Qui parla...**	prontoa. kooee pahrlah
I'd like to speak to...	**Vorrei parlare a...**	vorraiee pahrlaaray
When will he/she be back?	**Qundo ritornerà?**	kwahndoa reetoarnehrah

Time and date *Ore e data*

It's...	Sono le...	soanoa lay...
ten past two	**due e dieci**	**doo**ay ay dee**ai**chee
quarter past three	**tre e un quarto**	tray ay oon **kwahr**toa
twenty past four	**quattro e venti**	**kwaht**troa ay **vayn**tee
half past six	**sei e mezza**	se**hee** ay **mehd**dzah
twenty-five to eight	**sette e trenta-cinque**	**seht**tay ay trayntah**cheeng**kooay
ten to ten	**dieci meno dieci**	dee**ai**chee **mai**noa dee**ai**chee
noon/midnight	**mezzogiorno/mezzanotte**	mehdzoa**joar**noa/ mehdzah**not**tay
in the morning	**del mattino**	dayl maht**tee**noa
in the afternoon	**del pomeriggio**	dayl poamay**reed**joa
in the evening	**della sera**	**dayl**lah **say**rah
during the day	**durante il giorno**	doo**rahn**tay eel **joar**noa
at night	**la nottee**	lah **not**tay
yesterday/today	**ieri/oggi**	ee**ai**ree/**od**jee
tomorrow	**domani**	doa**maa**nee
spring	**la primavera**	lah preemah**vay**rah
summer	**l'estate**	lay**staa**tay
autumn	**l'autonno**	low**toon**noa
winter	**l'inverno**	leen**vehr**noa

Sunday	**domenica**	doa**may**neekah
Monday	**lunedì**	loonay**dee**
Tuesday	**martedì**	mahrtay**dee**
Wednesday	**mercoledì**	mehrkoalay**dee**
Thursday	**giovedì**	oavay**dee**
Friday	**venerdì**	vaynayr**dee**
Saturday	**sabato**	**saa**bahtoa
January	**gennaio**	jehn**naa**eeoa
February	**febbraio**	fehb**braa**eeoa
March	**marzo**	**mahr**tsoa
April	**aprile**	ah**pree**lay
May	**maggio**	**mahd**joa
June	**guigno**	**joo**ñoa
July	**luglio**	**loo**lyoa
August	**agosto**	ah**goa**stoa
September	**settembre**	sayt**tehm**bray
October	**ottobre**	oat**toa**bray
November	**novembre**	noa**vehm**bray
December	**dicembre**	dee**chehm**bray

NUMBERS, see page 110

Numbers *Numeri*

0	**zero**	dzehroa
1	**uno**	oonoa
2	**due**	dooay
3	**tre**	tray
4	**quattro**	kwahttroa
5	**cinque**	cheengkooay
6	**sei**	sehee
7	**sette**	sehttay
8	**otto**	ottoa
9	**nove**	nawvay
10	**dieci**	deeaichee
11	**undici**	oondeechee
12	**dodici**	doadeechee
13	**tredici**	traydeechee
14	**quattordici**	kwahttordeechee
15	**quindici**	kooeendeechee
16	**sedici**	saydeechee
17	**diciassette**	deechahssehttay
18	**diciotto**	deechottoa
19	**diciannove**	deechahnnawvay
20	**venti**	vayntee
21	**ventuno**	vayntoonoa
30	**trenta**	trayntah
40	**quaranta**	kwahrahntah
50	**cinquanta**	cheengkwahntah
60	**sesssanta**	sayssahntah
70	**settanta**	sayttahntah
80	**ottanta**	ottahntah
90	**novanta**	noavahntah
100	**cento**	chehntoa
1000	**mille**	meellay
1,000,000	**un milione**	oon meelyoanay
1,000,000,000	**un miliardo**	un meelyahrdo

first	**primo**	preemoa
second	**secondo**	saykoandoa
third	**terzo**	tehrtsoa
once	**una volta**	oonah voltah
twice	**due volte**	dooay voltay
a half	**un mezzo**	oon mehddzoa
a quarter	**un quarto**	oon kwahrtoa
a third	**un terzo**	oon tehrtsoa

Emergency *Emergenza*

Call the police	Chiami la polizia	keeaamee lah poaleetseeah
Get a doctor	Chiami un medico	keeaamee oon maideekoa
Go away	Se ne vada	say nay vaadah
HELP	AIUTO	aheeootoa
I'm ill	Mi sento male	mee sayntoa maalay
I'm lost	Mi sono perso(a)	mee soanoa pehrsoa(ah)
Leave me alone	Mi lasci in pace	mee laashee een paachay
LOOK OUT	ATTENZIONE	ahttayntseeoanay
STOP THIEF	AL LADRO	ahl laadroa
My... has been stolen.	Mi hanno rubato ...	mee ahnnoa roobaatoa
I've lost my...	Ho perso ...	oa pehrsoa
handbag	la mia borsetta	lah meeah boarsayttah
wallet	il mio portafogli	eel meeoa portahfoalyee
passport	il mio passaporto	eel meeoa pahssahpoartoa
Where can I find a doctor who speaks English?	Dove possso trovare un medico che parla inglese?	doavay possoa troavaaray oon maideekoa kay pahrlah eengglaysay

Guide to Italian pronunciation *Pronuncia*

Consonants

Letter	Approximate pronunciation	Symbol	Example	
b, d, f, k, l, m, n, p, q, t, v	as in English			
c	1) before **e** and **i**, like **ch** in **chip**	ch	**cerco**	**chayr**koa
	2) elsewhere, like **c** in **cat**	k	**conto**	**koant**oa
ch	like **c** in **cat**	k	**che**	kay
g	1) before **e** and **i**, like **j** in **jet**	j	**valigia**	vah**lee**jah
	2) elsewhere, like **g** in **go**	g	**grande**	**grahn**day

TELEPHONING, see page 108

gh	like **g** in go	g	**ghiaccio**	gee**ah**tchoa
gl	like **lli** in million	ly	**gli**	lyee
gn	like **ni** in onion	ñ	**bagno**	bah**ñ**oa
h	always silent		**ha**	ah
r	trilled like a Scottish **r**	r	**deriva**	deh**r**eevah
s	1) generally like **s** in sit	s	**questo**	koo**ay**stoa
	2) sometimes like **z** in zoo	z	**viso**	vee**z**oa
sc	1) before **e** and **i**, like **sh** in shut	sh	**uscita**	oo**sh**eetah
	2) elsewhere, like **sk** in skin	sk	**scarpa**	**sk**ahrpah
z/zz	1) generally like **ts** in hits	ts	**grazie**	graa**ts**eeay
	2) sometimes like **ds** in roads	dz	**romanzo**	roamahn**dz**oa

Vowels

a	1) short, like **a** in car, but shorter	ah	**gatto**	g**ah**ttoa
	2) long, like **a** in car	aa	**casa**	k**aa**sah
e	1) can always be pronounced like **ay** in way, but without moving tongue or lips	ay	**sera**	s**ay**rah
	2) in correct speech, it is sometimes pronounced like **e** in get or, when long, more like **ai** in hair	eh	**bello**	b**eh**lloa
i	like **ee** in meet	ee	**vini**	v**ee**nee
o	1) can always be pronounced like **oa** in goat, but without moving tongue or lips	oa	**sole**	s**oa**lay
	2) in correct speech, it is sometimes pronounced like **o** in got, or when long, more like **aw** in law	o aw	**notte** **rosa**	n**o**ttay r**aw**zah
u	like **oo** in foot	oo	**fumo**	f**oo**moa

Norwegian

Basic expressions *Vanlyige uttrykk*

Yes/No.	**Ja/Nei.**	yaa/næi
Please.	**Vær (så) snill å .../ ..., takk.**	væ (saw) snil aw/ ... tahk
Thank you.	**Takk.**	tahk
I beg your pardon?	**Unnskyld?**	ewnshewl

Introductions *Presentasjon*

Good morning.	**God morgen.**	goomawer'n
Good afternoon.	**God dag.**	goodaag
Good night.	**God natt.**	goonaht
Hello/Hi.	**Hallo/Hei!**	hahlōō/hæi
Goodbye.	**Adjø.**	ahdyūr
My name is...	**Mitt navn er...**	mit nahvn ær
Pleased to meet you.	**Hyggelig å treffes.**	hewgerli aw trehferss
What's your name?	**Hva heter du?**	vah hāyterr dew
How are you?	**Hvordan står det til?**	voo'dahn stawr deh til
Fine thanks. And you?	**Bare bra, takk. Og med deg?**	baarer braa tahk. o(g) meh(d) dæi
Where do you come from?	**Hvor kommer du fra?**	voor kommer dew fraa
I'm from...	**Jeg er fra...**	yæi ær fraa
Australia	**Australia**	oustraaleeah
Canada	**Kanada**	kahnahdah
Great Britain	**Storbritannia**	stoorbrittahneeah
United States	**USA**	ēw-ehss-aa
I'm with my...	**Jeg er her med...**	yæi æ hāēr meh(d)
wife/husband	**min kone/mann**	meen kōōner/mahn
family	**min familie**	meen fahmeelyer
boyfriend/girlfriend	**min venn/venninne**	meen vehn/vehninner
I'm here on business/vacation.	**Jeg er her i forretninger/ på ferie.**	yæi ær hāēr ee forrehtingerr/ paw fāyryer

114

Questions *Spørsmål*

When?	**Når?**	nor
How?	**Hvordan/Hvor?**	voo'dahn/voor
What?/Why?	**Hva?/Hvorfor?**	vaa/voorfor
Who?/Which?	**Hvem?/Hvilken?**	vehm/vilkern
Where is/are...?	**Hvor er...?**	voor ær
Where can I find...?	**Hvor finner jeg...?**	voor finnerr yæi
Where can I get...?	**Hvor kan jeg få tak i...?**	voor kahn yæi faw taak ee
How far?	**Hvor langt?**	voor lahngt
How long?	**Hvor lenge?**	voor lehnger
How much/many?	**Hvor mye/mange?**	voor mēwer/mahnger
Can I have...?	**Kan jeg få...?**	kahn yæi faw
Can you help me?	**Kan du hjelpe meg?**	kahn dew yehlper mæi
What does this mean?	**Hva betyr dette?**	vaa bertēwr dehter
I understand.	**Jeg forstår.**	yæi foshtawr
I don't understand.	**Jeg forstår ikke.**	yæi foshtawr ikker
Can you translate this for me?	**Kan du oversette dette for meg?**	kahn dew awversehter dehter for mæi
Do you speak English?	**Snakker du engelsk?**	snahkerr dew ehngerlsk
I don't speak (much) Norwegian.	**Jeg snakker ikke (så bra) norsk.**	yæi snahkerr ikker (saw braa) noshk

A few more useful words *Noen flere nyttige ord*

better/worse	**bedre/verre**	bāydrer/væer
big/small	**stor/liten**	stoor/leetern
cheap/expensive	**billig/dyr**	billi/dēwr
early/late	**tidlig/sen**	teeli/sāyn
good/bad	**bra/dårlig**	braa/dāw'li
hot/cold	**varm/kald**	vahrm/kahl
near/far	**nær/fjern**	nær/fyæ'n
old/new	**gammel/ny**	gahmerl/nēw
right/wrong	**riktig/feil**	rikti/fæil
vacant/occupied	**ledig/opptatt**	lāydi/optaht

Hotel–Accommodation *Hotell*

I have a reservation.	**Jeg har bestilt rom.**	yæi haar ber**stilt** room
Do you have any vacancies?	**Har dere noen ledige rom?**	haar **da̅y**rer **noo**ern **la̅y**deeyer room
I'd like a ...	**Jeg vil gjerne ha et ...**	yæi vil **yæ**'ner **haa** eht
single room	**enkeltrom**	**ehng**kerltroom
double room	**dobbeltrom**	**dobb**erltroom
with twin beds	**med to senger**	meh(d) **too sehng**err
with a double bed	**med dobbeltseng**	meh(d) **dobb**erltsehng
with a bath/shower	**med bad/dusj**	meh(d) baad/dewsh
We'll be staying ...	**Vi blir ...**	vee bleer
overnight only	**bare natten over**	**baa**rer **nah**tern **aw**verr
a few days	**et par dager**	eht pahr **daa**gerr
a week	**en uke (minst)**	ehn **e̅w**ker (minst)
Is there a camp site near here?	**Er det en camping-plass i nærheten?**	ær deh ehn **kæm**ping-plahss ee **næ̅r**hehtern

Decision *Beslutning*

May I see the room?	**Kan jeg få se rom-met?**	kahn yæi faw **sa̅y room**mer
That's fine. I'll take it.	**Det er bra. Jeg tar det.**	deh ær braa. yæi taar deh
No. I don't like it.	**Nei. Jeg liker det ikke.**	næi. yæ **lee**kerr deh **ik**ker
It's too ...	**Det er for ...**	deh ær for
dark/small/noisy	**mørkt/lite/ støyende**	murrkt/**lee**ter/**stoy**erner
Do you have any-thing ...?	**Har dere noe ...?**	haar **da̅y**rer **noo**er
better/bigger	**bedre/større**	**ba̅y**drer/**stur**rer
cheaper	**rimeligere**	**ree**merleeyerrer
quieter	**roligere**	**roo**leeyerrer
May I have my bill, please?	**Kan jeg få regnin-gen?**	kahn yæi faw **ræi**ningern
It's been a very enjoyable stay.	**Det har vært et meget hyggelig.**	deh haar væ'rt eht **ma̅y**gert **hew**gerli **op**hol

Eating out *Mat og drikke*

I'd like to reserve a table for 4.	**Jeg vil gjerne bestille et bord til 4.**	yæi vil **yǣ'**ner ber**still**er eht bŏor til 4
We'll come at 8.	**Vi kommer kl. 8.**	vee **kom**merr **klok**kern 8
I'd like breakfast/ lunch/dinner.	**Jeg vil gjerne ha frokost/lunsj/ middag.**	yæi vil **yǣ'**ner haa **frŏo**kost/**lurnsh middah(g)**
What would you recommend?	**Hva anbefaler du?**	vaa **ahn**berfaalerr dew
Do you have any vegetarian dishes?	**Har dere noen vegetariske retter?**	haar **day**rer **nŏo**ern vehger**taa**risker **reht**err

Breakfast *Frokost*

I'll have some...	**Jeg tar...**	yæi taar
bread	**litt brød**	lit brūr
butter	**litt smør**	lit smurr
cheese	**ost**	oost
ham and eggs	**egg og skinke**	ehg o(g) **shing**ker
jam	**syltetøy**	**sewl**tertoy
rolls	**et rundstykke**	eht **rewn**stewker

Starters and soups *Forretter og supper*

betasuppe	**bāy**tahsewper	thick meat and vegetable soup
blomkålsuppe	**blom**kawlsewper	cauliflower soup
fiskesppe	**fisker**sewper	fish soup
froskelår	**frosker**lawr	frog's legs
gåselever	**gawsser**lehverr	goose liver
hummersuppe	**hoom**merrsewper	lobster soup
neslesuppe	**nehsh**lersewper	nettle soup
snegler	**snæi**lerr	snails

Fish and seafood *Fisk og skalldyr*

cod	**torsk**	toshk
crab	**krabbe**	**krah**ber
eel	**ål**	awl
haddock	**kolje**	**kol**yer
herring	**sild**	sil
lobster	**hummer**	**hoom**merr
mussels	**blåskjell**	**blaw**shehl
oysters	**østers**	**urs**tersh
sole	**sjøtunge**	**shūr**toonger
trout	**ørret**	**ur**reht

NUMBERS, see page 126

baked/boiled	**bakt/kokt**	bahkt/kookt
fried/grilled	**stekt/grillet**	stehkt/**grill**ert
roasted	**ovnsstekt**	**ovns**stehkt
underdone (rare)	**råstekt**	**raw**stehkt
medium	**medium stekt**	**may**diewm stehkt
well-done	**godt stekt**	got stehkt

Meat *Kjøtt*

I'd like some...	**Jeg vil gjerne ha...**	yæi vil yǣ'ner haa
beef	**oksekjøtt**	**ook**serkhurt
chicken/duck	**kylling/and**	**khew**ling/ahn
lamb	**lammekøtt**	**lah**merkhurt
pork	**svinekjøtt**	**svee**nerkhurt
veal	**kalvekjøtt**	**kahl**verkhurt
fårikål	fawrikawl	lamb and cabbage stew
benløse fugler	**bayn**lürsser **few**lerr	veal or beef stuffed with forcemeat
stekt juleribbe/ribbe	stehkt **yew**lerribber/ribber	roast spareribs with sweet and sour cabbage

Vegetables *Grønnsaker*

beans	**bønner**	**bur**nerr
cabbage	**kål**	kawl
carrots	**gulrøtter**	**gewl**rurterr
cauliflower	**blomkål**	**blom**kawl
mushrooms	**sopp**	sop
onions	**løk**	lürk
peas	**erter**	**æ'**terr
potatoes	**poteter**	poo**tay**terr
tomatoes	**tomater**	too**maa**terr

Fruit and dessert *Frukt og dessert*

apple	**eple**	**ehp**ler
banana	**banan**	bah**naan**
cherries	**kirsebær**	**khish**erbǣr
lemon	**sitron**	sit**roon**
orange	**appelsin**	ahperl**seen**
pear	**pære**	**pǣ**rer
plums	**plommer**	**ploom**merr
strawberries	**jordbær**	**yoor**bǣr

Hoffdessert	hofdehssǣr	layered meringue and cream with chocolate sauce
is(krem)	**eess(krāym)**	ice-cream
jordbær-	yoorbǣr	strawberry
vanilje-	vahnilyer	vanilla
sjokoladepudding	shookoolaaderpewding	chocolate mousse
vafler med syltetøy	**vah**flerr meh(d) **sewl**tertoy	waffles with jam

Drinks *Drikkevarer*

beer	**en øl**	ehn url
(hot) chocolate	**(varm) sjokolade**	(vahrm) shookoolaader
coffee	**kaffe**	**kah**fer
a pot of	**en kanne**	ehn **kah**ner
with cream	**med fløte**	meh(d) **flur**ter
fruit juice	**en juice**	ehn yēwss
(glass of) milk	**(et glass) melk**	(eht glahss) mehlk
mineral water	**naturlig mineralvann**	nahtēw'li minerraalvahn
tea	**te**	tāy
wine	**vin**	veen
red/white	**rødvin/hvitvin**	**rūr**veen/**veet**veen

Complaints and paying *Klager og regningen*

This is too...	**Dette er for...**	**deh**ter ær for
bitter/sweet	**beskt/søtt**	behskt/surt
salty	**salt**	sahlt
That's not what I ordered.	**Dette er ikke det jeg bestilte.**	**deh**ter ær **ik**ker deh yæi ber**stil**ter
I'd like to pay.	**Jeg vil gjerne betale.**	yæi vil **yǣ'**ner ber**taa**ler
I think there's a mistake in this bill.	**Jeg tror det er en feil på regningen.**	yæi trōōr deh ær ehn fæil paw **ræi**ningern
Can I pay with this credit card?	**Kan jeg betale med dette kredittkortet?**	kahn yæi ber**taa**ler meh(d) **deh**ter kreh**dit**-ko'ter
Is everything included?	**Er alt inkludert?**	ær ahlt inklew**dāy**'t
We enjoyed it, thank you.	**Det var meget godt.**	deh vaar **māy**gert got

NUMBERS, see page 126

Travelling around *På reise*

Plane *Fly*

Is there a flight to...?	**Går det et fl til...?**	gawr eh eht flew til
What time should I check in?	**Når må jeg sjekke inn?**	nor maw yæi **sheh**ker in
I'd like to... my reservation.	**Jeg vil gjerne... reservasjonen.**	yæi vil **yæ^r**ner... rehssævah**shoo**nern
cancel	**annullere**	ahnew**lay**rer
change	**endre**	**ehn**drer
confirm	**bekrefte**	ber**krehf**ter

Train *Tog*

I'd like a ticket to...	**Jeg vil gjerne ha en billett til...**	yæi vil **yæ^r**ner haa ehn bil**leht** til
single (one-way)	**enkeltbillett**	**ehng**kerlt**billeht**
return (round trip)	**tur-returbillett**	tewr-reh**tewr**billeht
first class	**første klasse**	**fursh**ter **klah**sser
second class	**andre/annen klasse**	**ahn**drer/**aaern klah**sser
When's the... train to...?	**Når går... tog til...?**	nor gawr... tawg til
first/next/last	**første/neste/siste**	**fursh**ter/**nehs**ter/**sis**ter
Is this the train to...?	**Er dette toget til...?**	ær **deh**ter **tawg**er til

Bus–Tram (streetcar) *Buss–Trikk*

Which tram goes to the town centre?	**Hvilken trikk går til sentrum?**	**vil**kern trik gawr til **sehn**trewm
How much is the fare to...?	**Hvor mye koster det til...?**	voor **mew**er **kos**terr deh til
Will you tell me when to get off?	**Kan du si fra når jeg skal gå av?**	kahn dew see fraa nor yæi skahl gaw ahv

Taxi *Drosje/Taxi*

How much is the fare to...?	**Hva koster det til...?**	vaa **kos**terr deh til
Take me to this address.	**Kjør meg til denne adressen.**	khürr mæi til **deh**ner ah**drehs**sern
Please stop here.	**Stans her.**	**stahnss** hær

TELLING THE TIME, see page 125

| Could you wait for me? | **Kan du vente på meg?** | kahn dew **vehn**ter paw mæi |

Car hire (rental) *Bilutleie*

I'd like to hire (rent) a car.	**Jeg vil gjerne leie en bil.**	yæi vil **yææ'**ner **læi**er ehn beel
I'd like it for...	**Jeg vil ha den...**	yæi vil haa dehn
a day	**en dag**	ehn daag
a week	**en uke**	ehn $\overline{ew}$ker
Where's the nearest filling station?	**Hvor er nærmeste bensinstasjon?**	voor ær **nær**mehster behn**seen**stahsh$\overline{oo}$n
Fill it up, please.	**Full tank, takk.**	fewl tahngk tahk
Give me... litres of petrol (gasoline).	**... liter bensin, takk.**	... **lee**terr behn**seen** tahk
How do I get to...?	**Hvordan kommer jeg til...?**	**voo'**dahn k**o**mmerr yæi til
this place	**dette stedet**	**deh**ter **stay**der
this address	**denne adressen**	**deh**ner ah**dreh**ssern
I've had a break-down at...	**Jeg har fått motor-stopp ved...**	yæi haar fot **moo**tooshtop veh(d)
Can you send a mechanic?	**Kan du sende en mekaniker?**	kahn dew **seh**ner ehn meh**kaa**nikkerr
Can you mend this puncture (fix this flat)?	**Kan du reparere denne punkte-ringen?**	kahn dew rehpah**ray**rer **deh**ner poong**tay**-ringern

---

Du har kjørt feil.	You're on the wrong road.
Kjør rett frem.	Go straight ahead.
Det er der borte til...	It's down there on the...
høyre/venstre	left/right
midt imot/bak...	opposite/behind...
ved siden av/etter...	next to/after...
nord/sør/øst/vest	north/south/east/west

NUMBERS, see page 126

Sightseeing *Sightseeing*

Where's the tourist office?	**Hvor er turist-kontoret?**	voor ær tewrist-koontŏŏrer
Is there an English-speaking guide?	**Fins det en engelsk-talende guide der?**	finss deh ehn **ehng**erlsk-taalerner "guide" dæer
Where is/are the...?	**Hvor er...?**	voor ær
art gallery	**kunstgalleriet**	**kewnst**gahlerreeyer
castle	**slottet**	**shlot**ter
cathedral/church	**domkirken/kirken**	**dom**khirkern/**khir**kern
city centre	**sentrum**	**sehn**trewm
exhibition	**utstillingen**	**ewt**stillingern
harbour	**havnen**	**hahv**nern
market	**torghandelen**	**torg**hahnderlern
museum	**museet**	mewss**say**er
shopping area	**handlestrøket**	**hahn**dlerstrŭrker
square	**plassen/torget**	**plahs**sern/**tor**gger
tower	**tårnet**	taw'ner
When is it open?	**Når er det åpent?**	nor ær deh **aw**pernt
When does it close?	**Når stenger det?**	nor **stehng**err deh
How much is the entrance fee?	**Hva koster inn-gangsbilletten?**	vah **kos**terr **in**gahngs-billehtern

Relaxing *Underholdning*

What's playing at the... Theatre?	**Hva spilles på... Theatret?**	vah **spill**erss paw ... tāy**aat**rer
Are there any tickets for tonight?	**Fins det fremdeles billetter til i kveld?**	finss eh frehm**day**lerss bill**eh**terr til ee kvehl
How much are the tickets?	**Hvor mye koster billettene?**	voor **mew**er **kos**terr bill**eh**terner
Would you like to go out with me tonight?	**Skal vi gå ut i kveld?**	skahl vee gaw ewt ee kvehl
Is there a discoteque in town?	**Fins det et diskotek i byen?**	finss deh eht diskoo**tayk** ee **bew**ern
Would you like to dance?	**Skal vi danse?**	skahl vee **dahn**ser
Thank you, it's been a wonderful evening.	**Takk, det har vært en veldig hyggelig kveld.**	tahk deh haar væ't ehn **vehl**di **hew**gerli kvehl

TELLING THE TIME/DAYS OF THE WEEK, see page 125

Shops, stores and services *Butikker og servicenæringer*

Where's the nearest...?	**Hvor er nærmeste...?**	voor ær nærmehster
bakery	**et bakeri**	eht baakerree
bookshop/store	**en bokhandel**	ehn bookhahnderl
butcher's	**en slakter**	ehn shlahkterr
chemist's/drugstore	**et apotek**	eht ahpootayk
dentist	**en tannlege**	ehn tahnlayger
department store	**et stormagasin**	eht stoormahgahsseen
grocery	**en matvarehandel**	ehn maatvaarerhahnderl
hairdresser	**en frisør**	ehn frissurr
liquor store	**et vinmonopol**	eht veenmoonoopool
newsstand	**en aviskiosk**	ehn ahveeskhyosk
post office	**et postkontor**	eht postkoontoor
supermarket	**et supermarked**	eht sewperrmahrkerd
toilets	**toalettet**	tooahlehter

General expressions *Vanlige uttrykk*

Where's the main shopping area?	**Hvor er det største handlestrøket?**	voor ær deh sturshter hahndlerstrurker
Do you have any...?	**Har du noen...?**	har dew nooern
Can you show me...?	**Kan du vise meg...?**	kahn dew veesser mæi
this/that	**dette/det**	dehter/deh
Don't you have anything...?	**Har du ikke noe...?**	haar dew ikker nooer
cheaper/better larger/smaller	**rimeligere/bedre større/mindre**	reemerleeyerrer/baydrer sturrer/mindrer
Can I try it on?	**Kan eg få prøve den?**	kahn yæi faw prurver dehn
How much is this?	**Hvor mye koster dette?**	voor mewer kosterr dehter
Please write it down.	**Kan du skrive det?**	kahn dew skreever deh
I don't want to spend more than... kroner.	**Jeg vil ikke gi mer enn... kroner.**	yæi vil ikker yee mayr ehn... kroonerr
No, I don't like it.	**Nei, jeg liker det ikke.**	næi yæi leekerr deh ikker
I'll take it.	**Jeg tar det.**	yæi taar deh
Do you accept credit cards?	**Tar dere kreditt-kort?**	taar dayrer krehditko't
Can you order it for me?	**Kan du bestille det til meg?**	kahn dew berstiller deh til mæi

NUMBERS, see page 126

black	**svart**	svah't
blue	**blå**	blaw
brown	**brun**	brewn
green	**grønn**	grurn
orange	**oransje**	oorahngsh
red	**rød**	rūr
white	**hvit**	veet
yellow	**gul**	gewl
light...	**lyse-**	lewsser-
dark...	**mørke-**	murrker

I'd like a/an/some...	**Jeg vil gjerne ha...**	yæi vil yæ'ner haa
aspirin	**aspirin**	ahspirreen
battery	**et batteri**	eht bahterree
bottle opener	**en flaskeåpner**	ehn flahskerawpnerr
bread	**litt brød**	lit brūr
newspaper	**en avis**	ehn ahveess
American	**amerikansk**	ahm(eh)rikaansk
English	**engelsk**	ehngerlsk
postcard	**et postkort**	eht postko't
shampoo	**en sjampo**	ehn shahmpoo
soap	**en såpe**	ehn sawper
sun-tan oil	**en sololje**	ehn soololyer
toothpaste	**en tannpasta**	ehn tahnpahstah
half a kilo of tomatoes	**en halv kilo toma-ter**	ehn hahl kheeloo toomaaterr
litre of milk	**en liter melk**	ehn leeterr mehlk
I'd like a film for this camera.	**Jeg vil gjjerne ha en film til dette apparatet.**	yæi vil yæ'ner haa ehn film til dehter ahpahraater
black and white	**svart-hvitt**	svah't-vit
colour	**farge**	fahrgger
I'd like a hair-cut, please.	**Klipping, takk.**	kliping tahk

Souvenirs *Suvenirer*

I'd like a...	**Jeg vil gjerne ha...**	yæi vil yæ'ner haa
doll in native costume	**en dukke med bunad**	ehn dewker meh(d) bewnahd
drinking horn	**et drikkehorn**	eht drikkerhoo'n
troll	**et troll**	eht trol
Viking ship	**et vikingskip**	eht veekingsheep
wooden figurine	**en trefigur**	ehn trayfiggewr

At the bank / banken

Where's the nearest bank/currency exchange office?	**Hvor er nærmeste bank/vekslings-kontor?**	voor ær **nærmehster** bahngk/**vehk**shlings-koontoor
I want to change some dollars/pounds.	**Jeg vil gjerne veksle noen dollar/pund.**	yæi vil yæ͞ᵊrner **vehk**shler no͞oern **dollahr/pewn**
What's the exchange rate?	**Hva er vekslings-kursen?**	vaa ær **vehk**shlings-ke͞wshern
I want to cash a traveller's cheque.	**Jeg vil gjerne løse inn en reisesjekk.**	yæi vil yæ͞ᵊrner lür̄sser in ehn **ræi**ssershehk

At the post office / postkontoren

I'd like to send this by...	**Jeg vil gjerne sende dette...**	yæi vil yæ͞ᵊrner **seh**ner **deh**ter
airmail	**med fly**	meh(d) fle͞w
express	**ekspress**	ehk**sprehss**
A...-kroner stamp please.	**Et... -kroners frimerke, takk.**	eht... -**kro͞o**nersh **free**mærker tahk
What's the postage for a letter/postcard to the U.S.?	**Hva er portoen for et brev/postkort til USA?**	vah ær **poo**ʳtooern for eht brāyv/**post**koʳt til e͞w-ehss-**aa**
Is there any post/mail for me?	**Har det kommet noe post til meg?**	har deh **kom**mert no͞oer post til mæi
My name is...	**Mitt navn er...**	mit **nahv**n ær

Telephoning / Telefon

Where's the nearest telephone booth?	**Hvor er nærmeste telefonkiosk?**	voor ær **nærmehster** tehler**fo͞on**khyosk
May I use your phone?	**Kan jeg få låne telefonen?**	kahn yæi faw **law**ner tehler**fo͞o**nern
Hello. This is...	**Hallo. Dette er...**	hah**lo͞o**. **deh**ter ær
I'd like to speak to...	**Kan jeg få snakke med...?**	kahn yæi faw **snah**ker meh(d)
When will he/she be back?	**Når kommer han/hun tilbake?**	nor **kom**mer hahn/hewn til**baa**ker
Will you tell him that I called?	**Kan du si til ham at jeg har ringt?**	kahn dew see til hahm aht yæi haar ringt

Days and date *Dager og dato*

It's...	Den er...	dehn ær
five past one	**fem over ett**	fehm **aw**verr eht
quarter past three	**kvart over tre**	kvah'ʳt **aw**verr trāy
twenty past four	**tjue over fire/**	**khē̄w**er **aw**verr **fee**rer/
	ti på halv fem	tee paw hahl fehm
half-past six	**halv sju**	hahl shē̄w
twenty-five to seven	**fem over halv sju**	fehm **aw**verr hahl shē̄w
ten to ten	**ti på ti**	tee paw tee
noon/midnight	**klokken tolv/mid-**	**klok**kern tol/**mid**naht
	natt	
in the morning	**om morgenen**	om **maw**ʳnern
in the afternoon	**om ettermiddagen**	om **eh**terrmiddaagern
in the evening	**om kvelden**	om **kveh**lern
during the day	**om dagen**	om **daa**gern
at night	**om natten**	om **nah**tern
yesterday	**i går**	ee gawr
today	**i dag**	ee daag
tomorrow	**i morgen**	ee **maw**erʳn
spring	**vår**	vawr
summer	**sommer**	**som**merr
autumn (fall)	**høst**	hurst
winter	**vinter**	**vin**terr

Sunday	**søndag**	**surn**dah(g)
Monday	**mandag**	**mahn**dah(g)
Tuesday	**tirsdag**	**teesh**dah(g)
Wednesday	**onsdag**	**oons**dah(g)
Thursday	**torsdag**	**tawsh**dah(g)
Friday	**fredag**	**frāy**dah(g)
Saturday	**lørdag**	**lūr**ʳdah(g)
January	**januar**	yahne**waar**
February	**februar**	fehbre**waar**
March	**mars**	mahsh
April	**april**	ah**preel**
May	**mai**	maay
June	**juni**	**yēw**nee
July	**juli**	**yēw**lee
August	**august**	ouge**wst**
September	**september**	sehp**tehm**berr
October	**oktober**	ok**taw**berr
November	**november**	noo**vehm**berr
December	**desember**	deh**ssehm**berr

NUMBERS, see page 126

Numbers *Tall*

0	**null**	newl
1	**en**	āyn
2	**to**	tōo
3	**tre**	trāy
4	**fire**	feerer
5	**fem**	fehm
6	**seks**	sehkss
7	**sju**	shew
8	**åtte**	otter
9	**ni**	nee
10	**ti**	tee
11	**elleve**	ehlver
12	**tolv**	tol
13	**tretten**	**treh**tern
14	**fjorten**	fyoo'tern
15	**femten**	**fehm**tern
16	**seksten**	**sæis**tern
17	**sytten**	surtern
18	**atten**	ahtern
19	**nitten**	nittern
20	**tjue**	khēwer
30	**tretti**	trehti
40	**førti**	fur'ti
50	**femti**	fehmti
60	**seksti**	sehksti
70	**sytti**	surti
80	**åtti**	otti
90	**nitti**	nitti
100	**hundre**	hewndrer
1,000	**tusen**	tēwssern
first	**første**	furshter
second	**annen/andre**	aaern/ahndrer
once/twice	**en gang/to ganger**	ehn gahng/tōo gahngerr
a half	**en halv**	ehn hahl

Emergency *Nødsfall*

Call the police	**Ring til politiet**	ring til pooli**tee**yer
Get a doctor	**Hent en lege**	hehnt ehn **lay**ger
Go away	**Gå vekk**	gaw vehk
HELP	**HJELP**	yehlp
I'm ill	**Jeg er syk**	yæi ær sēwk
STOP THIEF	**STOPP TYVEN**	stop **tēw**vern
My... has been stolen.	**... er blitt stjålet.**	... ær blit **styaw**lert

I've lost my...	**Jeg har mistet...**	yæi haar mistert
handbag	**håndvesken**	honvehskern
wallet	**lommeboken**	loommerbōōkern
passport/baggage	**passet/bagasjen**	pahsser/bahgaashern
Where can I find	**Hvor kan jeg få**	voor kahn yæi faw
a doctor who speaks	**tak i en lege som**	taak ee ehn lāȳger som
English?	**snakker engelsk?**	snahkerr ehngerlsk

Guide to Norwegian pronunciation *Uttale*

Consonants

Letter	Approximate pronunciation	Symbol	Example	
b, c, d, f, h, l, m, n, p, q, t, v, x	as in English			
g	1) before **ei, i** and **y**, generally like **y** in **yes**	y	**gi**	yee
	2) before **e** and **i** in some words of French origin, like **sh** in **shut**	sh	**geni**	shehnee
	3) like **g** in **go**	g	**gått**	got
gj	like **y** in **yes**	y	**gjest**	yehst
j	like **y** in **yes**	y	**ja**	yaa
k	1) generally like **ch** in German **ich** (like **h** in **huge**)	kh	**kino**	**kh**eenoo
	2) like **k** in **kit**	k	**kaffe**	**k**ahfer
kj	like **ch** in German **ich**	kh	**kjøre**	**kh**ūrrer
r	rolled near the front of the mouth	r	**rare**	**r**aa**r**er
rs	like **sh** in **shut**	sh	**norsk**	noshk
s	like **s** in **sit**	s/ss	**spise**	**s**peesser
sj	generally like **sh** in **shut**	sh	**stasjon**	stah**sh**ōōn
sk	1) before **i, y** and **ø**, generally like **sh** in **shut**	sh	**ski**	shee
	2) elsewhere, like **sk** in **skate**	sk	**skole**	**sk**ōōler
skj	like **sh** in **shut**	sh	**skje**	shāy
w	like **v** in **vice**	v	**whisky**	**v**iski
z	like **s** in **sit**	s	**zoom**	**s**ōōm

Vowels

a	1) long, like **a** in **car**	aa	**dag**	daag
	2) when short, between **a** in **car** and **u** in **cut**	ah	**takk**	tahk

e	1) long, like **ay** in s**ay**	a͞y	**sent**	s**a͞y**nt
	2) when followed by **r,**	ǣ	**her**	h**ǣ**r
	often like **a** in man	æ	**herre**	**hæ**rer
	3) short, like **e** in get	eh	**penn**	p**eh**n
	4) unstressed, like **a** in about	er	**betale**	ber**taa**ler
i	1) long, like **ee** in b**ee**	ee	**hit**	h**ee**t
	2) short, like **i** in sit	i	**sitt**	s**i**t
o	1) when long, often like **oo** in s**oo**n, but with the lips more tightly rounded	o͞o	**ord**	**o͞o**rd
	2) short, like **oo** in foot	oo	**ost**	**oo**st
	3) long, like **aw** in saw	aw	**tog**	t**aw**g
	4) short, like **o** in got (British pronunciation)	o	**stoppe**	st**o**pper
u	1) someting like **ew** in few, or Scottish **oo** in good (long or short)	e͞w / oo	**mur**	m**e͞w**r
			busk	b**ew**sk
	2) like **oo** in foot	oo	**nummer**	n**oo**mmerr
y	very much like the sound described under **u** (1) above (long or short)	e͞w / ew	**by**	b**e͞w**
			bygge	b**ew**ger
æ	like **a** in act (long or short)	ǣ	**lære**	l**ǣ**rer
ø	like **ur** in fur, but with the lips rounded (long or short)	u͞r / ur	**dør**	d**u͞r**r
			sønn	s**ur**n
å	1) when long, like **aw** in s**aw**	aw	**såpe**	s**aw**per
	2) when short, like **o** in got (British pronunciation)	o	**sånn**	s**o**n

Diphthongs

au	rather like **ou** in loud, though the first part is the Norwegian **æ**-sound	ou	**sau**	s**ou**
ei, eg, egn	like **ai** in w**ai**t, though first part is the Norwegian **æ**-sound	æi	**geit**	y**æi**t
			jeg	y**æi**
øy	rather like **oy** in boy, though the first part is the Norwegian **ø**-sound	oy	**gøy**	g**oy**

Portuguese

Basic expressions *Expressões correntes*

Yes/No.	**Sim/Não.**	seeng/nahng^w
Please.	**Por favor/Se faz favor.**	poor fer**voar**/ser fahsh fer**voar**
Thank you.	**Obrigado(a).**	oabri**ggah**doo(-er)
I beg your pardon?	**Como disse?**	**koa**moo **dees**ser

Introductions *Apresentações*

Good morning.	**Bom dia.**	bawng **deeer**
Good afternoon.	**Boa tarde.**	boaer **tahr**der
Good night.	**Boa noite.**	boaer **noy**ter
Good-bye.	**Adeus.**	er**deh**oosh
My name is…	**Chamo-me…**	**sher**moo mer
Pleased to meet you.	**Muito prazer em conhecê-lo(-la).**	moong^ytoo prer**zayr** ahng^y koonyer**ssay** loo(ler)
What's your name?	**Como se chama?**	**koa**moo ser **sher**mer
How are you?	**Como está?**	**koa**moo ish**tah**
Fine thanks. And you?	**Bem, obrigado(-a). E o Senhor [a Senhora]?**	bahng^w oabri**ggah**doo(-er). ee oo sinn**yoar** [er sinn**yoar**er]
Where do you come from?	**Donde é?**	**dawng**der eh
I'm from…	**Sou de…**	soa der
Australia	**a Austrália**	er owsh**trah**lyer
Canada	**o Canadá**	oo kerner**dah**
Great Britain	**a Grã-Bretanha**	er grahng brer**ter**nyer
United States	**os Estados Unidos**	oosh ish**tah**doosh oo**nee**doosh
I'm with my…	**Estou com…**	ish**toa** kawng
wife	**a minha mulher**	er **mee**nyer moo**lyehr**
husband	**o meu marido**	oo **meh**oo mer**ree**doo
family	**a minha família**	er **mee**nyer fer**mee**lyer
boyfriend	**o meu namorado**	oo **meh**oo nermoo**rah**doo
girlfriend	**a minha namorada**	er **mee**nyer nermoo**rah**der
I'm here on vacation.	**Estou aqui de férias.**	ish**toa** er**kee** der **feh**ryersh

PRONUNCIATION, see page 143/EMERGENCIES, page 142

Questions *Perguntas*

When?	**Quando?**	**kwahng**doo
How?	**Como?**	**koa**moo
What?/Why?	**O quê/Porquê?**	oo kay/poor**kay**
Who?/Which?	**Quem?/Qual?**	kahng^y/kwahl
Where is...?	**Onde é/fica...?**	**awng**der eh/**fee**ker
Where are...?	**Onde são/ficam...?**	**awng**der sahng^w/**fee**kahng^w
Where can I find/ get...?	**Onde posso encontrar/arranjar...?**	**awng**der **po**sso ayng-kawng**trahr**/err**ahng**zhahr
How far?	**A que distância?**	er ker dish**tahng**syer
How long?	**Quanto tempo?**	**kwahng**too **tayng**poo
How much/many?	**Quanto/Quantos?**	**kwahng**too/**kwahng**toosh
May I?	**Pode...?**	**po**dder
Can I have...?	**Pode dar-me...?**	**po**dder dahr mer
Can you help me?	**Pode ajudar-me?**	**po**dder erzhoo**dahr** mer
What does this/that mean?	**O que quer dizer isto/aquilo?**	oo ker kehr di**zzayr** **eesh**too/erk**ee**loo
I understand.	**Compreendo.**	kawng**pryayng**doo
I don't understand.	**Não compreendo.**	nahng^w kawng**pryayng**doo
Can you translate this for me?	**Pode traduzir-me isto?**	**po**dder trerdoo**zeer** mer **eesh**too
Do you speak English?	**Fala inglês?**	**fah**ler eeng**glaysh**
I don't speak (much) Portuguese.	**Não falo (bem) português.**	nahng^w **fah**loo (bahng^y) poortoo**gaysh**

A few more useful words *Outras palavras úteis*

better/worse	**melhor/pior**	mi**llyor**/pyor
big/small	**grande/pequeno**	**grahng**der/perk**ay**noo
cheap/expensive	**barato/caro**	be**rrah**too/**kah**roo
early/late	**cedo/tarde**	**say**doo/**tahr**der
good/bad	**bom/mau**	bawng/mow
hot/cold	**quente/frio**	**kayng**ter/**free**oo
near/far	**perto/longe**	**pehr**too/**lawng**zher
old/new	**velho/novo**	**veh**lyoo/**noa**voo
right/wrong	**certo/errado**	**sehr**too/i**rrah**doo
vacant/occupied	**livre/ocupado**	**lee**vrer/okkoo**pah**doo

Hotel–Accommodation *Hotel*

I have a reservation.	**Mandei reservar.**	mahng**day** rerzerr**vahr**
We've reserved two rooms.	**Reservámos dois quartos.**	rerzerr**vah**moosh doysh **kwahr**toosh
Do you have any vacancies?	**Tem quartos vagos?**	tahng^y **kwahr**toosh **vah**goosh
I'd like a... room.	**Queria um quarto...**	kerr**eee**er oong **kwahr**too

single	**individual**	eengdivvi**dwahl**
double	**duplo**	**doo**ploo
with twin beds	**com duas camas**	kawng **doo**ersh ker**mer**sh
with a double bed	**de casal**	der ker**zahl**
with a bath/shower	**com banho/duche**	kawng **ber**nyoo/**doo**sher

| We'll be staying... | **Ficamos...** | fi**kker**moosh |

overnight only	**só esta noite**	saw **ehsh**ter **noy**ter
a few days	**alguns dias**	ahl**goong**sh **deee**ersh
a week	**uma semana**	**oo**mer ser**mer**ner

| Is there a campsite near here? | **Há um parque de campismo aqui perto?** | ah oong **pahr**ker der kahng**peezh**moo er**kee pehr**too |

Decision *Decisão*

May I see the room?	**Posso ver o quarto?**	**pos**soo vayr oo **kwahr**too
That's fine. I'll take it.	**Está bem. Fico com ele.**	ish**tah** bahng^y. **fee**koo kawng **ay**ler
No. I don't like it.	**Não, não gosto dele.**	nahng^w nahng^w **gosh**too **day**ler
It's too...	**É muito...**	eh **moong**^{y}too
dark/small	**escuro/pequeno**	ish**koo**roo/per**kay**noo
Do you have anything...?	**Tem alguma coisa...?**	tahng^y ahl**goo**mer **koy**zer
better/bigger	**melhor/maior**	mill**yor**/ma**yor**
cheaper	**mais barata**	mighsh ber**rah**ter
quieter	**mais sossegada**	mighsh soosser**gah**der
May I have my bill, please?	**Pode dar-me a conta, por favor?**	**pod**der dahr mer er **kawng**ter poor fer**voar**
It's been a very enjoyable stay.	**Tivemos uma estadia muito agradável.**	tiv**veh**moosh **oo**mer ishter**deee**er **moong**^{y}too ergrer**dah**vehl

Eating out *Restaurante*

I'd like to reserve a table for four.	**Queria reservar uma mesa para quatro pessoas.**	kerreeer rerzerr**vahr** oo**mer** **may**zer perrer **kwah**troo perss**oa**ersh
We'll come at 8.	**Viremos às 8.**	vir**ray**moosh ahsh 8
I'd like...	**Queria tomar...**	kerreeer too**mahr**
breakfast	**o pequeno almoço**	oo per**kay**noo ahl**moa**ssoo
lunch	**o almoço**	oo ahl**moa**ssoo
dinner	**o jantar**	oo zhahng**tahr**
What do you recommend?	**O que me recomenda?**	oo ker mer rerkoo**mayng**der
Do you have any vegetarian dishes?	**Tem pratos vegetarianos?**	tahng[y] **prah**toosh verzherter**ryer**noosh

Breakfast *Pequeno almoço*

May I have some...?	**Pode trazer-me...?**	podder trer**zayr** mer
bread	**pão**	pahng[w]
butter	**manteiga**	mahng**tay**ger
cereal	**cereais**	serr**yigh**sh
ham and eggs	**ovos estrelados com presunto**	**ov**voosh ishtrer**lah**doosh kawng prer**zoong**too
jam	**doce de fruta**	**doa**sser der **froo**ter
rolls	**papo-secos**	**pah**poo **say**koosh

Starters and soups *Acepipes e sopas*

carnes frias	**kahr**nersh **free**ersh	assorted cold cuts
canja	**kahng**zher	chicken soup with rice
espargos	ish**pahr**goosh	asparagus
pipis	pip**pee**sh	spicy giblet stew
sopa à pescador	**soa**per ah pishker**doar**	fish soup
sopa de abóbora	**soa**per der erbobb**boo**rer	pumpkin soup
sopa de feijão frade	**soa**per der fay**zhahng**[w] **frah**der	black-eyed bean soup
sopa de grão	**soa**per der grahng[w]	chick-pea soup

caldo verde
(**kahl**doo **vayr**der)

thick potato and kale soup with sausage

chouriço
(shoaree**sso**o)

smoked pork sausage with paprika and garlic

gaspacho
(gersh**pah**shoo)

chilled soup with tomatoes, peppers, onions, cucumber and croutons

TELLING THE TIME, see page 141/NUMBERS, page 142

Fish and seafood *Peixes e mariscos*

crab	**caranguejo**	kerrahnggayzhoo
lobster	**lavagante**	lervergahngter
prawns	**gambas**	gahngbersh
sardines	**sardinhas**	serrdeenyersh
sole	**linguado**	leenggwahdoo
squid	**lulas**	loolersh
tuna	**atum**	ertoong

caldeirada (kahldayrahder)	various fish simmered with onions, tomatoes, potatoes and olive oil

baked	**no forno**	noo **foar**noo
boiled	**cozido**	koo**zee**doo
fried/roast	**frito/assado**	**free**too/er**ssah**doo
grilled	**grelhado**	grill**yah**doo
stewed	**guisado**	gizz**ah**doo
underdone (rare)	**mal passado**	mahl pers**sah**doo
medium	**meio passado**	**may**oo pers**sah**doo
well-done	**bem passado**	bahng[y] pers**sah**doo

Meat *Carnes*

I'd like some...	**Queria...**	ker**ree**er
bacon	**toucinho**	toa**ssee**nyoo
beef	**carne de vaca**	**kahr**ner der **vah**ker
chicken/duck	**frango/pato**	**frahng**goo/**pah**too
lamb	**borrego**	boor**ray**goo
pork	**carne de porco**	**kahr**ner der **poar**koo
sausage	**salsicha**	sahl**see**sher
steak	**bife**	"beef"
turkey	**peru**	per**roo**
veal	**vitela**	vit**teh**ler

churrasco misto (shoorrahskoa meestoa)	mixed barbecue (beef, sausage, pork)

Vegetables *Legumes*

beans (green)	**feijão verde**	fayz**hahng**[w] **vayr**der
carrots	**cenouras**	ser**noa**rersh
mushrooms	**cogumelos**	koogoo**meh**loosh
onions	**cebolas**	ser**boa**lersh
peas	**ervilhas**	irr**vee**lyersh
potatoes	**batatas**	ber**tah**tersh
spinach	**espinafres**	ishpin**nah**frersh
tomatoes	**tomates**	too**mah**tish

Fruit–Dessert–Pastries *Frutas–Sobremesas–Pastelaria*

apple	maçã	merssahng
cherries	cerejas	serrayzhersh
lemon	limão	limmahng^w
orange	laranja	lerrahngzher
pear	pêra	payrer
plums	ameixas	ermayshersh
strawberries	morangos	moorahnggoosh
arroz doce	erroash doasser	rice pudding
bolinhos de canela	booleenyoosh der kernehler	cinnamon biscuits
pastel de nata/de Belém	pershtehl der nahter/ der berlahng^y	small cream tart
pudim flam	poodeeng flahng	creme caramel
tarte de amêndoa	tahrter der ermayngdwer	almond tart

Drinks *Bebidas*

beer	cerveja	serrvayzher
coffee	um café	oong kerfeh
black	sem leite	sahng^y layter
with milk	com leite	kawng layter
fruit juice	um sumo de fruta	oong soomoo der frooter
(glass of) milk	(um copo de) leite	(oong koppoo der) layter
mineral water	uma água mineral	oomer ahgwer minnerrahl
tea	um chá	oong shah
wine	vinho	veenyoo
red/white	tinto/branco	teengtoo/brahngkoo

Complaints and paying *Reclamações e a conta*

This is too...	Isto está... demais.	eeshtoo ishtah... dermighsh
bitter/sweet	amargo/doce	ermahrgoo/doasser
That's not what I ordered.	Não é o que eu encomendei.	nahng^w eh oo ker ehoo ayngkoomayngday
I'd like to pay.	Queria pagar.	kerreeer pergahr
I think there's a mistake in this bill.	Creio que se enganou na conta.	krayoo ker ser aynggernoa ner kawngter
Can I pay with this credit card?	Posso pagar com este cartão de cré-dito?	possoo pergahr kawng ayshter kerrtahng^w der krehdittoo
We enjoyed it, thank you.	Gostámos muito, obrigado(a).	gooshtahmoosh moong^ytoo oabriggahdoo (er)

Travelling around *Excursões*

Plane *Avião*

Is there a flight to...?	**Há um voo para o...**	ah oong **voa**oo **per**rer oo
What time should I check in?	**A que horas devo apresentar-me?**	er ker **or**rersh **day**voo erprerzayng**tar** mer
I'd like to... my reservation.	**Queria... a marcação do meu lugar.**	ker**ree**er... er merrker-**ssahng**w doo **me**hoo loo**gahr**
cancel	**anular**	ernoo**lahr**
change	**mudar**	moo**dahr**
confirm	**confirmar**	kawngfirr**mahr**

Train *Comboio (trem)*

I'd like a ticket to....	**Quero um bilhete para...**	**keh**roo oon bill**yay**ter **per**rer
single (one-way)	**ida**	**ee**der
return (round trip)	**ida e volta**	**ee**der ee **voll**ter
first/second class	**primeira/segunda classe**	prim**may**rer/ser**goong**der **klah**sser
How long does the journey (trip) take?	**Quanto tempo demora a viagem?**	**kwahng**too **tayng**poo der**mor**rer er **vyah**zhahngy
When is the... train to...?	**Quando é o... comboio para...?**	**kwahng**doo eh oo... kawng**boy**oo **per**rer
first/next/last	**primeiro/próximo/último**	prim**may**roo/**pros**simmoo/ **ool**timmoo

Bus–Tram (streetcar) *Autocarro–Eléctrico*

Which tram goes to the town centre?	**Qual é o eléctrico que vai para o centro da cidade?**	kwahl eh oo illeh**trik**koo ker vigh **per**rer oo **sayng**troo der sid**dah**der
How much is the fare to...?	**Qual é o preço do bilhete para...?**	kwahl eh oo **pray**ssoo doo bill**yay**ter **per**rer
Will you tell me when to get off?	**Pode avisar-me quando devo descer?**	**pod**der erviz**zahr** mer **kwahng**doo **day**voo dish**sayr**

TELLING THE TIME, see page 141/NUMBERS, page 142

Taxi *Táxi*

How much is the fare to...?	**Qual é o preço do percurso para...?**	kwahl eh oo **prays**soo doo perr**koor**soo perrer
Take me to this address.	**Leve-me a este endereço.**	**leh**ver mer er **aysh**ter ayngder**rays**soo
Please stop here.	**Páre aqui, por favor.**	**pah**rer er**kee** poor fer**voar**
Could you wait for me?	**Pode esperar por mim?**	**po**dder ishper**rahr** poor meeng

Car hire (rental) *Aluguer de automóveis*

I'd like to hire (rent) a car.	**Queria alugar um automóvel.**	ker**reeer** erloo**gahr** oong owtoo**mo**vvehl
I'd like it for...	**Queria-o por...**	ker**reeer** oo poor
a day	**um dia**	oong **dee**er
a week	**uma semana**	**oo**mer ser**mer**ner
Where's the nearest filling station?	**Qual é a estação de serviço mais próxima?**	kwahl eh er ishter**ssahng**^w der serr**vee**ssoo mighsh **pross**immer
Give me... litres of petrol (gasoline).	**Dê-me... litros de gasolina.**	day mer... **lee**troosh der gerzoo**lee**ner
How do I get to...?	**Como se vai para...?**	**koa**moo ser vigh **perr**er
I've broken down at...	**Tive uma avaria em...**	**tee**ver **oo**mer erver**reeer** ahng^w
Can you send a mechanic?	**Pode mandar-me um mecânico?**	**po**dder mahng**dahr** mer oong merker**nik**koo
Can you mend this puncture (fix this flat)?	**Pode consertar este furo?**	**po**dder kawngserr**tahr** **aysh**ter **foo**roo

Enganou-se na estrada.	You're on the wrong road.
Vá sempre em frente.	Go straight ahead.
É ali...	It's down there on the...
à esquerda/à direita.	left/right
ao lado de/depois de...	next to/after...
norte/sul/(l)este/oeste	north/south/east/west

EMERGENCIES, see page 143

Sightseeing *Visitas turisticas*

Where's the tourist office?	**Onde é o turismo?**	awng̃der eh oo tooreezhmoo
Is there an English-speaking guide?	**Há algum guia que fale inglês?**	ah ahlgoong gheeer ker fahler eengglaysh
Where is/are...?	**Onde fica/ficam...?**	awng̃der feeker/feekahng̃ʷ
art gallery	**o galeria de arte**	er gerlerreeer der ahrter
castle	**o castelo**	oo kershtehloo
cathedral	**a sé/catedral**	er seh/kerterdrahl
church	**a igreja**	er iggrayzher
city centre	**o centro da cidade**	oo sayngtroo der siddahder
exhibition	**a exposição**	er ishpoozissahng̃ʷ
harbour	**o porto**	oo poartoo
market	**o mercado**	oo merrkahdoo
museum	**o museu**	oo moozehoo
shopping area	**a zona comercial**	er zoaner koomerrsyahl
square	**a praça**	er prahsser
tower	**a torre**	er toarrer
zoo	**o jardim zoológico**	oo zherrdeeng zoolozhikkoo
What are the opening hours?	**Quais são as horas de abertura?**	kwighsh sahng̃ʷ ersh orrersh der erberrtoorer
When does it close?	**A que horas fecha?**	er ker orrersh faysher
How much is the entrance fee?	**Quanto custa a entrada (o ingresso)?**	kwahng̃too kooshter er ayngtrahder (oo eenggrehssoa)

Relaxing *Distracções*

What's playing at the... Theatre?	**O que está em cena no teatro...?**	oo ker ishtah ahng̃ʸ sayner noo tyahtroo
Are there any seats for tonight?	**Há ainda bilhetes para hoje à noite?**	ah ereengder billyaytish perrer oazher ah noyter
How much are the seats?	**Qual é o preço dos lugares?**	kwahl eh oo prayssoo doosh loogahrersh
Would you like to go out with me tonight?	**Quer sair comigo hoje à noite?**	kehr sereer koomeegoo oazher ah noyter
Is there a disco-theque in town?	**Há alguma dis-coteca na cidade?**	ah ahlgoomer dishkoo-tehker ner siddahder
Would you like to dance?	**Quer dançar?**	kehr dahng̃sahr
Thank you, it's been a wonderful evening.	**Obrigado(a), passei uma noite maravil-hosa.**	oabriggahdoo(er) perssay oomer noyter merrervillyozzer

DAYS OF THE WEEK, see page 142

Shops, stores and services *Lojas e serviços*

Where's the nearest...?	**Onde é... mais próximo(-a)?**	awngder eh ... mighsh **pros**simmoo(-er)
bakery	**o padaria**	er pahder**reeer**
bookshop	**a livraria**	er livvrer**reeer**
butcher's	**o tahlo**	oo **tahl**yoo
chemist/drugstore	**a farmácia**	er ferr**mahs**syer
dentist	**o dentista**	oo dayng**teesh**ter
department store	**o grande armazém**	oo **grahng**der ahrmer**zahng**ᵛ
grocery	**a mercearia**	er merrsyer**reeer**
hairdresser	**o cabeleireiro**	oo kerberlayray**roo**
post office	**a estação de correios**	er ishter**ssahng**ʷ der koorra**yoosh**
supermarket	**o supermercado**	oo soopehrmerr**kah**doo
toilets/restrooms	**as cases de banho (os banheiros)**	ersh **kah**zersh der **ber**nyoo (oass bah**nyay**roass)

General expressions *Expressões gerais*

Where's the main shopping area?	**Onde é a zona comercial?**	awngder eh er **zoa**ner koomerr**syahl**
Do you have any...?	**Tem...?**	tahngᵛ
Can I show me this/that?	**Pode mostrar-me isto/aquilo?**	**po**dder moosh**trahr** mer **eesh**too/er**kee**loo
Haven't you anything...?	**Não tem nada...?**	nahngʷ tahngʸ **nah**der
cheaper	**mais barato**	mighsh ber**rah**too
better/larger	**melhor/maior**	mill**yor**/**may**or
smaller	**mais pequeno**	mighsh per**kay**noo
Can I try it on?	**Posso provar?**	**pos**soo proo**vahr**
How much is this?	**Quanto custa isto?**	**kwahng**too **koosh**ter **eesh**too
Please write it down.	**Pode escrever num papel?**	**po**dder ishkrer**vayr** noong perp**ehl**
I don't want to spend more than... escudos.	**Não quero gastar mais que... escudos.**	nahngʷ **keh**roo gersh**tahr** mighsh ker... ish**koo**doosh
No, I don't like it.	**Não, não gosto.**	nahngʷ nahngʷ **gosh**too
I'll take it.	**Fico com ele.**	**fee**koo kawng **ay**ler
Do you accept credit cards?	**Aceitam cartões de crédito?**	erss**ay**tahngʷ kerr**tawng**ʸsh der **kreh**dittoo
Can you order it for me?	**Pode encomen-darmo?**	**po**dder ayngkoomayng**dahr**moo

NUMBERS, see page 142

black	preto	praytoo
blue	azul	erzool
brown	castanho	kershternyoo
green	verde	vayrder
grey	cinzento	seengzayngtoo
orange	cor-de-laranja	koar der lerrahngzher
red	vermelho	verrmaylyoo
white	branco	brahngkoo
yellow	amarelo	ermerrehloo
light...	... claro	... klahroo
dark...	... escuro	... ishkooroo

I want to buy a/an/ some...	Quero comprar...	kehroo kawngprahr
aspirin	aspirinas	ershpirreenersh
bottle-opener	um abre-garrafas	oong ahbrer gerrahfersh
newspaper American/English	um jornal americano/inglês	oong zhoornahl ermerri- kkernoo/eengglaysh
postcard	um bilhete postal	oong billyayter pooshtahl
shampoo	um shampoo	oong shahngpoa
soap	um sabonete	oong serboonayter
sun-tan cream	um creme para bronzear	oong krehmer perrer brawngzyahr
toothpaste	uma pasta de dentes	oomer pahshter der dayngtish
a half-kilo of tomatoes	meio-quilo de tomates	mayoo keeloo der toomahtish
a litre of milk	um litro de leite	oong leetroo der layter
I'd like a film for this camera.	Queria um rolo para esta máquina.	kerreeer oong roaloo perrer ehshter mahkinner
black and white	a preto e branco	er praytoo ee brahngkoo
colour	a cores	er koarersh
I'd like a hair-cut, please.	Quero cortar o cabelo, por favor.	kehroo koortahr oo kerbayloo poor fervoar

Souvenirs *Lembranças*

china	a porcelana	er poorserlerner
corkware	os artigos de cortiça	oosh errteegoosh der koorteesser
lace	as rendas	ersh rayngdersh
pottery	a loiça de barro	er loysser der bahrroo
tiles	os azulejos	oosh erzoolayzhoosh

At the bank *Banco*

Where's the nearest bank/currency exchange office?	Onde é o banco/a agência de câmbio mais próximo/a?	awngder eh oo **bahng**koo/ er er**zhayng**syer der **kahng**byoo mighsh **prossimmoo/**er
I want to change some dollars/pounds.	Quero trocar dólares/libras.	**keh**roo troo**kahr** **doll**ersh/**lee**brersh
What's the exchange rate?	A como está o câmbio?	er **koa**moo ish**tah** oo **kahng**byoo
I want to cash a traveller's cheque.	Quero levantar um cheque de viagem.	**keh**roo lervahng**tahr** oong **sheh**ker der vyah**zhahng**ʸ

At the post office *Correio*

I want to send this by...	Quero mandar isto...	**keh**roo mahng**dahr** **eesh**too
airmail	por avião	poor er**vyahng**ʷ
express	por expresso	poor ish**preh**ssoo
A... escudo stamp, please.	Um selo de... escudos, por favor.	oong **say**loo der... ish-**koo**doosh poor fer**voar**
What's the postage for a postcard/letter to United States?	Qual é a franquia de um bilhete postal/uma carta para os Estados Unidos?	kwahl eh er frahng**keee**r der oong bil**yay**ter poosh**tahl**/**oo**mer **kahr**ter perrer oosh ish**tah**doosh oo**nee**doosh
Is there any post/mail for me?	Há correio para mim?	ah koo**rray**oo **per**rer meeng

Telephoning *Telefones*

Where is the nearest telephone booth?	Onde fica e cabine telefónica mais próxima?	awngder **fee**ker er kah**bee**-ner terler**fon**nikker mighsh **pross**immer
I want to reverse the charges (call collect).	Quero uma comunicação pagável no destino.	**keh**roo **oo**mer koomoo-nikker**ssahng**ʷ per**gah**vehl noo dish**tee**noo
May I use your phone?	Posso utilizar o seu telefone?	**poss**oo ootilli**zahr** oo **seh**oo terler**fon**ner
Hello. This is... speaking.	Está. Aqui fala...	ish**tah**. er**kee fah**ler
I'd like to speak to...	Queria falar com...	ker**reee**r fer**lahr** kawng
When will he/she be back?	Quando é que ele/ela estará de volta?	**kwahng**doo eh ker **ay**ler/**eh**ler ish**terrah** der **voll**ter

Time and date *Horas e data*

It's one o'clock.	**É uma hora.**	eh **oo**mer orrer
It's two o'clock.	**São duas horas.**	sahng^w **doo**ersh **orr**ersh
five past...	**... e cinco**	... ee **seeng**koo
quarter past...	**... e um quarto**	... ee oong **kwahr**too
twenty past...	**... e vinte**	... ee **veeng**ter
half past...	**... e meia**	... ee **may**er
twenty-five to ...	**vinte e cinco para as ...**	**veeng**ter ee **seeng**koo **perr**er ersh ...
ten to...	**dez para as ...**	dehsh **perr**er ersh...
noon/midnight	**meio-dia/meia-noite**	**may**oo **deeer**/**may**er **noy**ter
in the morning/ afternoon/evening	**da manhã/da tarde/da noite**	der mer**nyahng**/der **tahr**der/der **noy**ter
during the day	**durante o dia**	doo**rahng**ter oo **deeer**
at night	**à noite**	ah **noy**ter
yesterday/today	**ontem/hoje**	**awng**tahng^y/**oa**zher
tomorrow	**amanhã**	ahmer**nyahng**
spring	**a Primavara**	er primmer**veh**rer
summer	**o Verão**	oo ver**rahng**^w
autumn (fall)	**o Outono**	oo oat**oa**noo
winter	**o Inverno**	oo eeng**vehr**noo

Sunday	**domingo**	doo**meeng**goo
Monday	**segunda-feira**	ser**goong**der **fay**rer
Tuesday	**terça-feira**	**tayr**ser **fay**rer
Wednesday	**quarta-feira**	**kwahr**ter **fay**rer
Thursday	**quinta-feira**	**keeng**ter **fay**rer
Friday	**sexta-feira**	**saysh**ter **fay**rer
Saturday	**sábado**	**sah**berdoo
January	**Janeiro**	zher**nay**roo
February	**Fevereiro**	fer**ver**rayroo
March	**Março**	**mahr**soo
April	**Abril**	er**breel**
May	**Maio**	**migh**oo
June	**Junho**	**zhoo**nyoo
July	**Julho**	**zhool**yoo
August	**Agosto**	er**goash**too
September	**Setembro**	ser**tayng**broo
October	**Outubro**	oat**oo**broo
November	**Novembro**	noo**vayng**broo
December	**Dezembro**	der**zayng**broo

NUMBERS, see page 142

Numbers *Números*

0	**zero**	zehroo
1	**um, uma**	oong **oo**mer
2	**dois, duas**	doysh **doo**ersh
3	**três**	traysh
4	**quatro**	**kwah**troo
5	**cinco**	**seeng**koo
6	**seis**	saysh
7	**sete**	**seh**ter
8	**oito**	**oy**too
9	**nove**	**nov**ver
10	**dez**	dehsh
11	**onze**	**awng**zer
12	**doze**	**doa**zer
13	**treze**	**tray**zer
14	**catorze**	ker**toar**zer
15	**quinze**	**keeng**zer
16	**dezasseis**	derzer**ssaysh**
17	**dezassete**	derzer**sseh**ter
18	**dezoito**	der**zoy**too
19	**dezanove**	derzer**nov**ver
20	**vinte**	**veeng**ter
21	**vinte e um**	**veeng**ter ee oong
30	**trinta**	**treeng**ter
40	**quarenta**	kwer**rayng**ter
50	**cinquenta**	seengk**wayng**ter
60	**sessenta**	serss**ayng**ter
70	**setenta**	ser**tayng**ter
80	**oitenta**	oy**tayng**ter
90	**noventa**	noo**vayng**ter
100	**cem/cento**	sahng^y/**sahng**^{y}too
1,000	**mil**	meel
first	**primeiro**	prim**mayr**oo
second	**segundo**	ser**goong**doo
once/twice	**uma vez/duas vezes**	**oo**mer vaysh/**doo**ersh **vay**zersh
a half	**uma metade**	**oo**mer mer**tah**der

Emergency *Urgências*

Call the police	**Chame a polícia**	**sher**mer er poo**lee**ssyer
Get a doctor	**Chame um médico**	**sher**mer oong **meh**dikkoo
Go away	**Vá-se embora**	vah ser ayng**bor**rer
HELP	**SOCORRO**	soo**koa**rroo
I'm ill	**Estou doente**	ish**toa** dway**ng**ter
I'm lost	**Perdi-me**	perr**dee** mer
LOOK OUT	**ATENÇÃO**	ertayng**sahng**^{w}

TELEPHONING, see page 140

My...has been stolen.	Roubaram-me...	roabahrahng^w mer
I've lost my...	Perdi...	perrdee
handbag	a mala de mão	er mahler der mahng^w
wallet	a minha carteira	er meenyer kerrtayrer
passport	o passaporte	o persserporrter
luggage	a minha bagagem	er meenyer bergahzhahng^y
Where can I find a doctor who speaks English?	Onde posso encontrar um médico que fale inglês?	awngder possoo ayngkawngtrahr oong mehdikkoo ker fahler eengglaysh

Guide to Portuguese pronunciation *Pronúncia*
Consonants

Letter	Approximate pronunciation	Symbol	Example	
f, l, p, t, v	as in English			
b	as in English, but less decisive	b	boca	boaker
c	1) before a, o, u or consonant, as in kill	k	casa	kahzer
	2) before e, i, like sit	s	cedo	saydoo
ç	like s in sit	s	começar	koomerssahr
ch	like sh in shut	sh	chamar	shermahr
d	as in English but less decisive	d	dia	deeer
g	1) like g in go	g/gh	garfo	gahrfoo
			guia	gheeer
	2) like s in pleasure	zh	gelo	zhayloo
h	always silent		homem	ommahng^y
j	like s in pleasure	zh	já	zhah
lh	like lli in million	ly	olho	oalyoo
m	1) like m in met	m	mais	mighsh
	2) nasalizes preceeding vowel; usually silent	ng	tempo	tayngpoo
		ng^y	tem	tayng^y
n	1) like n in no	n	novo	noavoo
		ng	branco	brahngkoo
	2) nasalizes preceeding vowel; usually silent	ng^y	homens	ommahng^ysh
nh	like ni in onion	ny	vinho	veenyoo
q	like k in kill	k	querer	kerrayr
r	strongly trilled	r	rua	rooer
s	1) like s in sit	s/ss	saber	serbayr
	2) like z in razor	z	casa	kahzer
	3) like sh in shut	sh	país	pereesh
	4) like s in pleasure	zh	cisne	seezhner

x	1) like **sh** in shut	sh	**baixo**	**bigh**shoo
	2) like **z** in razor	z	**exacto**	izzahtoo
	3) like **x** in exit	ks	**táxi**	tahksi
z	1) like **z** in razor	z	**zero**	zehroo
	2) like **sh** in shut	sh	**feliz**	ferleesh
	3) like **s** in pleasure	zh	**luz da**	loozh der

Vowels

a	1) mix of cut and party	ah	**nado**	**nah**doo
	2) like **a** in about	er	**porta**	**por**ter
e	1) like **e** in get	eh	**perto**	**pehr**too
	2) like **a** in late	ay	**cabelo**	ker**bay**loo
	3) like **er** in other	er	**pesado**	per**zah**doo
	4) like **i** in hit	i	**exacto**	izzahtoo
é	like **e** in get	eh	**café**	ker**feh**
ê	like **a** in late	ay	**mês**	maysh
i	1) like **ee** in seed	ee	**riso**	**ree**zoo
	2) as **o** in coming	i	**final**	finnahl
o	1) like **o** in rod	o	**fora**	**for**rer
	2) like **o** in note	oa	**voltar**	voal**tahr**
	3) like **oo** in foot	oo	**caso**	**kah**zoo
ô, ou	like note, but not diphthong	oa	**pôs**	poash
u	1) like **oo** in soon	oo	**número**	**noo**merroo
	2) silent in **gu**, **qu** before **e**, **i**		**querer**	ker**rayr**

Nasal vowels

ã, am, an	like **ung** in lung or **an** in French dans	ahng	**maçã**	merssahng
em, en	mix of **ing** in sing and **a** in late	ayng	**cento**	sayngtoo
im, in	nasalized **ee** as in feet	eeng	**cinco**	seengkoo
om, on	like **orn** in corncob or **on** in French bon	awng	**bom**	bawng
um, un	nasalized **oo** in foot	oong	**um**	oong

Semi-nasalized diphthongs

em, final **en**(s), usually final **em**				
	as **ã** followed by **y** in yet	ahng^y	**sem**	sahng^y
ão, final unstressed **am**				
	as **ã** followed by **w**	ahng^w	**mão**	mahng^w
õe	as **on** in French bon, followed by **y** in yet	awng^y	**põe**	pawng^y

Spanish

Basic expressions *Expresiones generales*

Yes/No.	**Sí/No.**	see/noa
Please.	**Por favor.**	por fah**bhor**
Thank you.	**Gracias.**	**grah**thyahss
I beg your pardon?	**¿Perdóneme?**	payr**doa**naymay

Introductions *Presentaciones*

Good morning.	**Buenos días.**	**bway**noass **dee**ahss
Good afternoon.	**Buenas tardes.**	**bway**nahss **tahr**dayss
Good night.	**Buenas noches.**	**bway**nahss **noa**chayss
Good-bye.	**Adiós.**	ah**dhyoss**
My name is...	**Me llamo...**	may **lyah**moa
Pleased to meet you.	**Encantado(-a) de conocerle.**	aynkahn**tahdhoa(-ah) day koanoa**thayr**lay
What's your name?	**¿Cómo de llama?**	**koa**moa say **lyah**mah
How are you?	**¿Cómo está usted?**	**koa**moa ay**stah** oo**staydh**
Fine thanks. And you?	**Bien, gracias. ¿Y usted?**	byayn **grah**thyahss. ee oo**staydh**
Where do you come from?	**¿De dónde es used?**	day **doan**day ayss oo**staydh**
I'm from...	**Soy de...**	soy day
Australia	**Australia**	ow**strah**lyah
Canada	**Canadá**	kahnah**dhah**
Great Britain	**Gran Bretaña**	grahn bray**tah**ñah
United States	**Estados Unidos**	ay**stah**dhoass oo**nee**dhoass
I'm with my...	**Estoy con mi...**	ay**stoy** kon mee
wife	**mujer**	moo**khehr**
husband	**marido**	mah**ree**dhoa
family	**familia**	fah**mee**lyah
boyfriend	**amigo**	ah**mee**goa
girlfriend	**amiga**	ah**mee**gah
I'm on my own.	**Estoy venido solo(-a).**	ay**stoy** bay**nee**dhoa **soa**loa(-ah)
I'm here on vacation.	**Estoy aquí para las vacaciones.**	ay**stoy** ah**kee** pah**rah** lahss bahkah**thyon**ayss

PRONUNCIATION/EMERGENCIES, page 159

Questions *Preguntas*

When?	¿Cuándo?	kwahndoa
How?	¿Cómo?	koamoa
What?/Why?	¿Qué/Por qué?	kay/por kay
Who?	¿Quién?	kyayn
Which?	¿Cuál/Cuáles?	kwahl/kwahlayss
Where is ...?	¿Dónde está ...?	doanday aystah
Where are ...?	¿Dónde están ...?	doanday aystahn
Where can I find/ get ...?	¿Dónde puedo encontrar ...?	doanday pwaydhoa aynkontrahr
How far?	¿A qué distancia?	ah kay deestahnthyah
How long?	¿Cuánto tiempo?	kwahntoa tyaympoa
How much/many?	¿Cuánto/s?	kwahntoa/ss
May I?	¿Puedo?	pwaydhoa
Can I have ...?	¿Puede darme ...?	pwaydhay dahrmay
Can you help me?	¿Puede usted ayudarme?	pwaydhay oostaydh ahyoodharmay
I understand.	Comprendo/ Entiendo.	koamprayndoa/ ayntyayndoa
I don't understand.	No comprendo.	noa koamprayndoa
Can you translate this for me?	¿Puede usted traducírmelo?	pwaydhay oostaydh trahdhootheermayloa
Do you speak English?	¿Habla usted inglés?	ahblah oostaydh eenglayss
I don't speak (much) Spanish.	No hablo (mucho) español.	noa ahbloa (moochoa) ayspahñol

A few more useful words *Algunas palabras útiles*

better/worse	mejor/peor	mahkhor/pehor
big/small	grande/pequeño	grahnday/paykayñoa
cheap/expensive	barato/caro	bahrahtoa/kahroa
early/late	temprano/tarde	taymprahnoa/tahrday
good/bad	bueno/malo	bwaynoa/mahloa
hot/cold	caliente/frío	kahlyayntay/freeoa
near/far	cerca/lejos	thehrkah/lehkhoss
old/new	viejo/nuevo	byaykhoa/nwaybhoa
right/wrong	correcto/incorrecto	koarrehktoa/ eenkoarrehktoa
vacant/occupied	libre/occupado	leebray/oakoopahdhoa

Hotel–Accommodation *Hotel*

I have a reservation.	**He hecho una reserva.**	eh **ay**choa **oo**nah rey**ssayr**bah
We've reserved two rooms.	**Hemos reservado dos habitaciones.**	**eh**moass rayssayr**bah**dhoa doss ahbheetah**thyo**nayss
Do you have any vacancies?	**¿Tiene habitaciones libres?**	**tyay**nay ahbheetah**thyo**nayss **lee**bhrayss
I'd like a ... room.	**Quisiera una habitacón ...**	kees**syay**rah **oo**nah ahbheetah**thyon**
single/double	**sencilla/doble**	sayn**thee**lyah/**doa**blay
with twin beds	**con dos camas**	kon doss **kah**mahss
with a double bed	**con una cama matrimonial**	kon **oo**nah **kah**mah mahtreemoan**yahl**
with a bath/shower	**con baño/ducha**	kon **bah**ñoa/**doo**chah
We'll be staying ...	**Nos quedaremos ...**	noss kaydhah**ray**moass
overnight only	**sólo una noche**	**soa**loa **oo**nah **noa**chay
a few days	**algunos días**	ahl**goo**noass **dee**ahss
a week	**una semana**	**oo**nah say**mah**nah

Decision *Decisión*

May I see the room?	**¿Puedo ver la habitación?**	**pway**dhoa behr lah ahbheetah**thyon**
That's fine. I'll take it.	**Muy bien, la tomaré.**	mwee byayn lah toama**ray**
No. I don't like it.	**No, no me gusta.**	noa noa may **goos**tah
It's too ...	**Es demasiado ...**	ayss deymah**ssyah**dhoa
dark/small	**oscura/pequeña**	os**koo**rah/pay**kay**ñah
noisy	**ruidosa**	rweedhoa**ssah**
Do you have anything ...?	**¿Tiene usted algo ...?**	**tyay**nay oos**taydh ahl**goa
better/bigger	**mejor/más grande**	meh**khor**/mahss **grahn**day
cheaper	**más barato**	mahss bah**rah**toa
quieter	**más tranquilo**	mahss trahn**kee**loa
May I have my bill, please?	**Por favor, ¿puede darme mi cuenta?**	por fah**bhor pway**dhay **dahr**may mee **kwayn**tah
It's been a very enjoyable stay.	**Ha sido una estancia muy agradable.**	ah **see**dhoa **oo**nah ays**tahn**thyah mwee ahgrah**dhah**blay

NUMBERS, see page 158/DAYS OF THE WEEK, see page 157

Eating out *Comidas y bebidas*

I'd like to reserve a table for four.	**Quiero reservar una mesa para cuatro.**	kyayroa rehssayrbahr oonah mayssah pahrah kwahtroa
We'll come at 8.	**Vendremos a las ocho.**	bayndraymoass ah lahss oachoa
I'd like...	**Quisiera...**	keessyayrah
breakfast	**el desayuno**	ayl dayssahyoonoa
lunch	**el almuerzo**	ayl ahlmwayrthoa
dinner	**la cena**	lah thaynah
What do you recommend?	**¿Qué me aconseja?**	kay may ahkoansehkhah
Do you have any vegetarian dishes?	**¿Tiene plataos vegetarianos?**	tyaynay plahtoass baykhaytahryahnoass

Breakfast *Desayuno*

May I have...	**Quisiera...**	keessyayrah
boiled egg	**huevo cocido**	waybhoa koatheedhoa
bread	**pan**	pahn
butter	**mantequilla**	mahntaykeelyah
cereal	**cereales**	thayrayahlayss
coffee	**café**	kahfay
jam	**mermelada**	mahrmaylahdhah
rolls	**panecillos**	pahnaytheelyoass
tea	**té**	tay

Starters (Appetizers) *Entremeses*

avocado	**aguacate**	ah wahkahtay
ham omelette	**tortilla de jamón**	toarteelyah day khamon
spiced meatballs	**albóndigas**	ahlbondee ahss
spicy sausage	**chorizo**	choareethoa
squid	**calamares**	kahlahmahrayss

Soups *Sopas*

fish soup	**sopa de pescado**	soapah day payskahdhoa
onion soup	**sopa de cebolla**	soapah day thayboalyah
vegetable soup	**sopa de verduras**	soapah day bayrdoorahss

caldo gallego (**kahl**doa gah**lyeh**goa)	meat and vegetable broth
gazpacho (gahth**pah**choa)	cold soup of tomato, cucumber, green pepper bread, onion and garlic

Fish and seafood *Pescado y mariscos*

cod	**bacalao**	bahkah**lah**oa
lobster	**langosta**	lahn**goas**tah
oysters	**ostras**	**ostr**ahss
snails	**caracoles**	kahrah**koa**layss
swordfish	**pez espada**	payth ays**pah**dhah
trout	**trucha**	**troo**chah
tuna (tunny)	**atún**	ah**toon**
zarzuela (thahr**thway**lah)	spicy fish and seafood stew	

baked	**al horno**	ahl **oar**noa
boiled	**hervido**	ayr**bheed**hoa
fried/roast	**frito/asado**	**free**toa/ah**ssah**dhoa
grilled	**a la parrilla**	ah lah pah**rree**lyah
stewed	**estofado**	aysto**afah**dhoa
underdone (rare)	**poco hecho**	**poa**koa **ay**choa
medium	**regular**	reh**goo**lahr
well-done	**muy hecho**	mwee **ay**choa

Meat *Carne*

I'd like some...	**Quisiera...**	kee**ssyay**rah
bacon	**tocino**	toa**thee**noa
beef	**carne de buey**	**kahr**nay day bway
chicken/duck	**pollo/pato**	**poal**yoa/**pah**toa
chops	**chuletas**	choo**lay**tahss
lamb	**carne de cordero**	**kahr**nay day koar**day**roa
pork	**carne de cerdo**	**kahr**nay day **thehr**doa
sausages	**salchichas**	sahl**chee**chahss
steak	**filete**	fee**lay**tay
veal	**carne de ternera**	day tehr**nay**rah

Vegetables *Verduras*

beans (green)	**judías verdes**	khoo**dhee**ahss **behr**dayss
cabbage	**repollo**	rey**poal**yoa
lettuce	**lechuga**	lay**choo**gah
mushrooms	**setas**	**say**tahss
onions	**cebollas**	thay**boal**yahss
potatoes	**patatas**	pah**tah**tahss
tomatoes	**tomates**	toa**mah**tayss
paella (pah**ay**lyah	golden saffron rice garnished with meat, fish, seafood and/or vegetables	

Fruit and dessert *Fruta y postre*

apple	**manzana**	mahn**thah**nah
cherries	**cerezas**	thay**ray**thahss
lemon	**limón**	lee**mon**
orange	**naranja**	nah**rahn**khah
peach	**melocotón**	mayloakoa**ton**
pear	**pera**	**peh**rah
plums	**ciruelas**	theer**way**lahss
strawberries	**fresas**	**fray**ssahss
crema catalana	**kray**mah kahtah**lah**nah	caramel pudding
fritos	**free**toass	fritters
helado	ay**lah**dhoa	ice-cream
pastel	pah**stayl**	cake
tarta de manzana	**tahr**tah day mahn**thah**nah	apple tart

Drinks *Bebidas*

beer	**cerveza**	thayr**bhay**thah
(hot) chocolate	**un chocolate (caliente)**	oon choakoa**lah**tay (kah**lyayn**tay)
coffee	**un café**	oon kah**fay**
black	**solo**	**soa**loa
with cream	**con crema**	kon **kray**mah
fruit juice	**un jugo de fruta**	oon **khoo**goa day **froo**tah
milk	**leche**	**lay**chay
mineral water	**agua mineral**	**ah**gwah meenay**rahl**
tea	**un té**	oon tay
wine	**vino**	**bee**noa
red/white	**tinto/blanco**	**teen**toa/**blahn**koa

Complaints and paying *Reclamaciones y la cuenta*

This is too…	**Esto está…**	**ay**stoa ay**stah**
bitter/sweet	**amargo/dulce**	ah**mahr**goa/**dool**thay
salty	**salado**	sah**lah**dhoa
That's not what I ordered.	**Esto no es lo que he pedido.**	**ay**stoa noa ayss loa kay ay peh**dhee**dhoa
I'd like to pay.	**Quisiera pagar.**	kees**syay**rah pah**gahr**
I think you made a mistake in this bill.	**Creo que se ha equivocado usted en esta cuenta.**	**kreh**oa kay say ah aykee-bhoa**kah**dhoa oo**staydh** ayn **ay**stah **kwayn**tah
Do you accept this credit card?	**¿Acepta esta tarjeta de crédito?**	ah**thayp**tah **ay**stah tahr-**khay**tah day **kray**dheetoa
We enjoyed it, thank you.	**Nos ha gustado, gracias.**	noss ah goo**stah**dhoa, **grah**thyahss

Travelling around *Excursiones*

Pláne *Avión*

Is there a flight to...?	¿Hay algún vuelo a...?	igh ahl**goon bway**loa ah
What time should I check in?	¿A qué hora debo presentarme?	ah kay **oarah day**bhoa prayssayn**tahr**may
I'd like to... my reservation.	Quisiera... mi reserva.	kees**syay**rah... mee ray**ssayr**bah
cancel	anular	ahnoo**lahr**
change	cambiar	kahm**byahr**
confirm	confirmar	konfeer**mahr**

Train *Tren*

I'd like a ticket to...	Quiero un billete para...	**kyay**roa oon beel**yay**tay **pah**rah
single (one-way)	ida	**ee**dhah
return (roundtrip)	ida y vuelta	**ee**dhah ee **bwehl**tah
first/second class	primera/segunda clase	pree**may**rah/say**goon**dah **klah**ssay
How long does the journey (trip) take?	¿Cuánto dura el viaje?	**kwahn**toa **doo**rah ayl **byah**khay
When is the... train to...?	¿A qué hora sale el ... tren para...?	ah kay **oarah sah**lay ayl... trayn **pah**rah
first/next/last	primer/próximo/ último	pree**mayr**/**prok**seemoa/ **ool**teemoa
Is this the train to...?	¿Es éste el tren para...?	ayss **ays**tay ayl trayn **pah**rah

Bus *Autobús*

Which bus do I take for the town centre?	¿Qué autobús debo tomar para el centro?	kay owtoa**bhooss day**bhoa toa**mahr pah**rah ayl **thayn**troa
How much is the fare to...?	¿Cuánto es la tarifa para...?	**kwahn**toa ayss lah tah**ree**fah **pah**rah
Will you tell me when to get off?	¿Me diría usted cuándo tengo que apearme?	may dee**ree**ah oos**taydh kwahn**doa **tayn**goa kay ahpay**ahr**may

Taxi *Taxi*

How much is the fare to...?	¿Cuánto es la tarifa a...?	**kwahn**toa ayss lah tah**ree**fah rah

NUMBERS, see page 158

Take me to this address.	Lléveme a estas señas.	**lyay**bhaymay ah **ays**tahss **say**ñahss
Please stop here.	Pare aquí, por favor.	**pah**ray ah**kee** por fah**bhor**
Could you wait for me, please?	¿Puede esperarme, por favor?	**pway**dhay ayspay-**rahr**may por fah**bhor**

Car hire (rental) *Alquiler de coches*

I'd like to hire/rent a car.	Quisiera alquilar un coche.	kee**ssyay**rah ahlkee**lahr** oon **koa**chay
I'd like it for...	Lo quisiera para...	loa kee**ssyay**rah **pah**rah
a day	un día	oon **dee**ah
a week	una semana	**oo**nah say**mah**nah
Where's the nearest filling station?	¿Dónde está la gasolinera más cercana?	**doan**day ays**tah** lah gahssoalee**nay**rah mahss thehr**kah**nah
Full tank, please.	Llénelo, por favor.	**lyay**nayloa por fah**bhor**
Give me... litres of petrol (gasoline).	Déme... litros de gasolina.	**day**may... **lee**troass day gahssoa**lee**nah
How do I get to...?	¿Cómo se va a...?	**koa**moa say bah ah
I've broken down at...	Tengo un coche estropeado en...	**tayn**goa oon **koa**chay aystroapay**ah**dhoa ayn
Can you send a mechanic?	¿Puede usted mandar un mecánico?	**pway**dhay oos**taydh** mahn**dahr** oon may**kah**neekoa
Can you mend this puncture (fix this flat)?	¿Puede arreglar este pinchazo?	**pway**dhay ahrray**glahr** **ays**tay peen**chah**thoa

Se ha equivocado usted de carretera.	You're on the wrong road.
Siga todo derecho.	Go straight ahead.
Es hacia allí...	It's down there...
a la izquierda/derecha	on the left/right
junto a/después de...	next to/after...
norte/sur/este/oeste	north/south/east/west

EMERGENCIES, see page 158

Sightseeing *Visitas turísticas*

Where's the tourist office?	**¿Dónde está la oficina de turismo?**	doanday aystah lah oafeetheenah day tooreesmoa
Is there an English-speaking guide?	**¿Hay algún guía que hable inglés?**	igh ahlgoon geeah kay ahblay eenglayss
Where is/are ...?	**¿Dónde está/ están ...?**	doanday aystah/aystahn
art gallery	**la galería de arte**	lah gahlayreeah day ahrtay
castle	**el castillo**	ayl kahsteelyoa
cathedral	**la catedral**	lah kahtaydrahl
church	**la iglesia**	lah eeglayssyah
city centre/downtown	**el centro de la ciudad**	ayl thayntroa day lah thyoodhahdh
harbour	**el puerto**	ayl pwayrtoa
market	**el mercado**	ayl mehrkahdhoa
museum	**el museo**	ayl moossayoa
square	**la plaza**	lah plahthah
tower	**la torre**	lah torray
When does it open/ close?	**¿A qué hora abren/ cierran?**	ah kay oarah ahbrayn/ thyayrrahn
How much is the entrance fee?	**¿Cuánto vale la entrada?**	kwahntoa bahlay lah ayntrahdhah

Relaxing *Diversiones*

What's playing at the ...Theatre?	**¿Qué ponen en el teatro ...?**	kay poanehn ayn ayl tayahtroa
Are there any seats for tonight?	**¿Quedan locali-dades para esta noche?**	kaydhahn loakahleedhah-dhayss pahrah aystah noachay
How much are the seats?	**¿Cuánto valen las localidades?**	kwahntoa bahlayn lahss loakahleedhahdhayss
Would you like to go out with me tonight?	**¿Quisiera usted salir conmigo esta noche?**	keessyayrah oostaydh sahleer konmeegoa aystah noachay
Is there a disco-theque in town?	**¿Hay alguna disco-teca en la ciudad?**	igh ahlgoonah deeskoatay-kay ayn lah thyoodhahdh
May I have this dance?	**¿Me permite este baile?**	may payrmeetay aystay bighlay
Thank you for the evening. It was great.	**Muchas gracias por la velada. Ha sido estupenda.**	moochahss grahthyahss por lah baylahdhah. ah seedhoa aystoopayndah

TELLING THE TIME, see page 157

Shops, stores and services *Comercios y servicios*

Where's the nearest...	¿Dónde está... más cercano/cercana?	doanday aystah ... mahss thayrkahnoa/thayrkahnah
bakery	la panadería	lah pahnahdhayreeah
bookshop	la librería	lah leebrayreeah
butcher's	la carnicería	lah kahrneethayreeah
chemist/drugstore	la farmacia	lah fahrmahthyah
dentist	el dentista	ayl daynteestah
department store	los grandes almacenes	loss grahndayss ahlmahthaynayss
grocery	la tienda de comestibles	lay tyayndah day koamaysteeblayss
hairdresser (ladies)	la peluquería	lah paylookayreeah
news-stand	el quiosco de periódicos	ayl kyoskoa day payryodheekoass
post office	la oficina de correos	lah oafeetheenah day korrehoass
supermarket	el supermercado	ayl soopayrmayrkahdhoa
toilets/restrooms	los servicios	loass sayrbeethyoass

General expressions *Locuciones básicas*

Where's the main shopping area?	¿Dónde está la zona de tiendas más importante?	doanday aystah lah thoanah day tyayndahss mahss eempoartahntay
Do you have any...?	¿Tiene usted...?	tyaynay oostaydh
Haven't you anything...?	¿No tiene usted algo...?	noa tyaynay oostaydh ahlgoa
cheaper/better larger/smaller	más barato/mejor más grande/más pequeño	mahss bahrahtoa/mehkhor mahss grahnday/mahss paykayñoa
Can I try it on?	¿Puedo probármelo?	pwaydhoa probahrmayloa
How much is this?	¿Cuánto cuesta esto?	kwahntoa kwaystah aystoa
Please write it down.	Escríbamelo, por favor.	ayskreebhahmayloa por fahbhor
I don't want to spend more than...	No quiero gastar más de...	noa kyayroa gahstahr mahss day
No, I don't like it.	No, no me gusta.	noa noa may goostah
I'll take it.	Me lo llevo.	may loa lyaybhoa
Do you accept credit cards?	¿Acepta usted tarjetas de crédito?	ahthayptah oostaydh tahrkhaytahss day kraydheetoa

NUMBERS, see page 158

black	**negro**	**neh**groa
blue	**azul**	ahth**ool**
brown	**marrón**	mahr**ron**
green	**verde**	**behr**day
orange	**naranja**	nah**rahn**khah
red	**rojo**	**roa**khoa
white	**blanco**	**blahn**koa
yellow	**amarillo**	ahmah**ree**lyoa
light...	**... claro**	**klah**roa
dark...	**... oscuro**	oas**koo**roa

I want to buy...	**Quisiera comprar...**	kee**ssyay**rah kom**prahr**
aspirins	**unas aspirinas**	**oo**nahss ahspee**ree**nahss
bread	**pan**	pahn
newspaper	**un periódico**	oon payr**yo**dheekoa
American	**americano**	ahmayree**kah**noa
English	**inglés**	een**glayss**
postcards	**unas tarjetas postales**	**oo**nahss tahr**khay**tahss poas**tah**layss
shampoo	**un champú**	oon chahm**poo**
soap	**jabón**	khah**bhon**
sun-tan cream	**una crema solar**	**oo**nah **kray**mah soa**lahr**
toothpaste	**pasta de dientes**	**pahs**tah day **dyayn**tayss
a half kilo of tomatoes	**medio kilo de tomates**	**may**dhyoa **kee**loa day toa**mah**tayss
a litre of milk	**un litro de leche**	oon **lee**troa day **lay**chay
I'd like a film for this camera.	**Quisiera un rollo para esta cámara.**	kee**ssyay**rah oon **roal**yoa **pah**rah **ays**tah **kah**mahrah
black and white	**en blanco y negro**	ayn **blahn**koa ee **nay**groa
colour	**en color**	ayn koa**loar**
I'd like a haircut, please.	**Quiero un corte de pelo, por favor.**	**kyay**roa oon **kor**tay day **pay**loa por fah**bhor**

Souvenirs *Recuerdos*

castanets	**las castañuelas**	lahss kahstah**ñway**lahss
copperware	**objetos de cobre**	oab**khay**toass day **koa**bray
doll	**la muñeca**	lah moo**ñay**kah
fan	**el abanico**	ayl ahbhah**nee**koa
guitar	**la guitarra**	lah geet**ahr**rah
lace	**los encajes**	loss ayn**kah**khayss
poncho	**el poncho**	ayl **pon**choa

At the bank *En el banco*

Where's the nearest currency exchange office?	**¿Dónde está la oficina de cambio más cercana?**	doanday aystah lah oafeetheenah day kahmbyoa mahss thehrkahnah
I want to change some dollars/pounds.	**Quiero cambiar unos dólares/unas libras esterlinas.**	kyayroa kahmbyahr oonoass doalahrayss/ oonahss leebrahss aystayr-leenahss
What's the exchange rate?	**¿A cómo está el cambio?**	ah koamoa aystah ayl kahmbyoa
I want to cash a traveller's cheque.	**Quiero cobrar un cheque de viajero.**	kyayroa koabrahr oon chaykay day byahkhayroa

At the post office *Correos*

I want to send this...	**Quiero mandar esto...**	kyayroa mahndahr aystoa
airmail express	**por correo aéreo urgente**	por korrehoa ahayrehoa oorkhayntay
I want... ...-peseta stamps.	**Quiero... sellos para... pesetas.**	kyayroa... saylyoass pahrah ... payssaytahss
What's the postage for a letter to United States?	**¿Cuál es el franqueo para una carta para los Estados Unidos?**	kwahl ayss ayl frahnkayoa pahrah oonah kahrtah pahrah loass aysahd hoass ooneedhoass
Is there any post/mail for me? My name is...	**¿Hay correo para mí? Me llamo(-a)...**	igh korrehoa pahrah mee. may lyahmoa(-ah)

Telephoning *Teléfonos*

Where is the nearest telephone?	**¿Dónde está el teléfono más cercano?**	doanday aystah ayl taylayfoanoa mahss thehrkahnoa
May I use your phone?	**¿Puedo usar su teléfono?**	pwaydhoa oossahr soo taylayfoanoa
Hello. This is... speaking.	**Oiga. Aquí habla con...**	oygah. ahkee ahblah kon...
I'd like to speak to...	**Quiero hablar con...**	kyayroa ahblahr kon...
When will he/she be back?	**¿Cuándo estará de vuelta?**	kwahndoa aystahrah day bwayltah

NUMBERS, see page 158

Time and date *Horas y fechas*

It's...	Es/Son...	ayss/son
five past one	**la una y cinco**	lah **oo**nah ee **theen**koa
quarter past three	**las tres y cuarto**	lahss trayss ee **kwahr**toa
twenty past four	**las cuatro y veinte**	lahss **kwah**troa ee **bayn**tay
half past six	**las seis y media**	lahss sayss ee **may**dhyay
twenty-five to seven	**las siete menos veinticinco**	lahss **say**tay **may**noass baynte**theen**koa
ten to ten	**las diez menos diez**	lahss dyayth **may**noass dyayth
twelve o'clock	**las doce**	lahss **doa**thay
in the morning	**por la mañana**	por lah mah**ña**nah
in the afternoon	**por la tarde**	por lah **tahr**day
in the evening	**por la tarde**	por lah **tahr**day
during the day	**durante el día**	doo**rahn**tay ayl **dee**ah
at night	**por la noche**	por lah **noa**chay
yesterday/today	**ayer/hoy**	ah**yehr**/oy
tomorrow	**mañana**	mah**ña**nah
spring	**la primavera**	lah preemah**bhay**rah
summer	**el verano**	ayl bay**rah**noa
autumn (fall)	**el otoño**	ayl o**toa**ñoa
winter	**el invierno**	ayl een**byayr**noa

Sunday	**domingo**	doa**meen**goa
Monday	**lunes**	**loo**nayss
Tuesday	**martes**	**mahr**tayss
Wednesday	**miércoles**	**myayr**koalayss
Thursday	**jueves**	khway**bhay**ss
Friday	**viernes**	**byayr**nayss
Saturday	**sábado**	**sah**bhadhoa
January	**enero**	ay**nay**roa
February	**febrero**	feh**breh**roa
March	**marzo**	**mahr**thoa
April	**abril**	ah**breel**
May	**mayo**	**mah**yoa
June	**junio**	**khoon**yoa
July	**julio**	**khool**yoa
August	**agosto**	ah**goas**toa
September	**septiembre**	sehp**tyaym**bray
October	**octubre**	ok**too**bray
November	**noviembre**	noa**bhyaym**bray
December	**diciembre**	deeth**yaym**bray

NUMBERS, page 158

Numbers *Números*

0	**cero**	thayroa
1	**uno**	oonoa
2	**dos**	doss
3	**tres**	trayss
4	**cuatro**	kwahtroa
5	**cinco**	theenkoa
6	**seis**	sayss
7	**siete**	syaytay
8	**ocho**	oachoa
9	**nueve**	nwaybhay
10	**diez**	dyayth
11	**once**	onthay
12	**doce**	doathay
13	**trece**	traythay
14	**catorce**	kahtorthay
15	**quince**	keenthay
16	**dieciséis**	dyaytheessayss
17	**diecisiete**	dyaytheessyaytay
18	**dieciocho**	dyaytheeoachoa
19	**diecinueve**	dyaytheenwaybhay
20	**veinte**	bayntay
21	**veintiuno**	baynteeoonoa
30	**treinta**	trayntah
40	**cuarenta**	kwahrayntah
50	**cincuenta**	theenkwayntah
60	**sesenta**	sayssayntah
70	**setenta**	saytayntah
80	**ochenta**	oachayntah
90	**noventa**	noabhayntah
100	**cien/ciento**	thyayn/thyayntoa
1,000	**mil**	meel
10,000	**diez mil**	dyath meel
1,000,000	**un millón**	oon meelyon
first	**primero**	preemayroa
second	**segundo**	saygoondoa
third	**tercero**	tehrthayroa
once	**una vez**	oonah behth
twice	**dos veces**	doss baythayss
a half	**una mitad**	oonah meetahdh
a quarter	**un cuarto**	oon kwahrtoa
a third	**un tercio**	oon tehrthyoa

Emergency *Urgencia*

Call the police	**Llama a la policía**	**lyah**mah ah lah poaleetheeah
Get a doctor	**Busque un doctor**	**boos**kay oon doak**tor**
Go away	**Váyase**	**bah**yahssay
HELP	**SOCORRO**	so**koar**roa
I'm ill	**Estoy enfermo(-a)**	ay**stoy** ayn**fehr**moa(ah)
I'm lost	**Me he perdido**	may ay payr**dee**dhoa
Leave me alone	**Déjeme en paz**	**day**khaymay ayn pahth
LOOK OUT	**CUIDADO**	kwee**dhah**dhoa
STOP THIEF	**AL LADRÓN**	ahl lah**dron**
My ... has been stolen.	**Me han robado mi ...**	may ahn roa**bhah**dhoa mee
I've lost my ...	**He perdido mi ...**	ay pehr**dee**dhoa mee
handbag	**bolso**	**boal**soa
luggage	**equipaje**	aykee**pah**khay
passport	**pasaporte**	passah**por**tay
wallet	**cartera**	kahr**tay**rah
Where can I find a doctor who speaks English?	**¿Dónde puedo encontrar un médico que hable inglés?**	**doan**day **pway**dhoa aynkon**trahr** oon **meh**dheekoa kay **ah**blay een**glayss**

Guide to Spanish pronunciation *Pronunciación*

Consonants

Letter	Approximate pronunciation	Symbol	Example	
f, k, l, m, n, p, t, x, y	as in English			
b	1) generally as in English	b	**bueno**	**bway**noa
	2) between vowels, a sound between **b** and **v**	bh	**bebida**	bay**bhee**dhah

c	1) before **e**, **i** like **th** in **thin**	th	**centro**	**thayn**troa
	2) like **k** in **kit**	k	**como**	**ko**amoa
ch	as in English	ch	**mucho**	**moo**choa
d	1) like **d** in **dog** but weaker	d	**donde**	**doan**day
	2) between vowels and at end of word like **th** in **this**	dh	**edad**	ay**dhahdh**
g	1) before **e**, **i**, like **ch** in Scottish lo**ch**	kh	**urgente**	oor**khayn**tay
	2) between vowels, sometimes within word, weak version	g	**agua**	**ahg**wah
	3) like **g** in **go**	g	**ninguno**	neen**goo**noa
h	always silent		**hombre**	**om**bray
j	like **ch** in lo**ch**	kh	**bajo**	**bah**khoa
ll	like **lli** in million	ly	**lleno**	**lyay**noa
ñ	like **ni** in onion	ñ	**señor**	say**ñor**
qu	like **k** in **kit**	k	**quince**	**keen**thay
r	trilled, like Scottish **r**	r	**río**	**ree**oa
rr	strongly trilled	rr	**arriba**	ahr**ree**bhah
s	like **s** in **sit**, with a slight lisp	s/ss	**vista** **cuantos**	**bees**tah **kwahn**toass
v	1) like **b** in **bad** but lighter	b	**viejo**	**byay**khoa
	2) between vowels like English **v**	bh	**rival**	ree**bhahl**
z	like **th** in **thin**	th	**brazo**	**brah**thoa

Vowels

a	like **ar** in **cart**, but fairly short	ah	**gracias**	**grah**thyahss
e	1) like **a** in **late**	ay	**de**	day
	2) like **e** in **get**	eh	**llover**	lyoa**bhehr**
i	like **ee** in **feet**	ee	**sí**	see
o	1) like **oa** in **boat**, but pronounced without a movement of tongue or lips	oa	**sopa**	**soa**pah
	2) like **o** in **got**	o	**dos**	doss
u	like **oo** in **loot**	oo	**una**	**oo**nah
y	like **ee** in **feet**, at end of word	ee	**y**	ee

Swedish

Basic expressions *Användbara uttryck*

Yes/No.	**Ja/Nej.**	yaa/nay
Please.	**Var snäll och .../**	vaar snehl ok/
	..., tack.	tahk
Thank you.	**Tack.**	tahk
I beg your pardon?	**Förlåt?**	fur'lawt

Introductions *Presentation*

Good morning.	**God morgon.**	goo(d) **mo**rron
Good afternoon.	**God middag.**	goo(d) **mi**ddah(g)
Good night.	**God natt.**	goo(d) naht
Good-bye.	**Adjö.**	ahy**ur**
My name is...	**Mitt namn är ...**	mit nahmn ǣr
Pleased to meet you.	**Trevligt att träffas.**	**trayv**lli(g)t aht **treh**fahss
What's your name?	**Vad heter ni/du?**	vaad **hay**terr nee/dew
How are you?	**Hur står det till?**	hewr stawr day(t) til
Fine thanks.	**Bra, tack.**	braa tahk.
And you?	**Och du?**	ok dew
Where do you come from?	**Varifrån kommer du?**	**vaa**rifrawn **ko**mmer dew
I'm from...	**Jag är från ...**	yaa(g) ǣr frawn
Australia	**Australien**	aaew**straa**liern
Canada	**Kanada**	**kah**nahdah
Great Britain	**Storbritannien**	**stoor**brittahniern
United States	**USA**	**ew**ehssaa
I'm with my...	**Jag är här med ...**	yaa(g) ǣr hǣr mayd
wife	**min fru**	min frew
husband	**min man**	min mahn
family	**min familj**	min fah**mil**y
boyfriend	**min pojkvän**	min **poyk**vehn
girlfriend	**min flickvän**	min **flik**vehn
I'm here on business/vacation.	**Jag är här i affärer/på semester.**	yaa(g) ǣr hǣr ee ah**fǣ**rerr/paw seh**mehs**terr

GUIDE TO PRONUNCIATION/EMERGENCIES, page 175

Questions *Frågor*

When?	**När?**	nær
How?	**Hur?**	hewr
What?/Why?	**Vad?/Varför?**	vaad/**vahr**furr
Who?	**Vem?**	vehm
Which?	**Vilken?**	**vil**kern
Where is/are...?	**Var är/Var finns/ Var ligger...?**	vaar ær/vaar finss/ vaar **li**gerr
Where can I find...?	**Var hittar jag...?**	vaaar **hi**ttahr yaa(g)
Where can I get...?	**Var kan jag få tag på...?**	vaar kahn yaa(g) faw taag paw
How far?	**Hur långt?**	hewr longt
How long?	**Hur länge?**	hewr **leh**nger
How much/many?	**Hur mycket/ många?**	hewr **mew**ker(t)/**mong**ah
Can I have...?	**Kan jag få...?**	kahn yaa(g) faw
Can you help me?	**Kan ni hjälpa mig?**	kahn nee **yehl**pah may
What does this mean?	**Vad betyder det här?**	vaa(d) ber**tew**derr day(t) hær
I understand.	**Jag förstår.**	yaa(g) fur'**stawr**
I don't understand.	**Jag förstår inte.**	yaa(g) fur'**stawr** inter
Can you translate this for me?	**Kan ni översätta det här för mig?**	kahn nee ūrver'sehtah day(t) hær fūrr may
Do you speak English?	**Talar ni engelska?**	**taa**lahr nee **ehng**erlskah
I don't speak (much) Swedish.	**Jag talar inte (så bra) svenska.**	yaa(g) **taa**lahr inter (saw braa) **svehn**skah

A few more useful words *Några fler användbara ord*

better/worse	**bättre/sämre**	**beh**trer/**sehm**rer
big/small	**stor/liten**	stoor/**lee**tern
cheap/expensive	**billig/dyr**	**bi**lli(g)/dewr
early/late	**tidig/sen**	**tee**di(g)/sayn
good/bad	**bra/dålig**	braa/**daw**li(g)
hot/cold	**varm/kall**	vahrm/kahl
near/far	**nära/långt (bort)**	**næ**rah/longt (bo't)
old/new	**gammal/ny**	**gah**mahl/new
right/wrong	**rätt/fel**	reht/fayl
vacant/occupied	**ledig/upptagen**	**lay**di(g)/**ewp**taagern

Hotel–Accommodation *Hotell*

I/We have a reservation.	**Jag/Vi har beställt rum.**	yaa(g)/vee haar ber**stehlt** rewm
Do you have any vacancies?	**Har ni några lediga rum?**	har nee **naw**grah **lay**diggah rewm
I'd like a ..	**Jag skulle vilja ha ett ...**	yaa(g) **skew**ler **vil**yah haa eht
single room	**enkelrum**	**ehn**kerlrewm
double room	**dubbelrum**	**dew**berlrewm
with twin beds	**med två sängar**	mayd tvaw **sehng**ahr
with a double bed	**med dubbelsäng**	mayd **dew**berlsehng
with a bath/shower	**med bad/dusch**	mayd baad/dewsh
We'll be staying ...	**Vi tänker stanna ...**	vee **tehn**kerr **stah**nah
overnight only	**bara över natten**	**baa**rah **ūr**verr **nah**tern
a few days	**några dagar**	**naw**grah **daa**(gah)r
a week	**en vecka**	ehn **veh**kah
Is there a camp site near here?	**Finns det någon campingplats i närheten?**	finss day(t) **naw**gon **kahm**pingplahtss ee **nǣr**haytern

Decision *Beslut*

May I see the room?	**Kan jag få se på rummet?**	kahn yaa(g) faw say paw **rew**mert
That's fine. I'll take it.	**Det är bra. Jag tar det.**	day(t) ǣr braa. yaa(g) taar day(t)
No. I don't like it.	**Nej. Jag tycker inte om det.**	nay. yaa(g) **tew**kerr **in**ter om day(t)
It's too ...	**Det är för ...**	day(t) ǣr fūrr
dark/cold	**mörkt/kallt**	murrkt/kahlt
Do you have anything ...?	**Har ni något ...?**	haar nee **naw**got
better/bigger	**bättre/större**	**beht**rer/**stur**rer
cheaper	**billigare**	**bil**liggahrer
quieter	**tystare**	**tews**tahtrer
May I have my bill, please?	**Kan jag få räkningen, tack?**	kahn yaa(g) faw **raik**ningern tahk
It's been a very enjoyable stay.	**Det har varit en mycket trevlig vistelse.**	day(t) haar **vaa**rit ehn **mew**ker(t) **trayv**li(g) **vis**terlser

DAYS OF THE WEEK, see page 172/NUMBERS, see page 173

Eating out *Mat och dryck*

I'd like to reserve a table for 4.	**Jag skulle vilja beställa ett bord för 4.**	yaa(g) **skewler vil**yah ber**steh**lah eht boo'd fur 4
We'll come at 8.	**Vi kommer klockan 8.**	vee **kom**merr **klok**kahn 8
I'd like some...	**Jag skulle vilja ha...**	yaa(g) **skew**ler **vil**yah haa
breakfast/lunch/ dinner	**frukost/lunch/ middag**	**frew**kost/lewnsh/ **mid**dah(g)
What would you recommend?	**Vak rekommen- derar ni?**	vaad rehkommern**day**rahr nee
Do you have any vegetarian dishes?	**Har ni några vegetariska rätter?**	haar nee **naw**grah vehger**taa**riskah **reh**terr

Breakfast *Frukost*

May I have some...	**Kan jag få...?**	kahn yaa(g) faw
bread	**lite bröd**	**lee**ter brürd
butter	**lite smör**	**lee**ter smürr
cheese	**ost**	oost
ham and eggs	**skinka och ägg**	**shin**kah ok ehg
jam	**lite sylt**	**lee**ter sewlt
rolls	**ett småfranska**	eht **smaw**frahnskah

Starters *Förrätter*

färska räkor	**fæ'skah rai**koor	unshelled prawns with toast and butter
grodlår	**grood**lawr	frog's legs
gåslever	**gaws**lay̆verr	goose liver
smör, ost och sill	smürr, oost ok sil	herring with bread, butter and cheese

Soups *Sopper*

buljong	**bewl**yong	consommé
grönsakssoppa	**grürn**saakssoppah	vegetable soup
kålsoppa	**kawl**soppah	cabbage soup
nässelsoppa	**nehs**serlsoppah	nettle soup
ärtsoppa	**æ't**soppah	yellow pea soup

Fish and seafood *Fisk och skaldjur*

cod	**torsk**	to͡rsk
crab	**krabba**	krahbah
eel	**ål**	awl
herring	**sill**	sil
lobster	**hummer**	hewmerr
mullet	**multe**	mewlter
oysters	**ostron**	oostron
smoked herring	**böckling**	burkling

gubböra	marinated sprats, onions and hard-boiled
(gewbrü͞rrah)	eggs, fried
lättrökt lax	smoked salmon with creamed spinach and
(lehtrü͞rkt lahks)	poached egg
sotare	Baltic herring grilled until black, with dill
(so͞otahrer)	butter

baked	**ugnstekt**	ewngnsta͞ykt
boiled	**kokt**	kookt
fried	**stekt**	sta͞ykt
grilled (broiled)	**halstrad, grillad**	hahlstrahd, **g**rillahd
roasted	**helstekt**	ha͞ylsta͞ykt
underdone (rare)	**blodig**	blo͞odig
medium	**medium**	ma͞ydeeyewn
well-done	**genomstekt**	ya͞ynomsta͞ykt

Meat *Kött*

I'd like some...	**Jag skulle vilja ha...**	yaa(g) **s**kewler **v**ilyah haa
beef/lamb	**oxkött/lamm**	ookskhurt/lahm
chicken/duck	**kyckling/anka**	khewkling/ahnkah
pork/veal	**fläskkött/kalv**	flehskkhurt/kahlv

dillkött	dilkhurt	veal in lemon and dill sauce
lövbiff	lü͞rvbif	fried sliced beef and onions
slottsstek	slotssta͞yk	pot roast with sprats and golden syrup

Vegetables *Grönsaker*

beans	**böner**	bü͞rnoor
carrots	**morötter**	mo͞orurterr
mushrooms	**svamp**	svahmp
onions	**lök**	lü͞rk

peas	**ärtor**	æ'toor
potatoes	**potatis**	pootaatiss
tomatoes	**tomater**	toomaaterr

Fruit and dessert *Frukt och Efterrätter*

apple	**äpple**	ehpler
banana	**banan**	bahnaan
cherries	**bigarråer**	biggahrawerr
lemon	**citron**	sitroon
orange	**apelsin**	ahperlseen
pear	**päron**	pǣron
plums	**plommon**	ploomon
strawberries	**jordgubbar**	yoo'dgewbahr

Drinks *Drycker*

apple juice	**äppeljuice**	ehperlyōōss
beer	**öl**	ūrl
(hot) chocolate	**(varm) choklad**	(vahrm) shoklaa(d)
coffee	**kaffe**	kahfer
a pot of	**en kanna**	ehn kahnah
with cream	**med grädde**	mǟyd grehder
milk	**mjölk**	myurlk
mineral water	**mineralvatten**	minerraalvahtern
tea	**te**	tǟy
wine	**vin**	veen
red/white	**rött/vitt**	rurt/vit

Complaints and paying *Klagomål och notan*

This is too...	**Det här är för...**	dǣy(t) hǟr ǟr fūrr
bitter/sweet	**beskt/sött**	behskt/surt
salty	**salt**	sahlt
That's not what I ordered.	**Det där har jag inte beställt.**	dǣy(t) dǟr haar yaa(g) inter berstehlt
I'd like to pay.	**Får jag betala.**	fawr yaa(g) bertaalah
I think there's a mistake in this bill.	**Jag tror att det är ett fel på notan.**	yaa(g) trōōr aht dǣy(t) ǟr eht fǟyl paw nōōtahn
Can I pay with this credit card?	**Kan jag betala med det här kreditkortet?**	kahn yaa(g) bertaalah mǟyd dǣy(t) hǟr krehdeetkoo'tert
Is everything included?	**Är allting inräknat?**	ǟr ahlting inraiknaht
We enjoyed it, thank you.	**Det var mycket gott.**	dǣy(t) vaar mewker(t) got

Travelling around *På resa*

Plane *Flyg*

Is there a flight to...?	**Finns et något flyg till...?**	finss dāy(t) **naw**got flēwg til
What time should I check in?	**Hur dags måste jag checka in?**	hēwr dahgss **mos**ter yaa(g) **kheh**kah in
I'd like to... my reservation.	**Jag skulle vilja... min reservation.**	yaa(g) **skew**ler **vil**yah min rehsehrvah**shōōn**
cancel	**annullera**	ahnew**lāy**rah
change	**ändra**	**ehn**drah
confirm	**bekräfta**	ber**krehf**tah

Train *Tåg*

I'd like a ticket to...	**Jag skulle vilja ha en bilett till...?**	yaa(g) **skew**ler **vil**yah haa ehn bily**eht** til
single (one-way)	**enkel**	**ehn**kerl
return (round trip)	**tur och retur**	tēwr ok reh**tēwr**
first/second class	**första/andra klass**	fur'stah/**ahn**drah klahss
What time does the train arrive in...?	**Hur dags är tåget framme i...**	hēwr dahgss ār **taw**gert **frah**mer ee
When is the... train to...?	**När går... tåget till...?**	nār gawr... **taw**gert til
first/last/next	**första/sista/nästa**	fur'stah/**sis**tah/**nehs**tah
Is this the train to...?	**Är det här tåget till...?**	ār dāy(t) hār **taw**gert til

Bus–Tram (streetcar) *Buss–Spårvagn*

Which tram goes to the town centre?	**Vilken spårvagn går till centrum?**	**vil**kern **spawr**vahngn gawr til **sehn**trewm
How much is the fare to...?	**Hur mycket kostar det till...?**	hēwr **mew**ker(t) **kos**tahr dāy(t) til
Will you tell me when to get off?	**Kan ni säga till när jag skall stiga av?**	kahn nee **seh**yah til nār yaa(g) skah(l) **stee**gah aav

Taxi *Taxi*

How much is the fare to...?	**Hur mycket kostar det till...?**	hēwr **mew**ker(t) **kos**tahr dāy(t) til
Take me to this address.	**Kör mig till den här adressen.**	khūr may til dehn hār ah**dreh**ssern
Please stop here.	**Var snäll och stanna här.**	vaar snehl ok **stah**nah hār

TELLING THE TIME, see page 172/NUMBERS, page 173

Car hire (rental) *Biluthyrning*

I'd like to hire (rent) a car.	**Jag skulle vilja hyra en bil.**	yaa(g) **skew**ler **vil**yah **hēw**rah ehn beel
I'd like it for...	**Jag vill ha den...**	yaa(g) vil haa dehn
a day/a week	**en dag/en vecka**	ehn daa(g)/ehn **veh**kah
Where's the nearest filling station?	**Var ligger närmaste bensin-station?**	vaar **ligg**err **nær**mahster behn**seen**stahsh**ōo**n
Fill it up, please.	**Full tank, tack.**	fewl tahnk tahk
Give me... litres of petrol (gasoline).	**Kan jag få... liter bensin.**	kahn yaa(g) faw... **lee**terr behn**seen**
How do I get to this place/this address?	**Hur kommer jag till den här platsen/ adressen?**	hēwr **komm**err yaa(g) til dehn **här plaht**sern/ ahd**reh**ssern
I've had a break-down at...	**Jag har fått motorstopp vid...**	yaa(g) haar fot **mōo**to'stop veed
Can you send a mechanic?	**Kan ni skicka en mekaniker?**	kahn nee **shi**kkah ehh meh**kaa**nikkerr
Can you mend this puncture (fix this flat)?	**Kan ni laga den här punkteringen?**	kahn nee **laa**gah dehn här pewngt**āy**ringern

Ni har kört fel.	You're on the wrong road.
Kör rakt fram.	Go straight ahead.
Det är där nere till...	It's down there on the...
vänster/höger	left/right
bredvid/efter...	next to/after...
norr/söder/öster/väster	north/south/east/west

Sightseeing *Sightseeing*

Where's the tourist office?	**Var ligger turistbyrån?**	vaar **ligg**err tew**rist**bēw**rawn
Is there an English-speaking guide?	**Finns det någon engelsktalande guide?**	finss dāy(t) **naw**gon **ehng**erlsktaalahnder "guide"
Where is/are the...?	**Var ligger...?**	vaar **ligg**err
art museum	**konstmuseet**	**konst**mewss**āy**ert
castle	**slottet**	**slott**ert

cathedral	**domkyrkan**	**doom**khewrkahn
church	**kyrkan**	**khewr**kahn
city centre/downtown	**(stads)centrum**	**(stahds)sehn**trewm
harbour	**hamnen**	**hahm**nern
museum	**museet**	mewss**ay**ert
square	**torget**	**tor**yert
tower	**tornet**	too'nert

When is it open?	**När är det öppet?**	nær ær day(t) **ur**pert
When does it close?	**När stänger det?**	nær **stehng**err day(t)
How much is the entrance fee?	**Vad kostar det i inträde?**	vaad **kos**tahr day(t) ee **in**traider

Relaxing *Nöjen*

What's playing at the... Theatre?	**Vad går det på... teatern?**	vad gawr day(t) paw... **tay**aater'n
Are there any tickets for tonight?	**Finns det några biletter till i kväll?**	finss day(t) **naw**grah bily**eht**err til ee kvehl
How much are the seats?	**Hur mycket kostar biljetterna?**	hewr **mew**ker(t) **kos**tahr bily**eht**er'nah
Would you like to go out with me tonight?	**Skall vi gå ut i kväll?**	skah(l) vee gaw **ewt** ee kvehl
Would you like to dance?	**Skall vi dansa?**	skah(l) vee **dahn**sah
Thank you, it's been a wonderful evening.	**Tack, det har varit en underbar kväll.**	tahk day(t) haar **vaa**rit ehn **ewn**derrbaar kvehl

Shops, stores and services *Affärer och service*

Where's the nearest ...?	**Var ligger närmaste...?**	vaar **li**ggerr **nær**mahster
bakery	**ett bageri**	eht baager**ree**
bookshop	**en bokhandel**	ehn **book**hahnderl
butcher's	**en slaktare**	ehn **slahk**tahrer
chemist's/drugstore	**ett apotek**	eht ahpoo**tayk**
dentist	**en tandläkare**	ehn **tahn(d)**laikahrer
department store	**ett varuhus**	eht **vaa**rewhewss
grocery	**en livsmedelsaffär**	ehn livs**may**derlsahfær
hairdresser	**en frisör**	ehn fri**surr**
newsstand	**en tidningskiosk**	ehn **tee(d)**ningskhiosk
post office	**ett postkontor**	eht **post**kontoor
supermarket	**ett snabbköp**	eht **snahb**khurp
toilets	**toaletten**	tooah**leht**tern

TELLING THE TIME, see page 172

General expressions *Allmänna uttryck*

Where's the main shopping area?	**Var ligger affärscentrum?**	vaar liggerr ahfæ'ssehntrewm
Do you have any...?	**Har ni några...?**	haar nee nawgrah
Don't you have anything...?	**Har ni inter någonting...?**	haar nee inter nawgonting
cheaper/better larger/smaller	**billigare/bättre större/mindre**	billiggaher/behtrer sturrer/mindrer
Can I try it on?	**Kan jag få prova den?**	kahn yaa(g) faw prōōvah dehn
Where's the changing room?	**Var är provhytten?**	vaar ār prōōvhewtern
How much is this?	**Hur mycket kostar det här?**	hewr mewker(t) kostahr dāy(t) hār
Please write it down.	**Kan ni skriva det?**	kahn nee skreevah dāy(t)
I don't want to spend more than... crowns.	**Jag vill inte lägga ut mer än... kroner.**	yaa(g) vil inter lehgah ēwt māyr ehn... krōōner
No, I don't like it.	**Nej, jag tycker inte om det.**	nay yaa(g) tewkerr inter om dāy(t)
I'll take it.	**Jag tar det.**	yaa(g) taar dāy(t)
Do you accept credt cards?	**Tar ni kreditkort?**	taar nee krehdeetkoo't

black	**svart**	svah't
blue	**blå**	blaw
brown	**brun**	brēwn
green	**grön**	grūrn
orange	**orange**	orahnsh
red	**röd**	rūrd
white	**vit**	veet
yellow	**gul**	gēwl
light...	**ljus...**	yēwss
dark...	**mörk...**	murrk

I want to buy a/an/ some...	**Jag skulle vilja köpa...**	yaa(g) skewler vilyah khūrpah
aspirin	**aspirin**	ahspireen
battery	**batteri**	bahterree
newspaper	**en dagstidning**	ehn dahgstee(d)ning
American	**amerikansk**	ahm(eh)rikaansk
English	**engelsk**	engerlsk

NUMBERS, see page 173

postcard	**ett vykort**	eht ve͞ekoo't
shampoo	**ett shampo**	eht **shahm**poo
soap	**en tvål**	ehn tvawl
sun-tan oil	**en sololja**	ehn so͞ololyah
toothpaste	**en tandkräm**	ehn **tahn(d)**kraim
half-kilo of tomatoes	**ett halvt kilo tomater**	eht hahlft **khee**loo too**maa**terr
litre of milk	**en liter mjölk**	ehn **lee**terr myurlk
I'd like a... film for this camera.	**Jag skulle vilja ha film till den här kameran.**	yaa(g) **skew**ler **vil**yah haa film til dehn hǣr **kaam**(er)rahn
black and white	**svart-vit**	svah't-veet
colour	**färg**	færy

Souvenirs *Souvenirer*

I'd like a/some...	**Jag skulle vilja ha...**	yaa(g) **skew**ler **vil**yah haa
ceramics	**keramik**	khehrah**meek**
glassware	**glas**	glaass
Lapp handicrafts	**sameslöjd**	**saa**mersluryd
silverware	**något i silver**	**naw**got ee **sil**verr
woodwork	**något i trä**	**naw**got ee trǣ

At the bank *Bank*

Where's the nearest bank/currency exchange office?	**Var ligger närmaste bank/ växelkontor?**	vaar **lig**gerr **næ**rmahster bahnk/**veh**kserlkontoo̅r
I want to change some dollars/pounds.	**Jag skulle vilja växla några dollar/ pund.**	yaa(g) **skew**ler **vil**yah **vehks**lah **naw**grah **dol**lahr/ pewnd
What's the exchange rate?	**Vilken är växelkursen?**	**vil**kern ǣr **veh**kserlkew'sern
I want to cash a traveller's cheque.	**Jag skulle vilja lösa in en rese- check.**	yaa(g) **skew**ler **vil**yah **lu̅r**ssah in ehn **ray**sserkhehk

At the post office *Post*

I'd like to send this by...	**Jag vil skicka det här...**	yaa(g) vil **shik**kah **day**(t) hær
airmail	**med flyg**	**may**d flewg
express	**express**	ehk**sprehss**

A...-öres stamp, please.	Ett... -öres frimärke, tack.	eht... ūrrerss freemærker tahk
What's the postage for a letter/postcard to the U.S.A.?	Vad är portot för ett brev/vykort till USA?	vaad ær po'tot fūrr eht brāyv/vewkoo't til ēwehssaa
Is there any post (mail) for me?	Finns det någon post till mig?	finss dāy(t) nawgon post til may.
My name is...	Mitt namn är...	mit nahmn ær

Telephoning *Telefon*

Where's the nearest telephone booth?	Var finns närmaste telefonkiosk?	vaar finss **nær**mahster tehleh**fawn**khiosk
May I use your phone?	Får jag låna telefonen?	fawr yaa(g) **law**nah tehleh**fawn**ern
Hello. This is...	Hallå, det här är...	hahlaw dāy(t) hær ær
I'd like to speak to...	Kan jag få tala med...?	kahn yaa(g) faw **taa**lah māyd
When will he/she be back?	När kommer han/ hon tillbaka?	nær **kom**merr hahn/ hoon **til**baakah
Will you tell him/her that I called?	Kan ni tala om för honom/henne att jag har ringt?	kahn nee **taa**lah om fūrr **hon**nom/**heh**ner aht yaa(g) haar ringt

Time and date *Klockan och datum*

It's...	Den är...	dehn ær
five past one	fem över ett	fehm **ūr**verr eht
quarter past three	kvart över tre	kvah't **ūr**verr trāy
twenty past four	tjugo över fyra	**khew**goo **ūr**verr **few**rah
half-past six	halv sju	hahlv shēw
twenty-five to seven	fem över halv sju	fehnm **ūr**verh hahlv shēw
ten to ten	tio i tio	**tee**oo ee **tee**oo
twelve o'clock	klockan tolv	**klok**kahn tolv
in the morning	på morgonen	paw **mor**ronern
in the afternoon	på eftermiddagen	paw **ehf**terniddahn
in the evening	på kvällen	paw **kveh**lern
during the day	under dagen	**ewn**derr **daa**gern
at night	på natten	paw **nah**tern
yesterday	i går	ee gawr
today	idag	ee**daa**(g)
tomorrow	i morgon	ee **mor**ron
spring/summer	vår/sommar	vawr/**som**mahr
autumn (fall)/winter	höst/vinter	hurst/**vin**terr

NUMBERS, see page 173

Sunday	**söndag**	**surn**daa(g)
Monday	**måndag**	mondaa(g)
Tuesday	**tisdag**	**tees**daa(g)
Wednesday	**onsdag**	**oons**daa(g)
Thursday	**torsdag**	**too'**sdaa(g)
Friday	**fredag**	**fray**daa(g)
Saturday	**lördag**	**lur'**daa(g)
January	**januari**	yahne**waa**ri
February	**februari**	fahbre**waa**ri
March	**mars**	mah'ss
April	**april**	ah**pril**
May	**maj**	mahy
June	**juni**	**yew**ni
July	**juli**	**yew**li
August	**augusti**	ah**gew**sti
September	**september**	seh**ptehm**berr
October	**oktober**	ok**too**berr
November	**november**	noo**vehm**berr
December	**december**	deh**ssehm**berr

Numbers *Räkneord*

0	**noll**	nol
1	**ett**	eht
2	**två**	tvaw
3	**tre**	tray
4	**fyra**	**few**rah
5	**fem**	fehm
6	**sex**	sehks
7	**sju**	shew
8	**åtta**	ottah
9	**nio**	**nee**oo
10	**tio**	**tee**oo
11	**elva**	**ehl**vah
12	**tolv**	tolv
13	**tretton**	**treh**ton
14	**fjorton**	**fyoo'**ton
15	**femton**	**fehm**ton
16	**sexton**	**sehks**ton
17	**sjutton**	**shew**ton
18	**arton**	**aa'**ton
19	**nitton**	**nit**ton
20	**tjuggo**	**khew**goo
30	**trettio**	**treh'**ti
40	**fyrtio**	**fur'**ti

50	**femtio**	fehmti
60	**sextio**	sehksti
70	**sjuttio**	shewti
80	**åttio**	otti
90	**nittio**	nitti
100	**(ett)hundra**	(eht)hewndrah
1,000	**(ett)tusen**	(eht)tewssern
first	**första**	fur'stah
second	**andra**	ahndrah
once/twice	**en gång/två gånger**	ehn gong/tvaw gongerr
a half	**eh halva**	ehn hahlvah

Emergency *Nödsituation*

Call the police	**Ring polisen**	ring poleessern
Get a doctor	**Hämta en läkare**	hehmtah ehn laikahrer
Go away	**Ge er i väg**	yay ayr ee vaig
HELP	**HJÄLP**	yehlp
I'm ill	**Jag är sjuk**	yaa(g) ær shewk
I'm lost	**Jag har gått vilse**	yaa(g) haar got vilser
LOOK OUT	**SE UPP**	say ewp
STOP THIEF	**STOPPA TJUVEN**	stoppah khewvern
My ... has been stolen.	**... har stulits.**	... haar stewlitss
I've lost my ...	**Jag har tappat ...**	yaa(g) haar tahpaht
handbag	**min handväska**	min hahn(d)vehskah
passport	**mitt pass**	mit pahss
wallet	**min plånbok**	min plawnbook
Where can I find a doctor who speaks English?	**Var kan jag få tag på en läkare som talar engelska?**	vaar kahn yaa(g) faw taag paw ehn laikahrer som taalahr engerlskah

Guide to Swedish pronunciation *Uttal*

Consonants

Letter	Approximate pronunciation	Symbol	Example	
b, c, d, f, h, l, m, n, p, v, w, x	as in English			
ch	at the beginning of words borrowed from French, like **sh** in **shut**	sh	**chef**	shayf
g	1) before stressed **i, e, y, ä, ö**, and sometimes after **l** or **r**, like **y** in yet	y	**ge**	yay

TELEPHONING, see page 172

Svensk

	2) before **e** and **i** in words of French origin, like **sh** in **sh**ut	sh	**geni**	sh**ay**nee
	3) elsewhere, like **g** in **g**o	g	**gaffel**	**gah**ferl
j, dj, g, lj, hj	at the beginning of words always like **y** in **y**et	y	**ja** **ljus**	yaa y**ew**ss
k	1) before stressed **i, e, y, ä, ö**, generally like **ch** in Scottish lo**ch**, but pronounced in the front of the mouth	kh	**köpa**	kh**ur**pah
	2) elsewhere, like **k** in **k**it	k	**klippa**	**kl**ippah
kj	like **ch** in lo**ch**, but pronounced in the front of the mouth	kh	**kjol**	kh**oo**l
qu	like **k** in **k**it followed by **v** in **v**at	kv	**Lindquist**	**lin**(d)kvist
r	rolled near the front of the mouth	r	**ryka**	**rew**kah
s	1) in the ending -**sion** like **sh** in **sh**ut	sh	**mission**	mi**shoo**n
	2) elsewhere, like **s** in **s**o	s/ss	**ses**	s**ay**ss
	3) the groups **sch, skj, sj, stj** are pronounced like **sh** in **sh**ut	sh	**schema**	**shay**mah
sk	1) before stressed **e, i, y, ä, ö**, like **sh** in **sh**ut	sh	**skänk**	shehnk
	2) elsewhere, like **sk** in **sk**ip	sk	**skola**	**skoo**la
t	1) in the ending -**tion** like **sh** in **sh**ut or **ch** in **ch**at	sh tsh	**station** **nation**	stah**shoo**n naht**shoo**n
	2) elsewhere, like **t** in **t**op	t	**tid**	teed
tj	like **ch** in Scottish lo**ch**, but pronounced in the front of the mouth; sometimes with a **t**-sound at the beginning	kh	**tjäna**	**khai**nah
z	like **s** in **s**o	s	**zenit**	**say**nit

Vowels

a	1) long, like a in car	aa	dag	daa(g)
	2) short, between a in cat and u in cut	ah	tack	tahk
e	1) long, like ay in say	a̅y̅	sen	sa̅y̅n
	2) when followed by r, like a in man	æ	erfara	æ̅rfaarah
	3) short, like e in get	eh	beck	behk
	4) like a in about	er	betala	bertaalah
ej	like a in mate	ay	nej	nay
i	1) long, like ee in bee	ee	vit	veet
	2) when short, between ee in meet and i in hit	i	hinna	hinnah
	3) like a in mate	ay	mig	may
o	1) when long, often like oo in soon, but with the lips more tightly rounded	o̅o̅	sko	sko̅o̅
	2) the same sound can be short	oo	solid	sooleed
	3) when long, sometimes like aw in raw, but with the tongue a little higher	aw	son	sawn
	4) like o in hot	o	korrekt	korrehkt
u	1) when long, like Swedish y, but with the tongue a little lower in the mouth	e̅w̅	hus	he̅w̅ss
	2) when short, a little more like the u of put	ew	full	fewl
y	like French u in une; round your lips and try to say ee as in bee	e̅w̅	vy	ve̅w̅
		ew	syster	sewsterr
å	1) when long, like aw in raw, but with the tongue a little higher in the mouth	aw	gå	gaw
	2) short, like o in hot	o	sång	song
ä	1) when followed by r, like a in man	æ	ära	æ̅rah
		æ	värka	værkah
	2) like e in get; long or short	ai	läsa	laissah
		eh	bäst	behst
ö	like ur in fur, but with the lips rounded and without any r-sound	u̅r̅	röd	ru̅r̅d
		ur	köld	khurld
			öra	u̅r̅rah

Turkish

Basic expressions *Önemli deyimler*

Yes/No.	**Evet/Hayır.**	ehveht/**hah**ʸır
Please.	**Lütfen.**	**lewt**fehn
Thank you.	**Teşekkür ederim.**	tehsheh**kk**ʸewr ehdehreem
I beg your pardon?	**Efendim?**	eh**fehn**deem

Introductions *Tanıştırmak*

Good morning.	**Günaydın.**	gʸewnah**ʸdın**
Good afternoon.	**İyi günler.**	eeyee gʸewn**lehr**
Good night.	**İyi geceler.**	eeyee gʸehjeh**lehr**
Good-bye.	**Allahaısmarladık.***	ahllahhahısmahrlahdık.
	Güle güle.**	gʸewleh gʸewleh
My name is ...	**Adım ... 'dir.**	ahdım ...deer
Pleased to meet you.	**Memnun oldum.**	**mehm**noom oldoom
What's your name?	**Adınız ne?**	ahdınız neh
How are you?	**Nasılsınız?**	nah**ssıl**sınız
Fine thanks.	**İyiyim, teşekkür ederim.**	eeyeeyeem tehsheh**kk**ʸewr ehdehreem
And you?	**Siz nasılsınız?**	seez nah**ssıl**sınız
Where do you come from?	**Nerelisiniz?**	neh**reh**leesseeneez
I'm from ...	**... denim/danım.**	... dehneem/dahnım
Australia	**Avustralya**	ahvoos**trahl**yah
Canada	**Kanada**	kah**nah**dah
Great Britain	**Büyük Britanya**	bew**yewk** breetahnyah
United States	**Amerika Birleşik Devletleri**	ahmehreekah beerleh**sheek** dehvlehtlehree
I'm with my ...	**... beraberim.**	... beh**rah**behreem
wife	**Karımla**	kahrımlah
husband	**Kocamla**	kojahmlah
family	**Ailemle**	aheelehmleh
friend	**Arkadaşımla**	ahrkahdahshımlah
I'm here on vacation.	**Burada izindeyim.**	**boo**rahdah eezeendehʸeem

---

* said by the one who is leaving; ** said by the one who remains.

PRONUNCIATION, see page 191/EMERGENCIES, see page 190

Questions *Sorular*

When?	**Ne zaman?**	neh zah**mahn**
How?	**Nasıl?**	**nah**ssıl
What?/Why?	**Ne?/Neden?**	neh/**neh**dehn
Who?	**Kim?**	kᵞeem
Which?	**Hangi?**	hahng**ᵞ**ee
Where is...?	**... nerededir?**	... **neh**rehdehdeer
Where are...?	**... nerededir?**	... **neh**rehdehdeer
Where can I find/get...?	**Nerede ... bulabilirim/alabilirim?**	**neh**rehdeh ... boolahbee**leer**eem/ahlahbee**leer**eem
How far?	**Ne uzaklıktadır?**	neh oozahklıktahdır
How long?	**Ne kadar zaman?**	neh kah**dahr** zah**mahn**
How much/many?	**Ne kadar?/Kaç tane?**	neh kah**dahr**/kahch **tah**neh
Can I have...?	**... rica edebilir miyim?**	... **ree**jah ehdehbee**leer** **mee**yeem
Can you help me?	**Yardım edebilir misiniz?**	**yahr**dım ehdehbee**leer** **mee**sseeneez
What does this/that mean?	**Bu/Şu ne demek?**	boo/shoo neh deh**mehk**
I understand.	**Anlıyorum.**	ahn**lıy**oroom
I don't understand.	**Anlamıyorum.**	ahn**lahmıy**oroom
Do you speak English?	**İngilizce biliyor musunuz?**	eeng**ᵞ**ee**leez**jeh beeleeyor **moo**ssoonooz
I don't speak (much) Turkish.	**(İyi) Türkçe bilmem.**	(eeyee) **tewrk**cheh beel**mehm**

A few more useful words *Birkaç önemli kelime*

better/worse	**daha iyi/daha kötü**	dah**hah** eeyee/dah**hah** kᵞur**tew**
big/small	**büyük/küçük**	bew**yewk**/kᵞew**chewk**
cheap/expensive	**ucuz/pahalı**	oo**jooz**/pah**hah**lı
early/late	**erken/geç**	ehr**k**ᵞ**ehn**/gᵞehch
good/bad	**iyi/kötü**	eeyee/kᵞur**tew**
hot/cold	**sıcak/soğuk**	sı**jahk**/**saw**ook
near/far	**yakın/uzak**	yah**kın**/oo**zahk**
old/new	**eski/yeni**	ehsk**ᵞ**ee/yeh**nee**
vacant/occupied	**serbest/meşgul**	sehr**behst**/mesh**gool**

Hotel–Other accommodation *Otel*

I have a reservation.	**Rezervasyonum var.**	rehzehrvahsyonoom **vahr**
We've reserved two rooms.	**İki odayı rezerve ettik.**	eek^yee odah^yı rehzehrveh **ehtteek**
Do you have any vacancies?	**Boş odanız var mı?**	bosh odahnız **vahr** mı
I'd like a... room.	**... bir oda istiyorum.**	... beer odah eesteeyoroom
single	**Tek yataklı**	tehk yah**tahk**lı
double	**Çift yataklı**	cheeft yah**tahk**lı
with twin beds	**İki yataklı**	eek^yee yah**tahk**lı
with a double bed	**Çift kişilik**	cheeft k^yeesheeleek
with a bath/shower	**Banyolu/Duşlu**	**bahn**yoloo/**doosh**loo
We'll be staying...	**... kalacağız.**	... kahlahjaaız
overnight only	**Sadece bir gece**	sahdehjeh beer g^yehjeh
a few days	**Birkaç gün**	**beer**kahch g^yewn
a week	**Bir hafta**	beer **hahf**tah

Decision *Karar*

May I see the room?	**Odayı görebilir miyim?**	odah^yı g^yurrehbeel**eer** meeyeem
That's fine. I'll take it.	**İyi. Alıyorum.**	eeyee. ahlıyoroom
No. I don't like it.	**Hayır, beğenmedim.**	**hah**^yır bayehnmehdeem
It's too...	**Çok...**	chok
dark	**karanlık**	kahrahnlık
small	**küçük**	k^yewchewk
noisy	**gürültülü**	g^yewrewltewlew
Do you have anything...?	**... birşeyiniz var mı?**	... **beer**sheh^yeeneez vahr mı
better	**Daha iyi**	**dah**hah eeyee
bigger	**Daha büyük**	**dah**hah bewyewk
cheaper	**Daha ucuz**	**dah**hah oojooz
quieter	**Daha sakin**	**dah**hah sahk^yeen
May I have my bill, please?	**Lütfen hesabı istiyorum?**	**lewt**fehn hehssahbı eesteeyoroom
It's been a very enjoyable stay.	**Burada çok hoş zaman geçirdik.**	**boo**rahdah chok hosh zahmahn g^yehcheerdeek

Eating out *Dışarda yemek*

I'd like to reserve a table for 4.	**Dört kişi için bir masa ayırtmak istiyorum.**	durrt k^yeeshee eecheen beer mahssah ah^yırt**mahk** eesteeyoroom
We'll come at 8.	**Saat 8 de geliriz.**	sahaht 8 deh g^yehleereez
I'd like...	... **istiyorum**	... eesteeyoroom
breakfast	**Kahvaltı**	kahhvahltı
lunch	**Öğle yemeği**	urleh yehmayee
dinner	**Akşam yemeği**	ahkshahm yehmayee
What do you recommend?	**Ne tavsiye edersiniz?**	neh tahvsseyeh ehdehrseeneez
Do you have any vegetarian dishes?	**Etsiz yemeğiniz var mı?**	ehtzeez yehmayeeneez vahr mı

Breakfast *Kahvaltı*

May I have some...	... **alabilir miyim?**	... ahlahbee**leer** meeyeem
bread	**Ekmek**	ehkmehk
butter	**Tereyağ**	tehrehyaa
cheese	**Peynir**	peh^yneer
ham and eggs	**Jambon ve yumurta**	zhahmbon veh yoomoortah
jam	**Reçel**	rehchehl
rolls	**Küçük ekmek**	k^yew**chewk** ehkmehk

Starters *Antreler*

chickpea dip	**humus**	hoomoos
creamed red caviar	**tarama**	tahrahmah
marinated artichoke	**enginar**	ehng^yeenahr
mussels	**midye**	**meed**yeh
oysters	**istiridye**	eesteereedyeh
sardines	**sardalya**	sahrdahlyah
seafood cocktail	**deniz mahsulleri kokteyli**	deh**neez** mahhssooll-ehree kokteh^ylee

Soup *Çorba*

chicken consomme	**tavuk suyu**	tahvook sooyoo
consomme	**et suyu (konsome)**	eht sooyoo (konsomeh)
French onion soup	**gratine soğan çorbası**	grahteeneh sawahn chorbahssı
noodle soup	**erişteli çorba**	ehreeshtehlee chorbah
tomato soup	**domates çorbası**	do**mah**tehss chorbahssı
vegetable soup	**sebze çorbası**	sehbzeh chorbahssı

NUMBERS, see page 189

Fish and seafood *Balık ve deniz hayvanları*

lobster	**ıstakoz**	ıstahkoz
plaice	**pisi**	peessee
prawns	**karides**	kʸehreedehss
salmon	**som balığı**	som bahlııı
sole	**dil balığı**	deel bahlııı
trout	**alabalık**	ahlahbahlık
tuna	**ton balığı**	ton bahlııı

baked	**fırında**	fırındah
boiled	**haşlama**	hahshlahmah
fried	**tavada kızarmış**	tahvah**dah** kızahrmısh
grilled	**ızgara**	ızgahrah
roast	**kızarmış**	kızahrmısh
stewed	**yahni**	yahnee
underdone (rare)	**az pişmiş**	**ahz** peeshmeesh
medium	**orta pişmi**	or**tah** peeshmeesh
well-done	**iyi pişmiş**	ee**yee** peeshmeesh

Meat *Et*

I'd like some...	**... istiyorum.**	... eesteeyoroom
beef/lamb	**Sığır/Kuzu**	sııır/koozoo
pork/veal	**Domuz/Dana**	domooz/dahnah
chicken/steak	**Tavuk/Biftek**	tahvook/beeftehk
fried meatballs	**kuru köfte**	kooroo kʸurfteh
lamb chops	**kuzu pirzolası**	koozoo peerzolahssı
stew	**haşlama**	hahshlahmah
kuzu dolması	lamb stuffed with savoury rice, liver and pis-	
(koozoo dolmahssı)	tachios	

Vegetables *Sebzeler*

beans	**fasulye**	fah**ssool**yeh
cabbage	**lâhana**	**laa**hahnnah
carrots	**havuç**	hahvooch ·
mushrooms	**mantar**	mahntahr
onions	**soğan**	sawahn
peas	**bezelye**	beh**zehl**yeh
potatoes	**patates**	pah**tah**tehss
tomatoes	**domates**	do**mah**tehss
... dolması	dolmahssı	stuffed...
biber	beebehr	peppers
patlıcan	pahtlıjahn	aubergine (eggplant)
yaprak	yahprahk	vine leaves

Fruit/dessert *Meyve/Tatlılar*

apple	**elma**	ehlmah
banana	**muz**	mooz
lemon	**limon**	leemon
melon	**kavun**	kahvoon
orange	**portakal**	portahkahl
pear	**armut**	ahrmoot
strawberries	**çilek**	cheelehk
baklava	bahklahvah	pastry with chopped nuts and syrup
börek	burrehk	fried pastry strips in sugar
kaymaklı ve sütlü dondurma	kah^ymahklı veh sewtlew dondoormah	ice-cream
lokum	lokoom	Turkish delight
peşmelba	pehshmehlbah	peach melba
turtalar	toortahlahr	tarts

Drinks *İçkiler*

beer	**bira**	beerah
coffee without sugar	**sade kahve**	sahdeh kahhveh
fruit juice	**meyve suyu**	meh^yveh sooyoo
milk	**süt**	sewt
mineral water	**maden suyu**	mahdehn sooyoo
fizzy/still	**gazlı/sade**	gahzlı/sahdeh
tea	**çay**	chah^y
wine	**şarap**	shahrahp
red/white	**kırmızı/beyaz**	kırmızı/beh^yahz
a bottle	**bir şişe**	beer sheesheh
a glass	**bir bardak**	beer bahrdahk

Complaints and paying *Şikayetler–Hesap*

This is too...	**Bu çok...**	boo chok
bitter/sweet	**acı/tatlı**	ahjı/tahtlı
That's not what I ordered.	**Bunu ısmarlama- mıştım.**	boonoo ısmahrlahmah- mıshtım
I'd like to pay.	**Ödemek istiyorum.**	urdehmehk eesteeyoroom
I think there's a mistake in this bill.	**Bu hesapta bir hata var galiba.**	boo hehssahptah beer hahtah vahr gahleebah
Can I pay with this credit card?	**Bu kredi kartı ile ödeyebilir miyim?**	boo krehdee kahrti eeleh urdeh^yehbeeleer meeyeem
We enjoyed it, thank you.	**Hoşumuza gitti, teşekkür ederiz.**	hoshoomoozah g^yeettee tehshehkk^yewr ehdehreez

Travelling around *Yolculukta*

Plane *Uçak*

Is there a flight to Antalya?	**Antalya'ya uçuş var mı?**	ahntahlyahyah oochoosh vahr mı
What time do I have to check in?	**Bagajların kaydını saat kaçta yapmam gerek?**	bahgahzhlahrın kah^ydını sahaht kahchtah yahpmahm g^yehrehk
I'd like to ... my reservation.	**Rezervasyo-numu ... istiyorum.**	rehzehrvahsyomoo ... eesteeyoroom
cancel	**iptal etmek**	eeptahl ehtmehk
change	**değiştirmek**	dayeeshteermehk
confirm	**konfirme etmek**	konfeermeh ehtmehk

Train *Tren*

I'd like a ticket to ...	**... 'ya bir bilet istiyorum.**	yah beer beeleht eesteeyoroom
single (one-way)	**gidiş**	g^yeedeesh
return (round trip)	**gidiş-dönüş**	g^yeedeesh-durnewsh
first class	**birinci mevki**	beereenjee mehvk^yee
second class	**ikinci mevki**	eek^yeenjee mehvk^yee
How long does the journey (trip) take?	**Yolculuk ne kadar zaman sürer?**	yoljoolook neh kahdahr zahmahn sewrehr
When is the ... train to Eskisehir?	**Eskişehir'e ... tren ne zaman?**	ehskeeshehheereh ... trehn neh zahmahn
first	**ilk**	eelk
next	**gelecek**	g^yehlehjehk
last	**son**	son
Is this the train to ...?	**... treni bu mudur?**	trehnee boo moodoor

Bus *Otobüs*

Which bus goes to the town centre?	**Şehir merkezine hangi otobüs gider?**	shehheer mehrk^yehzeeneh hahng^yee otobewss g^yeedehr
How much is the fare to Erzurum?	**Erzurum'a yolculuk kaça?**	ehrzooroomah yoljoolook kahchah
Will you tell me when to get off?	**Ne zaman inmem gerektiğini söyler misiniz?**	neh zahmahn eenmehm g^yehrehkteeeenee surlehr meesseeneez

TELLING THE TIME, see page 188/NUMBERS, see page 189

Taxi *Taksi*

How much is the fare to...?	**... a/e ücret ne kadardır?**	... ah/eh ewjreht neh kahdahrdır
Take me to this address.	**Beni bu adrese götürün.**	behnee **boo** ahdrehsseh g^yurtewrewn
Please stop here.	**Durabilir miyiz, lütfen?**	doorahbeeleer meeyeez lewtfehn
Could you wait for me?	**Lütfen beni bekler misiniz.**	lewtfehn behnee behklehr meesseeneez

Car hire (rental) *Araba kiralama*

I'd like to hire (rent) a car.	**Bir araba kiralamak istiyorum.**	beer ahrahbah k^yeerahlahmak eesteeyoroom
I'd like it for a day/a week.	**Bir gün/Bir hafta için istiyorum.**	beer g^yewn/beer hahftah eecheen esteeyoroom
Where's the nearest filling station?	**En yakın benzin istasyonu nerededir?**	ehn yahkın behnzeen eestahssyonoo nehrehdehdeer
Fill it up, please.	**Doldurun, lütfen.**	doldooroon lewtfehn
Could you give me... litres of petrol (gasoline).	**... litre benzin verir misiniz?**	... leehtreh behnzeen vehreer meesseeneez
How do I get to...?	**... 'e nasıl gidebilirim?**	... eh nahssıl g^yeedehbeeleerem
I've broken down at...	**... 'da/de arabam arızalandı.**	... dah/deh ahrahbahm ahrızahlahndı
Can you send a mechanic?	**Bir araba tamircisi gönderir misiniz?**	beer ahrahbah tahmeerjeessee g^yurndehreer meesseeneez

---

Yanlış yoldasınız.	You're on the wrong road.
Doğru gidin.	Go straight ahead.
Orada ileride...	It's down there on the...
solda/sağda	left/right
... ın yanında	next to
... den/dan sonra	after...
kuzey/güney/doğu/batı	north/south/east/west

Sightseeing *Gezi*

Where's the tourist office?	**Turizm bürosu nerededir?**	tooreezm bewrossoo nehrehdehdeer
Is there an English-speaking guide?	**İngilizce bilen bir rehber var mı?**	eeng'eeleezjeh beelehn beer rehhbehr vahr mı
Where is/are the...?	**... nerededir?**	... nehrehdehdeer
art gallery	**Sanat galerisi**	sahnaht gahlehreessee
botanical gardens	**Botanik bahçesi**	botahneek bahhchehssee
castle	**Şato**	shahto
city centre/downtown	**Şehir merkezi**	shehheer mehrk'ehzee
harbour	**Liman**	leemahn
market	**Pazar**	pahzahr
mosque	**Câmi**	jaamee
museum	**Müze**	mewzeh
square	**Meydan**	meh'dahn
tower	**Kule**	kooleh
zoo	**Hayvanat bahçesi**	hah'vahnaht bahhchehssee
What are the opening hours?	**Habgi saatlerde açıktır?**	hahng'ee sahahtlehrdeh ahchıktır
When does it close?	**Ne zaman kapanır?**	neh zahmahn kahpahnır
How much is the entrance fee?	**Giriş ücreti ne kadar?**	g'eereesh ewjrehtee neh kahdahr

Relaxing *Eğlence*

What's playing at the...Theatre?	**... tiyatrosunda ne oynuyor?**	... teeyahtrossoondah neh oynooyor
Are there any seats for tonight?	**Bu akşam için yer var mı?**	boo ahkshahm eecheen yehr vahr mı
How much are the tickets?	**Biletler ne kadar?**	beelehtlehr neh kahdahr
Would you like to go out with me tonight?	**Bu akşam benimle çıkar mısınız?**	boo ahkshahm behneemleh chıkahr mıssınız
Is there a disco-theque in town?	**Şehirde diskotek var mı?**	shehheerdeh deeskotehk vahr mı
Would you like to dance?	**Dans eder misiniz?**	dahns ehdehr meesseeneez
Thank you, it's been a wonderful evening.	**Teşekkür ederim, fevkalâde bir akşam geçirdim.**	tehshehkk'ewr ehdehreem fehvkahlaadeh beer ahkshahm g'ehcheerdeem

TELLING THE TIME, see page 188/NUMBERS, see page 189

Shops, stores and services *Dükkânlar ve hizmet*

Where's the nearest...?	**En yakın...** **nerededir?**	ehn yahkın ... nehrehdehdeer
bakery	**fırın**	fırın
bookshop	**kitabevi**	kᵞeetahbehvee
butcher's	**kasap dükkânı**	kahsahp dewkkaanı
chemist/drugstore	**eczane**	ehjzahneh
dentist	**dişçi**	deeshchee
department store	**büyük mağaza**	bewyewk maaahzah
grocery	**bakkal dükkânı**	bahkkahl dewkkaanı
hairdresser	**kuaför/berber**	kooahfurr/behrbehr
newsagent	**gazeteci**	gahzehtehjee
post office	**postane**	postahneh
supermarket	**süpermarket**	sewpehrmahrkᵞeht
toilets	**tuvaletler**	toovahlehtlehr

General expressions *Genel tabirler*

Where's the main shopping area?	**Asıl alış veriş merkezi nerededir?**	ahssıl ahlısh vehreesh mahrkᵞehzee nehrehdehdeer
Do you have any...?	**... var mı?**	... vahr mı
Haven't you anything...?	**... birşey yok mu?**	... beershehᵞ yok moo
cheaper/better	**Daha ucuz/Daha iyi**	dahhah oojooz/dahhah eeyee
larger/smaller	**Daha büyük/Daha küçük**	dahhah bewyewk/dahhah kᵞewchewk
Can I try it on?	**Bunu deneyebilir miyim?**	boonoo dehnehᵞehbeeleer meeyeem
How much is this?	**Bu ne kadar?**	boo neh kahdahr
Please write it down.	**Lütfen yazar mısınız.**	lewtfehn yahzahr mıssınız
I don't want to spend more than... lira.	**... liradan fazla harcamak istemiyorum.**	... leerahdahn fahzlah hahrjahmahk eestehmeeyoroom
No, I don't like it.	**Hayır, bunu beğenmedim.**	hahᵞır boonoo bayehnmehdeem
I'll take it.	**Bunu alacağım.**	boonoo ahlahjaaım
Do you accept credit cards?	**Kredi kartı kabul eder misiniz?**	krehdee kahrtı kahbool ehder meesseeneez
Can you order it for me?	**Bunu benim için ısmarlar mısınız?**	boonoo behneem eecheen ısmahrlahr mıssınız

black	**siyah**	seeyahh
blue	**mavi**	mahvee
brown	**kahverengi**	kahhvehrehng^yee
green	**yeşil**	yehsheel
orange	**portakal rengi**	portah**kahl** rehng^yee
red	**kırmızı**	kırmızı
white	**beyaz**	beh^yahz
yellow	**sarı**	sahrı
light...	**açik**	ahchık
dark...	**koyu**	koyoo

I want to buy a/an/ some...	**... istiyorum**	... eesteeyoroom
aspirin	**Aspirin**	ahspeereen
newspaper American/English	**Bir ... gazetesi Amerikan/İngiliz**	beer ... gahzehtehssee ahmehreekahn/ eeng^yeeleez
postcard	**Bir kartpostal**	beer kahrtpostahl
shampoo	**Şampuan**	shahmpooahn
soap	**Sabun**	sahboon
sun-tan cream	**Güneş kremi**	g^yewnehsh krehmee
toothpaste	**Diş macunu**	deesh mahjoonoo
a half kilo of tomatoes	**Yarım kilo domates**	yahrım k^yeelo domahtehss
a litre of milk	**Bir litre süt**	beer leetreh sewt
I'd like a film for this camera.	**Bu fotoğraf makinesı için film istiyorum.**	boo fotawrahf mahk^yeenehssı eecheen feelm eesteeyoroom
black and white	**siyah-beyaz film**	seeyahbeh^yahz feelm
colour	**renkli film**	rehnklee feelm
I'd like a hair-cut, please.	**Lütfen saçımı kesin.**	**lewt**fehn sahchımı k^yehsseen

Souvenirs *Hatıra*

carpet	**halı**	hahlı
chocolate	**çukolata**	chookolahtah
crystal	**kristal**	kreestahl
hubble-bubble pipe	**nargile**	nahrg^yeeleh
prayer mat	**namaz seccâdesi**	nahmahz sehjjaadehssee
Turkish delight	**lokum**	lokoom

NUMBERS, see page 189

At the bank *Banka*

Where's the nearest bank/currency exchange office?	En yakın banka/ kambiyo bürosu nerededir?	ehn yahkın **bahn**kah/ **kam**beeyo bewrossoo nehrehdehdeer
I want to change some dollars/pounds.	Birkaç dolar/sterlin çevirmek istiyo- rum.	**beer**kahch dolahr/ stehrleen chehveer**mehk** eesteeyoroom
What's the exchange rate?	Kambiyo kuru nedir?	**kahm**beeyo kooroo **neh**deer
I want to cash a traveller's cheque.	Traveller's çek boz- durmak istiyorum.	'traveller's' chehk bozdoor**mahk** eestee- **yo**room

At the post office *Postane*

A...-lira stamp, please	... liralık posta pulu lütfen.	... leerahlık **pos**tah pooloo **lewt**fehn
What's the postage for a postcard/letter to United States?	Amerika Birleşik Devletleri'e kart- postal/mektup kaça gider?	ahmehreekah beerleh- **sheek** dehvlehtlehree'eh kahrtpostahl/mehktoop **kah**chah g**y**eedehr
Is there any post/mail for me?	Benim için posta var mı?	behneem eecheen postah vahr mı

Telephoning *Telefon etmek*

Where is the nearest telephone?	En yakın telefon kulübesi nerededir?	ehn yahkın **teh**lehfon koolewbehssee **neh**reh- dehdeer
Hello. This is...	Alo, ben...	ahlo behn
I'd like to speak to...	... ile konuşmak istiyorum.	... eeleh konooshmahk eesteeyoroom
When will he/she be back?	Ne zaman geri döner?	**neh** zahmahn g**y**ehree dur**nehr**

Time and date *Saat ve tarih*

It's...

five past one	Biri beş geçiyor	beer**ee** behsh g**y**ehchee**yor**
quarter past three	Üçü çeyrek geçiyor	ewchew cheh**y**rehk g**y**ehchee**yor**
twenty past four	Dördü yirmi geçi- yor	durr**dew** yeermee g**y**ehchee**yor**
half past six	Altı buçuk	ahltı boochook
twenty-five to seven	Yediye yirmibeş var	yehdeeyeh yeermeebehsh vahr

ten to ten	**Ona on var**	onah on vahr
noon/midnight	**Öğle/Gece yarısı**	urley/g^yehjeh yahrıssı
in the morning	**sabahları**	sahbahhlahrı
in the afternoon	**öğleden sonra**	urlehdehn sonrah
in the evening	**akşamları**	ahkshahmlahrı
during the day	**gündüzleri**	g^yewndewzlehree
at night	**geceleri**	g^yehjehlehree
yesterday/today	**dün/bugün**	dewn/**boog**^yewn
tomorrow	**yarın**	yahrın
spring/summer	**ilkbahar/yaz**	**eelk**bahhahr/yahz
autumn/winter	**sonbahar/kış**	**son**bahhahr/kısh

Sunday	**Pazar**	pah**zahr**
Monday	**Pazartesi**	pah**zahr**tehssee
Tuesday	**Salı**	sahlı
Wednesday	**Çarşamba**	chahrshahm**bah**
Thursday	**Perşembe**	pehrshehm**beh**
Friday	**Cuma**	**joo**mah
Saturday	**Cumartesi**	**joo**mahrtehssee
January	**Ocak**	ojahk
February	**Şubat**	shoobaht
March	**Mart**	mahrt
April	**Nisan**	neessahn
May	**Mayıs**	mah^yıss
June	**Haziran**	hahzeerahn
July	**Temmuz**	tehmmooz
August	**Ağustos**	aaoostos
September	**Eylül**	eh^ylewl
October	**Ekim**	ehk^yeem
November	**Kasım**	kahssım
December	**Aralık**	ahrahlık

Numbers *Sayılar*

0	**sıfır**	sıfir
1	**bir**	beer
2	**iki**	eek^yee
3	**üç**	ewch
4	**dört**	durrt
5	**beş**	behsh
6	**altı**	ahltı
7	**yedi**	yeh**dee**
8	**sekiz**	sehk^yeez
9	**dokuz**	do**kooz**

10	**on**	on
11	**on bir**	on beer
12	**on iki**	on eek^yee
13	**on üç**	on ewch
14	**on dört**	on durrt
15	**on beş**	on behsh
16	**on altı**	on ahltı
17	**on yedi**	on yehdee
18	**on sekiz**	on sehk^yeez
19	**on dokuz**	on dokooz
20	**yirmi**	yeermee
21	**yirmi bir**	yeermee beer
30	**otuz**	otooz
40	**kırk**	kırk
50	**elli**	ehllee
60	**altmış**	ahltmısh
70	**yetmiş**	yehtmeesh
80	**seksen**	sehksehn
90	**doksan**	doksahn
100/1000	**yüz/bin**	yewz/been
first/second	**ilk/ikinci**	eelk/eek^yeenjee
once/twice	**bir kez/iki kez**	beer k^yehz/eek^yee k^yehz
a half	**yarım**	yahrım

Emergency *Tehlikeli durum*

Call the police	**Polis çağırın**	poleess chaaırın
Get a doctor	**Doktor çağırın**	doktor chaaırın
Go away	**Gidiniz**	g^yeedeeneez
HELP	**İMDAT**	eemdaht
I'm ill	**Hastayım**	hahstah^yım
I'm lost	**Kayboldum**	kah^yboldoom
LOOK OUT	**DİKKAT**	deekkaht
STOP THIEF	**HIRSIZI YAKA-LAYIN**	hırsızı yahkahlah^yın

My...has been stolen.	**... um/im/am çalındı.**	... oom/eem/ahm chahlındı
I've lost my...	**... kaybettim.**	... kah^ybehtteem
handbag	**El çantamı**	ehl chahntahmı
wallet	**Para cüzdanımı**	pahrah jewzdahnımı
passport	**Pasaportumu**	pahssahportoomoo
luggage	**Bagaj**	bahgahz
Where can I find a doctor who speaks English?	**İngilizce bilen bir doktor nerede bula-bilirim?**	eeng^yeeleezjeh beelehn beer doktor nehrehdeh boolahbeeleereem

TELEPHONING, see page 188